A Vast Amount of Trouble

John W. Davis

# A Vast Amount of Trouble
## A History of the Spring Creek Raid

University Press of Colorado

Copyright © 1993 by the University Press of Colorado

Published by the University Press of Colorado
P.O. Box 849
Niwot, Colorado 80544

The University Press of Colorado is a cooperative publishing enterprise supported, in part, by Adams State College, Colorado State University, Fort Lewis College, Mesa State College, Metropolitan State College of Denver, University of Colorado, University of Northern Colorado, University of Southern Colorado, and Western State College of Colorado.

Cover painting: *Night Riders of Nowood* by L. D. Edgar of Cody, Wyoming.

**Library of Congress Cataloging-in-Publication Data**

Davis, John W., 1943–
    A vast amount of trouble: a history of the Spring Creek Raid / John W. Davis.
      p.  cm.
    Includes bibliographical references and index.
    ISBN 0-87081-310-2 (acid-free paper)
    1. Brink, Herbert — Trials, litigation, etc. 2. Trials (Murder) — Wyoming — Basin. 3. Mass murder — Wyoming — Ten Sleep — History — 20th century. 4. Sheep ranchers — Crimes against — Wyoming — Ten Sleep — History — 20th century. I. Title.
    KF224.B75D38  1993
    345.787'02523 — dc20
    [347.87052523]
                                     93-33209
                                               CIP
                                             r93

10  9  8  7  6  5  4  3  2  1

# Contents

# Preface

This book arose out of a project of the Washakie County (Wyoming) Bar Association.

Nineteen ninety was the centennial year of Wyoming statehood, and events were held throughout the state to commemorate this 100-year anniversary. In Park County, District Judge Hunter Patrick sponsored a re-enactment of a territorial murder trial. Washakie County attorneys were invited to take part, but Powell and Cody (in Park County) were a good ways from Worland, the county seat. About the same time that I learned of Judge Patrick's project, however, I also learned that Clay Gibbons of Worland had a copy of the trial transcript of the case of *State v. Brink*.

*State v. Brink* is a fabled case in Washakie County, being the trial that arose out of the infamous Spring Creek raid. That 1909 sheep raid is still a topic of great interest and has been the subject of numerous writings. So Washakie County had its own famous trial appropriate for re-enactment.

Jeff Donnell (one of my law partners) and I used the 387-page transcript to create a one-day script. Then, on August 10, 1990, people gathered at the Washakie County Courthouse. Local lawyers played the *Brink* trial lawyers, and other citizens played the witnesses. Whenever we could, we used descendants of the actual participants. Tom Greet played his great-uncle Fred Greet, Kent Orchard his great-uncle Billy Goodrich, and Bill Simpson his great-grandfather William (Billy) Simpson. Though the transcript was abridged to show only the core evidence, we faithfully followed its exact words.

The presentation was well received and was great fun for the participants. I played Ridgely, the chief defense attorney, and although staging this trial was also enjoyable for me, my interest had become much deeper. In the course of working with the trial transcript, reading and re-reading it to create our script, then reading the 1909 Basin newspaper reports and some of the literature about the raid, I'd become captivated with the event. For all the writings there was no comprehensive, scholarly treatment of the raid, the trials that followed, and their aftermath. I decided to attempt such a project.

At first I worked with Clay Gibbons. Clay had been instrumental in having a monument and highway marker established at the site of the raid and was very knowledgeable and enthusiastic about it. From Clay I learned a great deal about the existing documentation, such as the tapes of the speeches of Percy Metz (the Big Horn county attorney in 1909) and the materials at the state archives offices in Cheyenne. This knowledge saved me many hours of initial research. I also learned from Clay and others about the key information that was missing.

For thirty years, people had been hunting for the minutes of the grand jury convened to investigate the raid. Percy Metz had tantalizingly waved them in front of his audiences in 1961 and 1962, but the papers had subsequently disappeared. It seemed, too, that key files were missing from the records of Big Horn County.

I set out to find everything I could. As an attorney who had practiced for eighteen years in the same district in which the trials were held, I felt I had an advantage in this research. At first, though, it did me little good. To locate the grand jury minutes, inquiries were made with remote relatives of Percy Metz and his wife, Cornelia, with retired clerks of court, and with former court reporters, to name only a few of the frustrating dead ends. A great deal of time was also spent rummaging through the records of the Big Horn County clerk of court, and although some progress was made, neither the key files nor the grand jury minutes were anywhere to be found. Not a clue. I should mention that throughout this effort, Donette Martin of the clerk of court's office was unfailingly courteous and helpful.

I went to Cheyenne to see what could be found in the historical offices of the state of Wyoming. They had wonderful materials and wonderfully helpful people, especially Jean Brainerd, and I believe I read every paper in their records. In Cheyenne I also found Lylas Skovgard, a former resident of Basin, who was of great assistance, not least by telling me of *The Sweet Smell of Sagebrush,* a chronicle written by a convict who knew all the Spring Creek defendants. After Cheyenne I went to the American Heritage Center in Laramie, where more interesting materials were found — but no grand jury minutes.

Returning to Worland, I started collecting all the contemporary newspaper accounts related to the raid, including those of the *Basin Republican, Big Horn County Rustler, Thermopolis Record, Worland Grit, Denver Post,* and *Cheyenne Daily Leader.* I tried to read everything that had ever been written about the raid and reviewed many books about the sheep and cattle wars.

My previous trip to Laramie had not allowed me enough time to review the entire Percy Metz collection at the Heritage Center. So I returned, determined to poke in all the eighty-eight cartons of that collection, convinced that somewhere in those boxes existed a lead to the grand jury minutes.

I remember a long day spent going through box after box. Interesting stuff, but after sixty or seventy cartons there was nothing even hinting of the grand jury minutes, and I was getting discouraged. The American Heritage people, though, kept feeding me materials and, when it looked as if the Percy Metz collection was not going to pan out, asked if I'd like to review a new, uncatalogued collection they had just received, one from the estate of Lola Homsher.

Jim Carlson brought me several boxes of materials that had little significance. Then he brought in a cardboard box with a lot of loose papers. More or less at random, I picked one of them out of the box and started reading it. It was testimony, the transcribed testimony of a very important witness, and I assumed it was from the trial. I was thoroughly familiar with that testimony, though, and this was not exactly what I remembered. In the trial, this witness told what happened during the raid. In *this* testimony, however, he seemed to be stating that he never left his home the evening of the raid. With mounting excitement, I read more. It didn't take long to conclude that it was not trial testimony I was reading but grand jury testimony, testimony given before this witness was indicted and turned state's evidence. That cardboard box was full of grand jury transcripts.

Through the rest of the afternoon I feverishly copied every page in that box, some 350 of them. In addition to grand jury testimony there were notes, some giving the prosecution's entire strategy and some of Percy Metz indicating the location in the Big Horn County records of all the files relating to the raid. Using the Metz notes, I returned to Basin and found every file. They hadn't been missing at all — they were just not placed where people expected them to be.

With the majority of my research completed, I could start writing. I wrote and wrote, month after month. During this time Milton Woods of Worland was of great assistance for his broad historical knowledge and, even more important, as a sounding board. My long-suffering law partners read most of the manuscript as it was being written, and although they may not have realized it, their comments and suggestions were much appreciated. To break the monotony of endless writing there were trips — to the Greybull Museum, to the Ten Sleep Cemetery, and to the Upper Nowood. I'll never forget that bright March day when Howard McClellan and I traveled all over the Upper Nowood country, going to the scene of the raid and to the sites of all those old ranches, those places where the ghosts of 1909 still play.

Finally, I completed a long manuscript of some 115,000 words, and this was read by Milton Woods, Debbie Hammons, and my brother, Jim Davis. Their comments led to a leaner manuscript, as I cut back on some of the broad background material that was initially included. I also collected additional photographs, and in this effort Jack Seaman and Georgia St. Clair were especially helpful.

One person whose help was invaluable in writing the manuscript was Caroline Hansen, one of my secretaries. Time and again when I encountered problems with the word processing program, she managed to find a solution. Another person providing invaluable help, although of a very different kind, was Professor Phil Roberts of the University of Wyoming. Professor Roberts has a profound knowledge of Wyoming history, and his encouragement and assistance were deeply appreciated.

But the one who helped the most, in more ways than I can count was Celia, my wife. Producing this book has taken a massive amount of time from my family, and Celia is alleged to have said: "Ada Allemand wasn't the only woman made a widow by the Spring Creek Raid." It would be understandable if she had said that, but she actually didn't. In truth, one of the endearing things about Celia is her commitment to protect my time for the crazy projects I sometimes pursue.

In writing this book, I had two purposes. One was not to get in the way of a remarkable story. Along these lines, I have quoted a great deal of material, some of which contains extensive misspellings. Unless it was confusing, I almost always chose to reproduce the original, incorrect spelling, and not clutter the document with the word "sic."

My second purpose was to write a true history, one faithful to the event. I hope the reader deems that I have.

JOHN W. DAVIS
*October 31, 1992*

A Vast Amount of Trouble

The man on the white horse stayed on the hill through most of the night, and the children were frightened. That figure was there for a reason; a man does not sit for hours on a horse through a cool night without a purpose.[1] He was only about a hundred yards away on a sharp rise, but it was far enough that the women in the ranch house could not identify him, and no one dared leave the house and confront him.

Tragedy had just struck this little house on Spring Creek, and the horseman and his white mount were grim reminders of the frailty of life and the finality of death.

Only a month before, this home had greeted a new and vibrant life when Ada Allemand gave birth to a son, the second for her and her husband, Joe. Joe and Ada had every reason to cherish life. Ada was a pretty young woman, and her husband was kind and gentle; they had been married about ten years in 1909. Their ranch was doing better now that Joe had taken on a new partner; indeed, it looked as if they would prosper. They had many friends in the valley. But when calamity struck, it was swift and complete. Only a few miles from the ranch house, Joe, his nephew, and his partner were slaughtered. Sheep and dogs were killed, and Joe's wagons were burned.

The night following Joe's funeral, the white horse was suddenly seen in the clear moonlight, and the rider's presence was surely meant to terrify Ada, to tell her that her husband had committed such an offense that she should leave the valley.

The rider slipped off as the sun rose, leaving in the new light of day ugly realities for Ada Allemand to consider. Beside the obvious message that she should go, there was the fact that it was not just a tiny baby and his brother who now depended on Ada; she had the whole burden of the ranch. Furthermore, she knew there would probably never be redress for the horrible wrongs done to her and her family; those who killed her husband would probably never face justice.

Such an awful event did not arise in a vacuum. It came from the collective experience and memories of people, from the anguish and joy of molding and melding with the land. Human beings live in the light of what they have known, and to understand why they act as they do we must know of the world in which they live.

The collective memory of the residents of the Big Horn Basin was only thirty years old in 1909. It could be traced to a very specific beginning: 1879. That is the year cattlemen first came to the Big Horn Basin. They came to the Basin when it was still an Eden, when it was still filled with buffalo and wolves and grizzly bears and when hunting bands of Crow and Shoshone still moved across the land. Those first cattlemen built empires, fighting the land, fighting the wild animals, fighting the weather, and they did it, more than anything, with an immense amount of hard work and courage. So it was understandable they would feel they had a prior claim to the land and its crop of grass and would resent and fight those who came later and intruded on their ranges.

In 1878, there was not a herd of cattle in the whole of the Big Horn Basin. But when the cattle started coming in 1879, it was as if a dam burst; for the next three years, cattle poured into the Basin.[2]

Charlie Russell lived in Montana during this time, and it was the primary inspiration for his art for the rest of his life. Russell painted Montana and its 1880s world with great fidelity, but his backdrop could just as easily have been Wyoming. The 1880s were the heyday of the cowboy, that glamorous figure painted by Russell and others, men on horseback chasing cattle, wearing outrageous accoutrements — chaps and spurs and those spectacular hats. The cowboy was remarkable, though, not just for his costume and his life but also for his character. To paraphrase Dickens, the cowboy was the best of men, he was the worst of men. Cowboys were, by and large, open, warm and generous young men, possessed of exceptional physical courage. But they could be intolerant, impetuous, and violent, ready to fight — literally — at the drop of a hat.

The Cattle Kings, as Paul Frison referred to them, had huge herds, as many as 25,000 cattle, and they ran their operations on the open range, on public lands.[3] That was not entirely a matter of choice. All of the land in the Big Horn Basin was public land, and there were statutory limitations on the amount that could be acquired from the federal government. Using all available legislation, the most land one could obtain was 1,120 acres.[4] Even to obtain this much acreage it was necessary to stretch the intent of the land acts. At the same time, it was estimated that in the West 2,560 acres were required for a herd of cattle sufficient to support only one family (at least 100 head).[5] The existing laws, so successful for distributing land in the wet eastern United States, were absurdly inadequate in the context of grazing in the dry West. Congressmen from the East could never come to terms with the dramatic difference in rainfall in the West and the practical significance of that fact.

The early 1880s in the Big Horn Basin were not marked by conflict. A few grangers moved into the stream valleys, and this settlement was no doubt irritating to the big ranchers. There really were not many of these newcomers, however, and, despite the annoyance caused by their presence, there was no serious trouble. There was no problem between sheepmen and cattlemen, either, because there were practically no sheep in the Basin. The first large herd of sheep did not arrive until 1886, when a man named "Dad" Worland drove in 7,700 head, and he was considerate enough to lose almost all of them in a blizzard in the spring of 1887.[6] For that matter, there was only scattered conflict between sheepmen and cattlemen in all of Wyoming until 1893.[7] That certainly was not the case elsewhere; in other parts of the West there had been very serious conflict. Sheepmen and cattlemen had been engaging in a particularly ugly series of guerilla skirmishes all over the Rocky Mountains, especially in the southern part. By 1892 there had been 44 reported incidents, with over 9,000 sheep and 27 men killed.[8] Wyoming was spared this terrible trouble in the 1880s and early 1890s for the simple reason that it had enough room for both animals.

So for several years, cattlemen had the Basin to themselves. They lived and worked in a kind of paradise. But paradise never lasts. People are less frequently driven from paradise than they debauch it themselves. Some of both happened in the Big Horn Basin. The magnificent parade of native animals the cattlemen first found was soon diminished.[9] The buffalo were nearly gone by the middle of 1885. There was no protection for any species, and a shameful slaughter began, perpetrated mainly by professional hunters although settlers and sportsmen also committed great waste.[10]

The ranchers were not distressed by the demise of the buffalo nor the onslaught against the wolf and the grizzly bear, but another event in the mid-1880s did bother them very much: Cattle prices began to slip. Beginning in the 1870s, cattle prices had swung upward strongly, peaking in 1882. They remained strong for the next two years, but in 1885 they started downward.[11] Because of that slippage, many cattle were left on the range, and they overburdened a range that was already becoming overstocked. A hot, dry summer further reduced the food available for each animal.[12] As a result, the cattle did not go into the winter of 1886–1887 in good shape.

That winter was the culminating catastrophe in this chain of events, a disaster that abruptly forced most of the big ranchers out of the Basin. The fury of that winter, the sheer savagery of it, has been described too many times to require treatment here.[13] The horrible winter of 1886–1887 was not the end for all the big ranches; a few of them survive today. The majority, however, were finished, and all of them were weakened. In 1887 another blow descended in the form of a ruinous drop in prices. There was a partial recovery in 1888, but it was only temporary, and prices remained poor into the 1890s.[14]

The bigger blow to the survivors, though, was not the price of cattle; it was the influx of settlers. The late 1880s witnessed a surge in the arrival of homesteaders, and some of the cowboys left the big ranching outfits (or were cast adrift when their employers went broke) and set up their own spreads. Almost all of these settlers, whether ranchmen or grangers, ran their own little herds. These people moved into many of the stream valleys, especially the Nowood and the Greybull; Henry Lovell's choice range on the floor of upper Shell Creek was almost completely removed from him.[15] The same trends occurred in other parts of Wyoming, most notably Johnson County east of the Big Horn Mountains.[16]

All over Wyoming, friction between the big ranchers and the small ranchers grew and grew, and it came to focus on one issue: mavericks, cattle born on the range and not yet branded. The open range system, with the presence of a lot of unbranded cattle on vast, empty tracts, certainly carried the potential for a serious problem with theft, and the large ranchers came to believe that the problem was *very* serious.

It is hard to say how much of the big cattlemen's resentment was rooted in anger toward the small cattlemen for having captured the best parts of the range. After all, if a man would take another man's range — if he would, in effect, steal his very livelihood, everything he had built over years — why wouldn't he also steal his cattle? Regardless of the origin of the feeling, the large ranchers finally came to believe that all small cattlemen were thieves, and they used the word "rustler" almost interchangeably with the phrase "small cattleman." They came to believe that in Johnson County, these rustlers had elected county officials, including the sheriff, who were little more than rustlers themselves and that it was virtually impossible to convict a cattle thief in that county, no matter how strong the evidence.[17]

Out of such feelings come extreme actions. In 1892, the large cattle-men of Wyoming committed the most extreme, the most outrageous action ever perpetrated in the state of Wyoming: They planned and carried out an invasion of Johnson County, the purpose of which was to assassinate county officials and small ranchers whom the large ranchers had identified as rustlers.[18]

Two small cattlemen were killed, but the attack was ultimately frus-trated as 200 local ranchers surrounded the 50 invaders (25 of whom were hired guns from Texas). The U.S. Cavalry came to the invaders' rescue and took them into custody. There followed an incredible series of events. Johnson County preferred charges against everyone in the invading army and asked the cavalry commander at Fort McKinney to turn these men over to county authorities for prosecution. The governor objected to this request on the grounds that the men would not be safe in Johnson County. They were taken instead to Cheyenne, and a change of venue was secured to Laramie County. The prisoners were allowed almost complete freedom, although Johnson County was being charged heavily for keeping them. In the middle of all this, Johnson County ran out of money; there was no help from the state. Johnson County was, in fact, bankrupt and had to turn all the prisoners loose on their own personal bonds. When the trial was finally convened in January, almost all of the Texans failed to appear. Worse, the chief witnesses for the prosecution had been kidnapped and taken to Nebraska. All the cases had to be dismissed.[19]

Only a few months after the invasion, another shocking event oc-curred that underlined how much the Big Horn Basin shared in the climate of conflict that brought about the Johnson County War. Two men, "Dab" Burch and Jack Bedford, were strongly suspected by the big ranchers of being very active rustlers. They lived on the Greybull River about six miles west of Otto, and their activities were watched constantly by range detectives. The big ranchers had employed many such detectives, and there were a lot of hard things said about what should be done about rustlers.

In September, Burch and Bedford were charged with stealing some horses, and a trial was to be held in Bonanza.[20] There was a hearing, but the trial was postponed. Three range detectives — Wickham, Rogers, and Peverly — attended this proceeding, and one of them, Peverly, provoked a fight with Bedford and Burch. This incident led in turn to other charges against the two men for disturbance of the peace. Convicted of these charges, both men were to be taken to Buffalo to serve time in jail.[21] Rogers was commissioned to accompany the prisoners, and Bedford had no objection, feeling that Rogers was a friend whom he could trust. Shortly after Rogers left Bonanza, however, he was joined by Wickham and Peverly. No one knows exactly what happened then, because there were no eyewitnesses, but all the circumstances indicate that the three range detectives gunned down Bedford and Burch in cold blood.[22]

There was evidence that at least one big rancher, Otto Franc, was involved in instigating this event. There is no doubt that Franc protected Rogers and Wickham from the wrath of the small ranchers and from arrest. Indeed, he assisted at least two of the men in fleeing to Montana; Franc took Rogers to Billings only a day ahead of a posse.[23] To people living through this period, the message from all these bloody events was abundantly clear: Men could take bold and violent actions in the name of protecting their property with virtual impunity.

## NOTES

1.  This incident is taken primarily from *Ten Sleep and No Rest* by Jack Gage (Casper: Prairie Publishing Company, 1958), 180.

2.  Charles Lindsay, *The Big Horn Basin* (Lincoln: University of Nebraska Press, 1932), 98. David John Wasden in *From Beaver to Oil* (Cody: Pioneer Printing & Stationery Company, 1973), notes at page 104 that J. D. Woodruff and Finn Burnett drove cattle across the Basin in the fall of 1878. Odds and ends of cattle had surely been driven through the Basin since the opening of the Montana goldfields, but these herds must have been very small. Woodruff's cattle were destined for the Shoshone Reservation.

3.  Paul Frison, *Great Days of The Cattle Kings, 1879–1886, Big Horn Basin, Johnson Co., Wyoming* (Worland: Paul Frison); Lindsay, *Big Horn Basin*, 100–103.

4.  George Watson Rollins, *The Struggle of the Cattlemen, Sheepmen and Settler for Control of Lands in Wyoming, 1867–1910* (New York: Arno Press, 1979), 182.

5.  Ibid, 169, 195, citing John Wesley Powell, *Report on the Lands of the Arid Region of the United States* (Washington: Government Printing Office, 1879), 29.

6.  Lindsay, *Big Horn Basin*, 133; John W. Davis, *Sadie and Charlie* (Worland: Washakie Publishing, 1989), 12.

7.  An ugly incident near Tie Siding in 1887, in which 2,600 sheep belonging to Charles Herbert were burned to death, is described in Edward Norris Wentworth, *America's Sheep Trails* (Ames: Iowa State College Press, 1948), 526. The description of the incident by Bill O'Neal, however, indicates that the fire was of "apparently accidental origins." Bill O'Neal, *Cattlemen v. Sheepherders* (Austin: Eakins Press, 1989), 121.

8.  O'Neal, *Cattlemen vs. Sheepherders*, 15.

9.  For a graphic description of the animal life in the Big Horn Basin in 1879, see Mrs. Bert Ainsworth, *To the Wilds of Wyoming, Pioneers of the Big Horn Basin in Wyoming* (College Place: Mrs. Bert Ainsworth, 1983), 55.

10. Bob Edgar, and Jack Turnell, *Brand of a Legend* (Cody: Stockade Publishing, 1978), 37. Edgar and Turnell write, "By 1890, the big game herds in the area had been reduced to almost nothing," 68. See also Wayne Gard, *The Great Buffalo Hunt* (Lincoln: University of Nebraska Press, 1959). Surprisingly, groups of buffalo were still encountered in the western part of the Basin into the 1890s and the last was not killed out of the Basin proper until the twentieth century. Interview of Tom Ball, Bureau of Land Management wildlife biologist, Worland, Wyoming, by author, March, 1991.

11. Lindsay, *Big Horn Basin*, 139, 140; Wasden, *Beaver to Oil*, 115.

12. Wasden, *Beaver to Oil*, 115; Rollins, *The Struggle of the Cattlemen*, 126.

13. For an excellent description of the fury of that winter in Wyoming, see Alfred Larson, "The Winter of 1886–87 in Wyoming," *Annals of Wyoming*, Vol. 14, No. 1 (January 1942), 5–9. See also Harold McCracken, *The Charles M. Russell Book* (Garden City, N. Y.: Doubleday & Company, Inc., 1957), 104, wherein Mr. McCracken tells of the origin of the famous watercolor sketch by Charlie Russell, *Waiting for a Chinook*.

14. Lindsay, *The Big Horn Basin*, 140; Larson, "The Winter of 1886–87 in Wyoming," 10.

15. Press Stephens and Gretel Ehrlich, eds., *The Shell Valley, an Oral History of Frontier Settlement* (The Shell Centennial Celebration, 1986), 84, 114, 234; Wasden, *Beaver to Oil*, 117; Lindsay, *Big Horn Basin*, 134–136.

16. That part of the Basin east of the Big Horn River but west of the mountains was also part of Johnson County.

17. There was a pretty good basis for this feeling. The presiding judge at an 1889 trial in which four men were acquitted of cattle stealing said: "Each of these four men who have been tried is guilty of the crime charged and it has been as clearly proved as any case that has come within my knowledge. And yet the jury has in each case set the prisoner free. I consequently refuse to go on with these cases. It might just as well be understood that there is no protection for property in Johnson County" (Wasden, *Beaver to Oil*, 125.) See also Helen Huntington Smith, *The War on Powder River, The History of an Insurrection* (New York: McGraw-Hill, 1966), 117.

    A factor that may have entered into juries' attitudes about stealing cattle was the widespread feeling that the Stock Grower's Association, through its control of roundups, was treating the small stockmen unfairly — was, in fact, appropriating mavericks to the large stockmen that should have gone to the small stockmen.

18. A. S. Mercer, *The Cattlemen's Invasion of Wyoming in 1892 (The Crowning Infamy of the Ages)*, (Norman: University of Oklahoma Press, 1954); Smith, *The War on Powder River*, 193, 194.

19. Smith, ibid, 246, 263, 264, 281, 282.

20. Bonanza no longer exists as a town; it was located about twenty miles upstream from Manderson, on the south bank of the Nowood River.

21. *Buffalo Bulletin*, 10/13/92; see also Wasden, *Beaver to Oil*, 128–131.

22. Lindsay, *Big Horn Basin*, 155, 156.

23. Lindsay indicates that at the time of the killings, Franc issued 5,000 rounds of ammunition to his crew and there was "extreme nervousness," as though a counter-attack was expected. Lindsay, *Big Horn Basin*, 131, 155, 156; Otto Franc diary, 12/16/92, 3/19, 3/20, and 3/30, 1893.

# 1909

## CHAPTER 2

By 1909, much had changed in Wyoming. The relentless pace of settlement meant that the day of the Cattle King was gone. A very few remained, but their importance was greatly diminished. In 1905, the governor of Wyoming, B. B. Brooks, described what had happened in the state: "Today, our cattle are owned by 5,000 different cattlemen and farmers, instead of by a few hundred outfits."[1]

The most profound change in the Big Horn Basin, though, was not the fading of the cattle barons but the coming of the farmer. After 1900, huge irrigation projects created hundreds of farms and new towns. The little ranch towns around the rim of the Basin, such as Ten Sleep, Hyattville, and Meeteetse, were eclipsed by these new agricultural communities in the dry center of the Basin. The Hanover and Big Horn canals produced Worland, the Garland Canal was responsible for Powell, and the Sidon and Elk canals were the genesis of Lovell. Towns such as Cody and Basin were greatly enlarged by the irrigation projects around them.

One thing that had not changed was the administration of the public lands by the federal government. There were no regulations and no restrictions except for those on outright sale of land. The fundamental problems associated with grazing on the public domain remained, and so did the fundamental sources of conflict.[2] The only difference was that it was no longer big cattlemen against small cattlemen — it was all cattlemen against all sheepmen. The sheep and cattle wars, which had avoided Wyoming for so many years, had arrived with a vengeance.

Through early 1909, there had been at least six killings in Wyoming in over twenty-nine incidents related to this conflict. More than 18,000 sheep had been slaughtered; they were shot, burned, or clubbed to death, driven over cliffs, dynamited, or poisoned. Sheepwagons had been burned and wrecked, and dogs were shot, clubbed to death, or burned.[3] This carnage — which is almost certainly understated — occurred in the vast majority of cases when cowboys raided sheep camps. Sheep camp raids were so common that the historical records of such attacks are surely incomplete. Information is usually available regarding the killings, but sometimes it is ambiguous. William O'Neal describes one incident that occurred in Natrona County in 1895. A man named Jacob Ervay shot two sheepmen, George E. Howard and William Kimberly, and from the description it seems that Mr. Kimberly should have died from the wounds he received, but apparently he did not. Also not included among the seven murder victims is fourteen-year-old Willie Nickell, who was killed by Tom Horn in 1901. The act did not occur as the result of a raid, although it was committed by a stock detective against the son of a sheepman who had been having a long-term feud with his cattle rancher neighbors.[4]

Tom Horn was hanged because a jury was convinced that he had executed a teenaged boy. Remarkably, though, out of all the many fights and raids in the whole state of Wyoming, there had been only one conviction of a crime. That occurred after the only shoot-out in which a cattleman was killed, an incident near Sheridan on June 7, 1893, when sheepman William Jones shot cattle rancher John D. Adams. A Johnson County jury rejected Jones' claim of self-defense and found him guilty of second-degree murder; he was sentenced to twenty-two years in the penitentiary and was not released until 1907.[5]

The obvious reason for all this conflict was the absence of law. The federal government made grazing land available to two groups when the grass was not sufficient for both, then failed to police the use of the land in any way. It was an invitation to conflict. But merely to make this observation is both to state too much and too little. The conflict between sheepmen and cattlemen also occurred for reasons beyond competition for grass, and this competition was a much more complex matter than it might initially appper.

The other reasons began with the cowboy's perception of himself. He was very proud of the athletic skills required in his occupation, of his ability to ride and rope and subdue a big, strong, contrary critter such as a longhorn steer. He relished the image of himself as a man on horseback. Next to this image, the lonely sheepherder shuffling along behind his docile little woollies was, in cowboys' minds, a contemptible figure.[6] There was another reason for this feeling of contempt. Sheepherders were, in the main, Mexicans or Basques. The turn of the century was a time of pervasive racial prejudice, and cowboys were as subject to it as those in any other part of society. Thus, sheepherders were cursed as "greasers," or "Boscoes."[7] Still another reason was religious prejudice, especially in southwestern Wyoming, where sheepmen were frequently Mormon.[8]

As to the complexity of the competition for grass, it must be remembered that the rivalry between cattlemen and sheepmen typically did not begin for ten, fifteen, or even twenty years after cattlemen had first settled a range. The idea that the first person to use a resource was entitled to priority was well established in the nineteenth century. That idea was embedded in the Homestead and Desert Land Entry acts. The distribution of water in Wyoming is governed by the concept of "prior appropriation"; the first to use water has the first right to it. Cattlemen developed concepts of "range rights" and "accustomed ranges," and these worked well to apportion the ranges between cattlemen long before sheep appeared on the scene.

The problem was that these concepts had absolutely no existence in law. As George Watson Rollins wrote, "there were no such things as 'range rights,' accustomed ranges, rights secured by prior discovery and utilization, or possessory rights due to occupation."[9] When sheepmen arrived, they felt, and were certainly correct as a matter of law, that they had just as much right to the grass on the public range as the cattleman. This feeling led sheepmen to "encroach" on established cattle ranges, and their actions led the cattlemen to see the sheepmen as the aggressors in the conflict. As the cattlemen saw it, they were simply minding their own business, tending their ranges, when sheepmen barged in on them.

Sheep grazed deeply into grass roots, and when large droves were driven on weaker grasslands, these pastures became useless for cattle until seasonal rains later fell. So when (to use the words of cattlemen) "predatory" flockmasters would "pirate" the winter range of cattlemen, it could have a devastating effect on a cattleman's operation. Such actions were usually taken by operators known as "tramp operators," sheepmen who just moved about on the range, were based nowhere, paid no local taxes, and contributed little to the local economy. These operators were a special target for the anger of cattlemen, but this anger spilled over to the resident sheepmen.[10]

Added to the very real harm sheep could cause were imagined damages, the sorts of allegations that always arise when people have emotional disagreements. These included the notion that whenever sheep grazed a range they tainted the ground so that cattle would not eat the remaining grass.[11] This idea persisted long after it was proven obviously fallacious by the many stockmen who began running both sheep and cattle.

Regardless of whether all their feelings were well based, cattlemen sincerely and deeply believed that sheep represented a threat to their whole way of life. This point of view was best expressed in a letter written by a Uinta County resident to the *Evanston News Register* in 1894. He spoke of how the range north of the Union Pacific Railroad had once been the finest cattle range in Wyoming, supporting 50,000 head, but how in the last five years that number had at least been halved. He blamed this whole situation on "the little tinkling sheep bell which has sounded the death knell of the cattle industry in this vicinity."[12]

The sheepmen's perspective was quite different. They believed the cattlemen to be the aggressors in the conflict, because so often it was the cattlemen who resorted to force. More than that, the force used by cowboys was vastly disproportionate to the alleged offense. Lurking just below the surface, cowboys had a deep and wide rowdy streak, and a raid on a sheep camp was a perfect excuse to release it.

The exact right and wrong of the sheep and cattle wars is a subject that is still debated, but no one has ever denied the seriousness of the problem — certainly not in the Big Horn Basin, which received more than its share of this terrible trouble.

Edward Norris Wentworth described a general pattern in range conflicts. They began with warnings for sheepmen to stay out; then the setting of "deadlines," boundaries that sheep could not cross; and finally violent confrontation.[13] Patterns very much like this occurred in the Big Horn Basin. It was made known early that much of the area along the Nowood River was considered cattle country and that sheep were not wanted. Then, in 1897, a committee of cattlemen consisting of "Bear" George McClellan (so named because of his skill at shooting grizzly bears in the Big Horn Mountains), G. E. Shaw, Dave Picard, and Joe Emge met with some sheep owners at Lost Cabin and divided the range; in other words, they established a deadline. It extended from the head of Kirby Creek north to the mouth of Paintrock Creek, from there to the summit of the Big Horn Mountains, from there back to Ten Sleep, then south along the base of the Big Horns to a point near Lone Tree Creek (near Nowood), and then back to the point of beginning. In the letter in which Bear George announced all this to Governor W. A. Richards (he was then managing Richards' ranch on the Nowood), McClellan also wrote, "I don't have much faith in the matter." But he hoped it would work as it could "prevent possible trouble of a serious nature."[14]

McClellan expressed the purpose of this exercise as one "to divide the range in some manner agreeable to both Sheep Men and the settlers."[15] Sheepmen, again, viewed the matter in quite a different light. Wentworth describes the attitude of sheepmen toward deadlines: "The method could scarcely be termed a 'division,' but rather the arbitrary setting aside of lands for the exclusive use of cattle."[16]

Once established, a deadline was taken very seriously. Indeed, contrary to the hope of McClellan, such lines seemed to aggravate hostilities; they became the focus of contention. As early as September 1897, some sheepmen disregarded the Nowood deadline, and shots were fired into their tents.[17] Frank Ainsworth had settled on Crooked Creek (almost twenty miles south of Ten Sleep) and started running 500 head of sheep before the deadline was set. The cattlemen allowed him to keep his herd, because it was already there, as long as he did not exceed roughly 500 head. The cowboys in the area did not like the situation, though, and for many years, Ainsworth remained apprehensive that this fragile arrangement would no longer be honored.[18]

On the west side of the Basin, the first stirrings of trouble also began in 1897. Otto Franc wrote about making visits to sheepmen in March 1897 as part of a delegation of cattlemen: "We are going to see the sheepmen to come to an agreement regarding a line on a reserved country for the cattleman." He added: "We succeed in getting them to agree." The "agreement" must have seemed shaky by August 1900, however, because Franc then wrote of going with a man named Anderson to Colonel Pickett's to discuss what to do "in case the sheepmen attempt to drive their sheep across our leases."[19]

The cattlemen of the upper Shoshone Valley organized in 1901, forming a Stockmen's Protective Association. Deadlines were established there and sheepmen threatened.[20]

The first major violent incidents involving cattle ranchers and sheepherders in the Big Horn Basin occurred in 1902 in the Wood River area:[21] Two bands of sheep were "rimrocked" (herded together and pushed over a steep incline) by unknown riders. Just two days later, a sheepman named John Sayles was confronted by thirteen masked riders. Sayles insisted on his right to graze his livestock on public lands during the summer, and for some reason the cowboys left him alone. But in another incident, three cowboys, Harvey Webb, Ezra Nostrum, and Herb Brink, pushed a sheepwagon off a knoll and watched it go "tail over double-trees into a coulee." Much worse was soon to come. During the winter of 1902–1903, William Minnick moved his sheep into a large basin between Black Mountain and the head of No Water Creek. The band was either inside the 1897 deadline or close enough that some of the sheep frequently grazed over the line.[22] One way or another, the presence of this herd was noted by cattlemen and created deep anger.

One night in the spring of 1903, William Minnick's brother Ben was in charge of the camp. He was only about twenty years old and was apparently a trusting young man; when a rider knocked on the door of his sheepwagon, he invited the visitor in. Instead of coming in, though, the rider shot Ben Minnick in the back, severing his spinal cord. Amazingly, when the rider realized that his victim was not William Minnick but Ben, he apologized for the shooting, said it was an accident, and helped place the wounded man on his bed. Then the rider was joined by two accomplices, and while Ben Minnick was suffering his death throes, the three of them shot and clubbed to death 200 sheep.

Ben Minnick died that night, and his body was taken to Nowood. The episode was not over, though. Two men were employed to skin the dead sheep, and while they were working they were surrounded by armed riders. One of the men, Henry Jensen, explained that they were just doing what they had been hired for, and the riders finally left.

There was great public indignation over this event, and three arrests were made. The charges were eventually dropped, however, because the killer could never be positively identified.

Only a year passed before there was another ugly incident in the Big Horn Basin. The June 4, 1904, issue of the *Thermopolis Record* reported the death of Lincoln A. Morrison, a prominent sheepman. Morrison was at his sheep camp near Kirby Creek, north of Thermopolis, when he was allegedly shot and killed without warning. The *Record* was mistaken, though — Morrison was very seriously wounded, but he was not killed. An old herder nursed him back to health. [23]

In the summer of 1905, Louis A. Gantz moved a large band of sheep into the Big Horn Basin. On August 24, 1905, ten masked men rode into his camp on Shell Creek; they shot, clubbed, and dynamited 4,000 sheep.[24] Two horses were shot and killed, other property worth $8,000 was burned (including three sheep wagons with harnesses and provisions), and the sheepdogs were tied to the burning wagons and burned to death.[25] The apparent offense warranting this severe penalty was that the herders were moving through the country too slowly and their sheep were eating all the grass. The herders were told to leave the country and never return.[26]

The *Garland Guard* published the day after the raid, and its headlines read: "Law Abiding be Damned! Lou Gantz suffers appalling loss of property on Big Horn Mountains at Hands of Unknown Devils."[27] It was not just property Gantz lost, either; he died a month later. The cause of his death is not known, but his shock and dismay at this horrible event surely contributed to it. It was generally felt that local cattlemen had conducted the raid, but once again there were no arrests.[28]

The friction continued in 1906. Ainsworth related how the cowboys would play "little jokes (?)" on the herders. When they found a herder away from his wagon, they would go in and help themselves to his food and then do something to tell the herder they had been there, such as spilling molasses all over his bed.[29] There were other raids in the Nowood area around this time that did not produce the huge damage of some of the more publicized raids. Marvin B. Rhodes wrote that the cowboys on one occasion clubbed sheep with rolling pins, which they then left at the scene. Afterwards, cattlemen sarcastically observed that the raid must have been the work of the neighborhood women.[30]

The slight lull of 1906 did not last long, for in 1907 there were three big raids. The first occurred in March in the Owl Creek valley northwest of Thermopolis. Fifteen local cattlemen had established a deadline on Owl Creek, but sheepmen entered the area anyway. The flock of a sheepman named Wisner was attacked; the camp was burned and 400 sheep killed. Only a week later, twelve masked riders hit a big camp; the herders were driven away, and 4,000 sheep owned by Hugh Dickey were destroyed.[31]

The third big raid in 1907 occurred on Shell Creek. J. L. Lynn had moved into this area, with his headquarters at the mouth of Shell Creek and his pasture on Trapper Creek, several miles east.[32] Lynn was not a passive character like some sheepmen were. He brought in a big herd, somewhere between 10,000 and 15,000 head, and employed gunmen to protect the operation. Lynn frequently moved his whole flock around and, as one cattlemen put it, "his sheep would just sweep an area like a horde of locusts."[33] The feelings against Lynn were especially strong, and when the cattlemen got their chance in early May, every man in the area except Arthur Flitner joined in a raid.[34] Lynn had pastured a band of about 3,000 head on Trapper Creek with only two men in charge. The cattlemen descended on the herd, and at gunpoint the herders were made to wade into the frigid waters of the creek. Then, with the help of dynamite, the entire flock was rimrocked into the creek. There is some dispute over the number of sheep killed, estimates ranging from 350 to 3,500, but from the description of the event, almost all of that herd must have been killed.[35]

David John Wasden asserts that law enforcement officials were only halfhearted in the matter and that the investigation was "casual," though his basis for this opinion is not revealed.[36] It is true, however, that even though the identity of the raiders was common knowledge in the area, no arrests were made.

The following year brought another lull in the Basin, although a Lander sheepman's flocks were hit just outside the Basin while grazing on the Shoshone Indian Reservation; 300 sheep were destroyed.[37]

After several years of triumphant hooliganism, one would expect sheepmen to have been deeply depressed about the future of their industry. In fact, quite the opposite attitude was building. The number of sheep in the state had been steadily increasing; the 1910 figures would show that the value of sheep was distinctly higher than the value of cattle.[38] More than that, the production from sheep was much greater, owing to the fact that two products came from sheep, wool, and mutton.[39]

So in 1909, sheep, not cattle, were ascendant in Wyoming, and woolgrowers had begun to flex their muscles. After several years of frustrating efforts, in 1905 a statewide sheepman's organization was finally founded, the Wyoming Woolgrower's Association. The association was created to combat sheep scab but very quickly started assisting sheep raid prosecutions.[40]

Even with this new development, however, it would have been hard to be optimistic about law enforcement in the Big Horn Basin in 1909, hard to believe that there could be much of an improvement over the dismal record of the last several years. The Big Horn Basin was then one big county and had been since 1897. Policing this huge and awkward political unit, with about 5,000 people settled over 12,000 square miles, was a daunting prospect.[41] And the officeholders in the county seat, Basin, would have undercut any feelings of optimism.

The county attorney was only twenty-five years old, had only practiced law a little over two years, and had just been elected to his post.[42] Percy Metz was so green that during the 1908 election campaign his father, an experienced and skilled attorney, promised that he would help his son without charge if Percy got in over his head, a sadly probable event.[43] It was surprising that Metz was elected at all; apparently his father's promise influenced the voters. Metz did have a few things going for him. He was a likable young man (his opponent derisively referred to him as "the high school kid") who was very energetic.[44] He campaigned hard, although his efforts were sometimes misdirected. He spent one whole day in what he thought was the northern part of the county and only later discovered that the voters he had been talking to were all in Montana.[45]

The sheriff, Felix Alston, had a little more seasoning, but his presence was still none too reassuring. Alston was an old Texas cowboy who had followed the longhorn steer into the country in 1892.[46] He was a smallish man, of medium height, but slender. Most people knew him simply as

"Felix." He had worked a few years as a deputy and was elected sheriff in 1906. He had many friends among the cattlemen, and they had supported him, thinking he would be friendly to their interests.[47]

Life, unfortunately, does not usually wait until people are fully pre- pared to handle every challenge. Both of these men, with all their limitations, were very soon to face the biggest challenge of their lives. Indeed, it would define and determine the rest of their lives. And it would arise in the Upper Nowood.

## NOTES

1. Gov. B. B. Brooks' message to Eighth State Legislature, 1/11/05.

2. This problem did not affect U.S. Forest Service lands, which were governed by leasing arrangements after 1905. Only one attack on sheep took place thereafter on National Forests. Edward Norris Wentworth, *America's Sheep Trails* (Ames: Iowa State College Press, 1948), 543.

3. This information was gleaned from several sources, including, in their approximate order of importance: O'Neal, *Cattlemen vs. Sheepherders;* Wasden, *Beaver to Oil;* Rollins, *The Struggle of the Cattlemen;* Wentworth, *America's Sheep Trails;* and Lindsay, *The Big Horn Basin.* The listing of the various incidents by these authors is not uniform, nor are the descriptions of the incidents themselves. To obtain a fair picture of the full scope of the conflict, however, all of these historians should be read. Even then, from various general allusions, one has to conclude that there were many "minor" episodes not described by any historian. In many instances, the reports are simply that sheep were destroyed or that a band was attacked, with no numbers given (O'Neal, at 92 and 118, Lindsay at 232, for instance). When totaling the number of sheep killed in Wyoming, no figures from any of these indefinite descriptions were included.

4. O'Neal, *Cattlemen vs. Sheepherders,* 93, 100–107.

5. Ibid, 92; Elnora L. Frye, *Atlas of Wyoming Outlaws of the Territorial Penitentiary* (Laramie: Jelm Mountain Publications, 1990), 149.

6. O'Neal, *Cattlemen vs. Sheepherders,* 2, 3; Rollins, *The Struggle of the Cattlemen,* 247, 248. Lowell H. Harrison, "The Cattle-Sheep Wars," *Mississippi Valley Historical Review,* Vol. 46, No. 4 (March 1960).

7. Rollins, *The Struggle of the Cattlemen,* 250; Harrison, "The Cattle-Sheep Wars," 24.

8. O'Neal, *Cattlemen vs. Sheepherders,* 95, 120.

9. Rollins, *The Struggle of the Cattlemen,* 286.

10. Wentworth, *America's Sheep Trails,* vii, 522, 526; Percy Metz speech before the Park County Historical Society, Cody, Wyoming, 6/9/61. Tapes of this speech and others by Metz are available from several sources, including the Washakie County Museum and Cultural Center in Worland and the Wyoming Division of Parks and Cultural Resources, Historical Research and Publications, in Cheyenne.

11. Wentworth, *America's Sheep Trails*, 523.

12. *Evanston News Register*, 3/30/94.

13. Wentworth, *America's Sheep Trails*, 524.

14. Notes of Paul Frison from an 1897 letter from George McClellan to Gov. W. A. Richards, papers of Paul Frison in the author's possession.

15. Ibid.

16. Wentworth, *America's Sheep Trails*, 524.

17. O'Neal, *Cattlemen vs. Sheepherders*, 97.

18. Ainsworth, *To the Wilds of Wyoming*, 155, 158–162, 176, 177.

19. Otto Franc diary, 3/22/97, 8/27/00.

20. Wasden, *Beaver to Oil*, 141.

21. The Wood River is a tributary of the Greybull River that runs into the Greybull about five miles west of Meeteetse. The following discussion of these Wood River incidents is taken from O'Neal, *Cattlemen vs. Sheepherders*, 118.

22. Ray Pendergraft, *Washakie: A Wyoming County History* (Basin: Saddlebag Books, 1985), 44 and O'Neal, *Ibid*, are the primary sources for the Minnick episode.

23. Bob Edgar and Jack Turnell, *Lady of Legend* (Cody: Stockade Publishing, 1979), 36–37. Morrison did not die until 1967.

24. Wentworth, *America's Sheep Trails*, 525.

25. Wasden, *Beaver to Oil*, 142; Wentworth, *America's Sheep Trails*, 525.

26. Wentworth, *America's Sheep Trails*, 525.

27. *Garland Guard*, 8/25/05.

28. Wasden, *Beaver to Oil*, 142.

29. Ainsworth, *To the Wilds of Wyoming*, 176.

30. Marvin B. Rhodes, *The Rest That Came, A History of the Ten Sleep Raid*, (unpublished manuscript available in the Miscellaneous Files on Ten Sleep Raids, Wyoming State Archives, Cheyenne), 11.

31. O'Neal, *Cattlemen vs. Sheepherders*, 126.

32. Ibid, 124.

33. Press Stephens and Gretel Ehrlich, eds., *The Shell Valley, an Oral History of Frontier Settlement* (Shell, Wyoming: A Project of the Shell Centennial Celebration, 1986), Richard Whaley, Stan Flitner, 89.

34. *Lovell Chronicle*, 5/4/07. The raiders stopped at the Flitner ranch but Arthur declined to join them. Interview of Dave Flitner, Shell, Wyoming, by the author, November 1991.

35. Wasden, *Beaver to Oil*, 141; O'Neal, *Cattlemen vs. Sheepherders*, 124; Lindsay, *Big Horn Basin*, 232; Stephens and Ehrlich, *The Shell Valley*, Paul Frison, 88, David Wasden, 141.

36. Wasden, *Beaver to Oil*, 141.

37. O'Neal, *Cattlemen vs. Sheepherders*, 126.

38. There were 736,872 cattle, as opposed to 5,408,241 sheep; this translated into a value for sheep of $29,724,310 and for cattle of $22,857,802. Rollins, *The Struggle of the Cattlemen*, 242.

39. George S. Walker, comp., *Sheep Owners of Wyoming, 1910 Directory* (Cheyenne: The S. A. Bristol Co., Printers, 1910), 5, 17; Rollins, *Struggle of the Cattlemen*, 246.

40. Rollins, *The Struggle of the Cattlemen*, 246; See Joe LeFors, *Wyoming Peace Officer, An Autobiography* (Laramie: Laramie Printing Company, 1953), 166, regarding wool-growers' assistance in Crook County. In 1907, the state woolgrowers established a standing reward of $1,000 for the arrest of any person implicated in a raid on a sheep camp. *Cheyenne Daily Leader*, 4/7/09.

41. *Alexander v. State*, 20 Wyo. 241, at 250, 123 P. 68.

42. Vera Saban, *He Wore a Stetson: The Story of Judge Percy W. Metz* (Basin: Big Horn Book Company, 1980), 2, 44; "Western Son," unattributed manuscript in the possession of the author, 2.

43. *Big Horn County Rustler*, 5/28/09.

44. Rhodes, *The Rest That Came*, 13; Percy W. Metz speech to the Park County Historical Society, 6/19/61.

45. Percy W. Metz speech to the Park County Historical Society, 6/9/61.

46. Rhodes, *The Rest That Came*, 4; Alston was about forty in 1909, which, in the Big Horn Basin at that time, was considered old. Idem, 16, Note 17.

47. *Sweet Smell of Sagebrush: A Prisoner's Diary, 1903–1912* (Rawlins: Friends of the Old Pen, 1990), 90; Rhodes, *The Rest That Came*, 26.

# The Upper Nowood CHAPTER 3

The Upper Nowood, as it has been known for over a century, is the part of the Nowood River drainage south of Ten Sleep. It runs almost due north and south for over fifty miles along the base of the Big Horn Mountains. The tributaries of the Nowood all come from the east, out of the Big Horns. There are draws on the west, draining the very dry badlands, but water flows only during infrequent heavy rains.

The Upper Nowood is an area of great natural beauty. Each of the little streams coming out of the Big Horns enters the lowlands through a gorge with sheer rock faces, which in the Upper Nowood is always referred to as a canyon. Some streams, such as Otter Creek, have carved a whole system of canyons emanating from the mountains. Otter Creek has Middle Fork and Dry Fork Canyons leading into North Fork Canyon and another pair of forks that become South Fork Canyon. North Fork and South Fork canyons reach the base of the Big Horns only about a quarter of a mile apart, where their two streams join in one of the most pleasing settings in the Big Horn Basin.

Some of these canyons — Deep Creek Canyon is the most startling example — have chiseled walls dropping straight down several hundred feet. Some broaden, such as upper Ten Sleep Canyon and the South Fork of Otter Creek immediately below the junction of its two branches. Some of the smaller canyons, such as Spring Creek and Crooked Creek, are compact and elegant. All of these canyons are unique, and are splendid instances of God's handiwork.

But the country west of the base of the Big Horns is even more distinctive because of the diversity of the terrain. There are buttes and bluffs and bumps in countless profusion. In one stretch south of Big Trails, there is an area known as the "Red Wall." For many miles, red buttes jut out, stretching back toward the mountains like great dust-red ocean liners lying at pier. Throughout the Upper Nowood, the hills and ridges and formations have such variety that they present the sun with an infinite variation of surfaces, so that the most remarkable thing about the place are the shadows, the play of the sun on the land.

Even in the shabby month of March, when the snow has left the land, revealing a disheveled brown and gray earth, the Upper Nowood is beautiful. When spring arrives in April and May, and the little valleys fill with kelly green grass and the streamside foliage leafs out and the Christmas colors of the green cedars against the red soil seem especially sharp, the Upper Nowood is resplendent.

Proceeding south (upstream) from Ten Sleep, the area can conveniently be separated into three parts. The distance from Ten Sleep to the village of Big Trails is about twenty miles, and a traveler crosses three streams: Spring Creek, six or seven miles south; Otter Creek, another five or six miles further south; and Crooked Creek, six more miles south. Two miles later one arrives at Big Trails, which sits near yet another stream, Little Canyon Creek.

The second part of the Upper Nowood extends from Big Trails to the town of No Wood, another twenty miles upstream. After Little Canyon Creek, no other creeks are met for three or four miles. A collection of streams is then encountered: Red Bank Creek, a spring stream about three miles long with a slight but steady flow, empties into Box Elder Creek, and a mile later Box Elder goes into Cherry Creek. These waters then flow into the Nowood only a half mile to the west. Five miles above this area is Mahogany Buttes, where the Nowood, just after being joined by Deep Creek, cuts through a huge fault.

Above Mahogany Buttes is the last third of the Upper Nowood, containing the headwaters of the stream. This was not cattle country in 1909 but sheep country. Only a few years after he settled his cattle on Ten Sleep Creek in 1880, W. P. Noble moved his ranch south, behind Mahogany Buttes, and formed a partnership with Fred Bragg. As Noble and Bragg, these two men had a very large operation, running both sheep and cattle.[1]

The people who lived in the Upper Nowood in 1909 knew their country well. Each of them carried a mental map of the area, and it was essentially a skeletal diagram of the streams. In this livestock country, everything people did revolved about the stream on which they lived, and so that mental map had all the ranches placed in their proper places along the proper streams.

On Ten Sleep Creek, the map would have included a number of ranches, starting with George Saban's Bay State Ranch. The Bay State was the biggest ranch in that area, and it had been there for over twenty years, having been formed by Massachusetts investors in 1888. It was one of the very few big ranches to come in after the 1886–1887 blizzard.[2]

George Saban was as curious a mixture of qualities as one is ever likely to find in a human being. Saban was born in Maine, but when he was six his family moved to Nebraska, and at only sixteen he came to Wyoming to work as a cowboy.[3] As an adult he was about medium height and rather stocky, with dark features, supposedly because of a great deal of Indian blood.[4] He first secured a job with the Embar in 1888, but it was only a few years before he took over that outfit's horse ranch, near Shell. In fact, this horse ranch was owned by Saban and Colonel J. L. Torrey as partners.[5] At the same time, Saban homesteaded land below Shell.[6]

In 1897 he married Bertha Whaley the daughter of W. T. Whaley, a Shell cattleman. They eventually had six children, although two died in childhood.[7]

Saban was athletic, a skilled cowboy, and a superb horseman. One historian wrote that "he sat his horse like a centaur" and told of a poem inspired by Saban's horsemanship, entitled "Saban, of Shell."[8] He was quiet and industrious, a nondrinker who rarely cursed. He did not even carry a gun (a distinct rarity in those days).[9] Saban was much admired and very popular among the cowboys, a man they almost instinctively looked to for leadership. He seemed to be the ideal embodiment of how the cowboys saw themselves, or at least how they wanted people to see them. Saban had many friends, including the man then occupying the sheriff's office in Basin. A few years later, when the relationship between them had changed from friendship to warden and prisoner, Felix Alston would still describe him as "square as a brick."[10]

Paul Frison said that George Saban "had the heartiest laugh of any man I ever knew. . . . George loved to ride among his cattle and he always had one of his children by his side."[11]

George Saban seemed almost too good to be true. And he was. For one thing, his quiet and solid exterior concealed a great deal of restlessness. At some point during his time with Torrey, he decided to move his life in a completely different direction. He went to Chicago, where he attended for a time the YMCA Business College.[12] Only two months after he was married, he went off to Florida to join Colonel Torrey's Rough Riders, a trip that became something of a fiasco; Saban never got to Cuba.[13]

But there was a much more disturbing aspect to George Saban. Living within this admirable man was another one, one with a very ugly side. Saban was one of the ringleaders of a lynch mob that hit the Basin jail in 1903. The mob killed three men, two of whom had committed murders

(J. P. Walters and Tom Gorman), and a deputy sheriff. Saban is supposed to have been identified when someone recognized his voice giving the command, as the mob was leaving, to "Fall in." Saban was indicted, along with six other men, but all of these charges were eventually dropped.[14] Saban was also almost certainly one of the riders who carried out the devastating raid against Lou Gantz in 1905 and was probably involved in other sheep raids as well.[15]

The odd thing is that Saban had himself run sheep in the northern part of the Basin. He lost about half of them in a storm near Garland some time around 1904 and then got out of the sheep business. Around 1906 or 1907, Saban dissolved the partnership with Torrey and for a brief time moved to a homestead in the Broken Back country, just north of Ten Sleep.[16] Shortly after that, he and his father-in-law purchased the Bay State.[17]

A number of men worked with and for the Bay State. In 1909 many landless men lived in the Upper Nowood and worked for ranches, but they did not always fit the traditional pattern of employees earning wages solely from one employer. Many ran their own small herds and were looking to obtain their own ranches. These hands would frequently work for just room and board and would move about where their labor was needed. The expression for this was "riding the grub line."[18] Then, too, men who did own ranches frequently traded labor with their neighbors. They did so not just for economic reasons but also because these men enjoyed one another's company. Out of an occupation that might have been a lonely one, the men of that time enjoyed very rich social lives.

Among the men associated with the Bay State was Wes Harvey, who stayed at the ranch but had his own herd, which he ranged around Ten Sleep. Sydney Ingram had been working at the Bay State only through the winter, and he also ran cattle of his own.[19] There were three or four other men who could be found at the Bay State, including Charles Runge and Earl Pickett, the son of area rancher George Pickett.[20] William C. Miller, who owned a ranch on Broken Back, was frequently at the Bay State, as was Milton Alexander, who owned a good-sized ranch fifteen miles up the Nowood. Still another man who spent a great deal of time at the Bay State was Ed Eaton. Eaton lived in a small cabin on the Nowood a couple of miles north of Ten Sleep.[21] Eaton had been a cattleman, the foreman of the Bay State, but then sold out, and he and a partner bought the Luxus bar in Basin. When the business did not work out, Eaton returned to the Nowood, and he was starting to build up another herd. He was a fifty-four- year-old bachelor then, tall and quite slender, with a reputation for being quarrelsome and moody.[22]

The Bay State was about a mile and a half east of Ten Sleep, and its headquarters were on the south bank of Ten Sleep Creek. About a quarter-mile further east and on the north side of the creek was Jake Frison's ranch. Frison brought his family to the Ten Sleep Valley in 1901; he had loaded all of them and all of their possessions in a wagon, left their home in Colorado, and driven north.[23] Frison was an intelligent and confident man. He had a distinctive speaking voice, high pitched with a rapid delivery.[24]

There were several small spreads closer to the town of Ten Sleep, which was then just a few businesses and a few residences. The most substantial business in Ten Sleep was the hardware store, owned by Walter Fiscus. It sold just about everything and was even the site of a central switchboard for the new telephone system, which extended all the way up the Nowood. There were two phone lines, the "granger," or "farmer's," line and the Redbank Telephone Company line. Both of them were all-party lines — that is, open to everybody on the line. They were superb conduits for gossip.[25]

One of the small ranches around Ten Sleep was the Paradise outfit, a name given to the combined lands of George Sutherland, Oscar Arnett, and James Richardson. These three men employed a hotheaded young man named Arthur McVay.[26]

Spring Creek, the next significant stream south, is much smaller than Ten Sleep Creek, but it was the location of almost as many ranches in 1909. When Spring Creek emerges from the mountain (in the Upper Nowood, "the mountain" refers to the Big Horn Mountains), at first it flows more north than west. After about a mile, it jogs west a short distance before heading northwest for three or four miles. This portion of the creek flows through a broad valley. It is not like the Ten Sleep Valley, where a large and relatively flat area is abruptly interrupted on both sides by hills and bluffs. Instead, this valley slopes steadily southward, away from Spring Creek. In the last half-mile before Spring Creek reaches the Nowood, the valley narrows as low ridges close in.

The Greet ranch sat near the mouth of Spring Creek. George Greet, who was English, came to Wyoming by way of Indiana and in 1891 homesteaded this spot. There were eight children in the family, the youngest of whom were twin boys named Fred and Frank.[27] During the Greets' first few years in Wyoming, many Indians still hunted and traveled in the area. One day, the men sharpened their axes on a grindstone and then went east to the mountain to cut corral poles, leaving Mrs. Greet with the twin boys. A number of Shoshone braves then approached the cabin; they were flashing knives around and speaking to Mrs. Greet in an animated manner. She knew nothing of the Shoshone language, but the situation frightened her, and she fled the cabin with the young boys, looking for her husband. When she and her husband returned several hours later, they found moccasin tracks all around the grindstone, but nothing else had been touched. It seems the Indians had been trying to tell Mrs. Greet they wanted to use the grindstone to sharpen their knives.[28]

In 1909, the Greet Ranch ran 500 to 600 head of cattle, which in those days was an average herd size , and the ranch was owned by the twin boys, Fred and Frank Greet, then twenty-three years old.[29] These two young bachelors had decided to expand their operation, however, and they had just purchased Joe Henry's ranch, about ten miles upstream on the Nowood. In turn, they were selling their Spring Creek place to a young couple from Lander, Porter and Lizzie Lamb.[30]

The next family upstream on Spring Creek was Elmer Chatfield's. Chatfield came to Spring Creek about the same time as the Greets, and he ran about the same number of cattle.[31] During early 1909, the Chatfields employed a cowhand named George Rogers.[32] The Chatfields sold out to the Taylor brothers in 1914 and moved to Worland, but the family contributed something to the area that remains today; they had two daughters, Helen and Marian, after whom two lakes in the Cloud Peak Wilderness Area were named.[33]

Just above the Chatfields were the Allemands, Joe and Ada. Joe was French; he was from St. Bonnet, a town in the Alps of southeastern France. As a young man he came across the Atlantic and was naturalized, and he had been in the United States for more than twenty years. He courted a local girl, Adeline Smith, whose father was the Big Trails postmaster; they were married in about 1900 and had since lived on Spring Creek.[34] Joe was at least ten years older than Ada, and it is not known why she selected him over other eligible men. There were many more men than women in the Big Horn Basin then; Ada was attractive, and she could have had her pick of fine, strong young men. Perhaps she chose Joe because he was gentle and easygoing, perhaps because she admired him for persevering and making something of his life in a country so far from the land of his birth.

There is a picture of Joe and Ada taken in 1908. Between them, their son, who was then seven or eight, leans comfortably on his parents' shoulders. Ada may have been pregnant then, because early in 1909 she presented Joe with another son.[35]

Joe and Ada were well liked in the Upper Nowood. That is surprising, not because of their characters but because of Joe's occupation. Joe Allemand was not a cattleman; he was a sheepman. He started grazing his herd on the east side of the Big Horn Mountains and then moved over the divide to the western slope.[36] He avoided the deadline by ranging his sheep above his ranch on the Big Horns and survived in a hostile atmosphere because of his ingratiating personality. But not even Joe Allemand could completely avoid the ire of the local cowboys.

Joe had also acquired a place on the Nowood about three miles south of Otter Creek, and sometimes he moved his sheep between his two places. Once, maybe in 1901, Allemand was taking his sheep to the mountain. At a place near Otter Creek he was stopped by several cattlemen, who warned him not to delay getting his sheep up the mountain. Ada was with him in a wagon, and their son was just a baby then. She became frightened and climbed down from the wagon with the baby, but one of the cowboys felt sorry for her and carried her baby. No serious trouble developed, probably because of the presence of Joe's wife and child, but it was an upsetting event.[37]

One of the cattlemen who confronted Allemand then was Joe Emge, and it was rumored that Emge later participated in a raid against Allemand.[38] All of that was behind him by 1909, though: He had quit the cattle business and had joined Joe Allemand running sheep. The speculation was that Allemand, who was having financial trouble, persuaded Emge that raising sheep would be more profitable than raising cattle. Emge was a very prosperous but ambitious man who always wanted to do better. Emge's home place was near Allemand's on Spring Creek, and Joe Allemand had frequent opportunities to bend Emge's ear.[39]

Still, their alliance was an odd one, if only because their personalities were so different. Emge was a pusher: hot-tempered, overtly aggressive and, unlike Allemand, disliked and unpopular. He was of a German family and people pigeonholed him as a "hot-headed Dutchman."[40]

He came to the Nowood in about 1885 from Evansville, Indiana, and first settled near Bonanza. From Bonanza, he wrote glowing letters back to his grandparents, telling them how beautiful the country was and how much they would love it. Emge finally persuaded them to come to Wyoming and built a seven-room house for them, an unusual residence for that day, when most of the homes were three-room log houses.[41]

When he was a cattleman, he was one of the most intolerant of the breed. He once built a fence ten miles long between Spring Creek and Otter Creek to keep all the sheepmen off the mountain. He also quarreled with other cattlemen. Emge was a strong, heavyset man, very skilled with guns, and he would never back down from a fight. People remembered that about him, of course, but they also remembered something else: His mouth was filled with gold fillings. When he would talk in his animated way, they would see flashing gold.[42]

Strange as the alliance between Emge and Allemand may have been, it was in earnest. In late February of 1909, the pair purchased Charlie Shaw's cattle ranch just outside of Ten Sleep, giving Shaw a $5,800 mortgage.[43] They employed a number of men, including Pete Cafferal and Charles David Helmer. Cafferal was French, a camp tender, and an older man, in his late forties or early fifties. Helmer, who would not have been recognized as "Charles David," was always known as "Bounce." He was eighteen or nineteen in 1909, a likable young man, although not terribly bright.[44] His father, Frank Helmer, and mother, Ade Goodrich, both lived in the Upper Nowood, but were divorced.

Otter Creek is the next stream south of Spring Creek. The north and south forks of Otter Creek are both larger than Spring Creek, and above the point where they issue from the Big Horns, back in the miles of dark canyons, they are excellent fisheries. The South Fork arises from springs and is rarely anything but brilliantly transparent — the kind of stream that makes Westerners misty-eyed with thoughts of cool, clear water. After the two forks come together, the creek undergoes a change in character; a slower, winding meadow stream emerges. The narrow valley through which it then flows makes a very direct westerly trip of about four miles to the Nowood. About a mile below the two forks, on the north side of the stream, is a towering red bluff. The spring sky behind that red bluff can be a piercing blue, a picture in praise of life itself. In 1894, though, George McClellan and Frank Warner were supposed to have found twenty-three human skulls at the base of that bluff. Paul Frison wrote: "The bleached skulls — was mute evidence of a tragic story of death — sealed forever in the lips of those yawning red cliffs of Otter Creek."[45]

Otter Creek was the site of several ranches in 1909. Mr. and Mrs. Al Coleman had a small place at the base of the Big Horns, at that pretty spot where the two Otter Creek canyons come together. Their son George was a freighter, and he was frequently away from home while freighting goods in and out of the Basin.[46]

Below Coleman lived Charlie Faris. Faris had been in the area at least eleven years but had only been on Otter Creek for two years. He was thirty-six and ran 250 to 300 cattle. Faris and his wife Eva had been quiet citizens; there is little mention of them in the historical record, although Charlie is reported to have had "a good reputation."[47]

Below Faris was Albert Keyes, who was known as Bill Keyes and whose last name was pronounced "Kize."[48] At forty-three, Keyes was a bit older than his friend Faris, although he had been in Big Horn County about as long. Like Faris, though, he had been on his own ranch on Otter Creek for just two years. He was in partnership with Charles Shaw, and they jointly ran about 400 head of cattle.[49] Two young cowboys, Farney Cole and Clyde Harvard, worked for Keyes.

Another ranch on Otter Creek was that of the Buckmasters, and their outfit sat downstream from Keyes' on the county road. The lands were adjacent, but the two ranch houses were about a mile apart. Johnny and Mary Buckmaster were old-timers on Otter Creek, having homesteaded there in 1887.[50]

One more ranch sat downstream of the Buckmasters', that of Mr. and Mrs. Billy Horton, whose place was at the mouth of Otter Creek. Horton was known as "Boston Billy," and he frequently worked as a surveyor with George McClellan's brother, Oscar.[51]

Where Otter Creek flows into the Nowood, it is still a fairly clear stream, but what remains of the mountain water is then swallowed by the muddy Nowood. About two miles upstream on the Nowood was the ranch of Jake and Ade Goodrich. As noted earlier, Ade Goodrich was Bounce Helmer's mother, divorced from his father, Frank. Their relationship had always been stormy. They had three boys, Bounce, Ben, and Bush, even before they were married. Frank was going to leave Ade when neighbors persuaded him that he ought to do the right thing and marry her.[52]

Above this ranch was Allemand's Nowood land, and above that was the ranch of Milton Alexander, which was one of the larger operations in the Upper Nowood. Alexander was a reserved and competent man and, at the age of forty-nine, a successful one, considered one of the more prominent cattleman in the area. Had he built a business in the Midwest, he probably would have been a quiet, rather dull fellow. But he put together his ranch on the frontier and had to develop abilities not required elsewhere. Alexander had the nickname of "Injun" because of his great skill with guns. In the coldest of weather he went without an overcoat or overshoes, with his shirt unbuttoned.[53]

Alexander was somewhat larger than average, maybe 5'11" and 185 pounds. His eyes did not mesh; one lid was droopy, the other wide open. In 1907 he was initiated into the Masons at Basin, and that same year his neighbor Joe Allemand also joined the Masons. He and his wife Myra had two little boys, and he was later said to be devoted to his family.[54]

Just above the Alexander ranch, on the Nowood, was Joe Henry's ranch, the one the Greet boys were purchasing. From an area on the county road known as the "double crossing," a road turned due west, following the Nowood, which briefly flows east and west. That road led, in less than half a mile, to a secluded area on the Nowood, the site of Joe Henry's ranch.[55] Henry was another old-timer who had come to the Basin to work for one of the big ranches; when it went out of business after the big winter, he found this spot on the Nowood in 1887.[56] He was considered tough and able and was well liked by the young cowboys in the area.

Upstream a short distance from Joe Henry's, Frank Helmer's ranch sat on Crooked Creek. Crooked Creek is a scrawny stream, and it is surprising anybody ever settled on it. Yet people established themselves on Crooked Creek very early (some of the very first water rights in the Big Horn Basin were taken on Crooked Creek, including one by Frank Ainsworth[57]), and people are still on Crooked Creek today. Frank Helmer's spread was called the Double H, and Helmer was so firmly identified with his ranch that he himself was known as "Double H."[58] His sons spent quite a lot of time with Frank even after he divorced their mother, although he was a gruff father. Helmer even questioned their paternity, but they probably were not aware of that.[59] Frank Helmer was a dedicated cattleman, and he must have been disappointed that Bounce was working as a sheepherder.

Not much more than a mile from the Double H, on Little Canyon Creek, there was a school, a store with a post office, and several families. This tiny settlement was known as Big Trails. Among those who lived there were Eliza and Frank Brown. The Browns had been at Big Trails for eleven years, with Frank doing some farming. He also acted as the assistant postmaster.[60]

Close by the Browns, on the east side of Little Canyon Creek, lived Billy and Anna Goodrich. The Goodriches had been married in 1904, when Billy was twenty-nine and Anna just twenty; he had been a cowboy in the Big Horn Basin about ten years before that. Goodrich owned a small ranch near Mahogany Buttes, but this Big Trails ranch was owned by his sister, Stella Hopkins. Her husband, John, had died, and Billy had been leasing the ranch for about a year.[61] Billy Goodrich was a small man, slight and only about 5'3" or 5'4". Anna was not a large woman, but she may have been a little taller than her husband. Goodrich got along with his neighbors, but he was not particularly well regarded. He was a talker and was not viewed as a man of great substance, unlike, for example, Joe Henry — he just did not have that kind of grit.[62]

In 1909 there were three cowboys who worked with the Goodrich ranch: Herbert Brink, Tommy Dixon, and Bill Garrison. All of them ran a few head of cattle on their own. Brink was only twenty-eight in 1909; he grew up in Colorado but had been in the Big Horn Basin for several years. He had first worked for George McClellan, then for Joe Henry for three years, and only recently had bunked at the Goodriches, helping out for his board.[63] Brink was 5'11" tall, weighed about 170 pounds, and was unusually strong because he had worked as a blacksmith.[64] He was regarded as a good, hard-working hand, but one who had a mean streak. In addition to the Meeteetse sheep raid, Brink was supposed to have been involved in raids in Colorado, but it was hard to be sure of that, because Brink liked to boast of such exploits, perhaps magnifying his part in them.[65] Like George Saban, though, he had unusually straight personal habits. He claimed not to drink at all and took pride in the fact that he had never been discharged from a job. In 1907 he even worked for a while as a deputy for Felix Alston.[66]

Brink was prematurely balding and had an open face, with eyes that stared at the world a bit too brightly. He and his bunkmate Tommy Dixon wanted to buy Billy Goodrich's ranch and were gathering money the winter of 1908–1909 for that purpose.[67]

At thirty-five, Dixon was older than Brink and had been a cowboy longer. He was from New York and was evidently estranged from his parents; in 1909, the only thing he knew about their location was that they lived somewhere in New York City. He didn't seem to be an unhappy man, though. Rhodes described him as "handsome and likeable," and people's statements about him leave the impression that he was a warm and decent man.[68]

A similar impression exists of Bill Garrison, who seemed more considerate and less aggressive than most cowboys. This is surprising, because Garrison was a very large man, 6'6" tall, and had been in the country since 1882, living through some rugged times. Coincidentally, Garrison was also from New York State, having been born in Genesee County. He looked after the cattle of Stella Hopkins in addition to his own.[69]

Roads leading from Big Trails in 1909 described a loop that generally followed the streams. From Big Trails there was a road west to the Nowood. This road and the Nowood then shot almost due south for several miles, going through a very narrow valley with high hills rising steeply on both sides — not quite a canyon, but formidable enough that a horse could only be ridden over these hills in a few places. They were especially steep on the east side, rising maybe 300 feet; they made up the western part of the Red Wall.

In 1909, the first ranch encountered on the Nowood was Oscar and Ella McClellan's. Oscar had followed his older brother, Bear George, into the Basin. Oscar was a small man, quiet and scholarly (a very different personality than his brother). He had even earned a college degree, a great rarity in those days, had taught school for thirteen years, and had been the headmaster of a school in Ontario, Canada. He had also learned skills as a surveyor, which he put to good use when he came west. Oscar married Ella in Ontario, where she was a trained nurse, and brought her to the Upper Nowood in the late 1890s.[70]

South of the McClellan's was the Rebidaux family. Abe Rebidaux was the patriarch, and there were two sons in their early twenties, Jack and Charlie. South of this ranch was the ranch of two single men, Charlie Goodall and Fred Widmeyer. The Goodall and Widmeyer place sat just north of where Cherry Creek comes into the Nowood, a place known in the Upper Nowood as the "turkey track," because Cherry Creek, Horse Creek (an intermittent stream coming in from the southwest), and the Nowood form something like a large bird track. These two men employed a man named W. G. Colethorpe, who was a brother-in-law of Joe Allemand.[71]

About two miles from Goodall and Widmeyer, proceeding upstream by way of Cherry Creek and Box Elder Creek, was the ranch of Charlie Wells. Wells was truly an old-timer, having already had an adventurous life in the West before coming to Wyoming in 1881 to work for the 76, Moreton Frewen's ranch on Powder River. In 1883 he rode for the WP ranch out of Ten Sleep and in 1884 for the Shield outfit.[72] Wells established his own ranch on Box Elder in the mid-1880s and later ran both sheep and cattle. His actions were not accepted at first, and shortly after he brought in sheep, someone fired at his house. A bullet went through the house and into the head of his sister's bed, although she wasn't there at the time. Despite such attempts at intimidation, Wells stuck with sheep and made a success of it.[73]

From Charlie Wells' ranch, following Red Bank Creek north for about three miles, leads to the 1/4, the large ranch owned by Bear George McClellan and former governor Richards. By 1909, it had been years since Bear George had shot a bear. Nevertheless, he kept his nickname, and would for the rest of his life. It fit McClellan: He was a big bear of a man. He was not only large but also assertive, and he spoke in stentorian tones.[74] Such a man might have been considered pompous, but he was not. George McClellan was widely admired; indeed, he was the Wyoming state senator from Big Horn County, having been elected in 1908.[75]

Beside those who ranched in the Upper Nowood, there were others who made their living there. John Callahan was a trapper who worked through the area, and Sam Brant carried the mail by stage up and down the Nowood.[76]

All of these people were a family. There were only 200 or so people in the Upper Nowood, and their social activities centered on each other. There was no television, no radio, and no movies, and they spent an uncommon amount of time socializing; dances were major events. As in many families, though, their lives covered a substrata of dispute and irritation and resentment. Unresolved differences had festered and created such a cloud of anger and mistrust that brothers harbored murderous intentions.

Before that very dark cloud was dispelled from the Upper Nowood, their society was shattered. Four men died, five were imprisoned, and three more families were driven from the valley, leaving many of those who remained with scars lasting a lifetime.

## NOTES

1.  Rhodes, *The Rest That Came*, 8.

2.  Notes of Paul Frison in the possession of the author.

3.  Stephens and Ehrlich, *The Shell Valley*, Vera Saban, 106.

4.  According to the Wyoming Penitentiary Records, Saban weighed 183 pounds in 1909. Wyoming Department of Commerce, Archives and Records Division, George Saban (No. 1441) Penitentiary file, "Description of Convict." Rhodes, *The Rest That Came*, 9.

5.  Colonel Jay L. Torrey was Captain R. A. Torrey's brother and ranch successor.

6.  Stephens and Ehrlich, *The Shell Valley*, Vera Saban, 106.

7.  W. T. Whaley came to the Shell Valley in 1890 from Texas. He was always known as "By Dumb," because he habitually used this expression. *The Shell Valley*, 106, 112, 116, 117.

8.  Rhodes, *The Rest That Came*, 9.

9.  Wyoming Department of Commerce, Archives and Records, Cheyenne, Gov. Joseph M. Carey Petition for Pardon (George Saban) File, 1/15/13 letter from Rev. Frank L. Moore to Governor Carey. See also grand jury testimony of Sydney Ingram, 12. A

grand jury met in April 1909 in Basin to investigate the Spring Creek raid, and the testimony of the witnesses was transcribed. Percy Metz kept these transcriptions and they later went to his niece, Lola Homsher. They can be found in the Lola Homsher Collection at the American Heritage Center, University of Wyoming.

10. Gov. Carey Saban Pardon File, 7/7/13 letter from John Donovan to Governor Carey.

11. Stephens and Ehrlich, *The Shell Valley,* Paul Frison, 108.

12. Gov. Carey Saban Pardon File, 11/15/13 letter from Rev. Frank L. Moore to Governor Carey.

13. Stephens and Ehrlich, *The Shell Valley,* Vera Saban, 106.

14. Rhodes, The Rest That Came, 11.

15. As noted in Chapter 2, the local cattlemen were considered the perpetrators of this raid, and Saban didn't move from the Shell area until after 1905. Later events showed Saban to be very knowledgeable about conducting sheep raids.

16. Broken Back Creek empties into the Nowood only three or four miles north of Ten Sleep.

17. Stephens and Ehrlich, *The Shell Valley,* Vera Saban, 106; Wasden, *Beaver to Oil,* 137. The initial deed was from Roe Emory to George Saban in 1908, but on May 11, 1909, Saban conveyed the ranch to W. T. Whaley. Records of the Washakie County Clerk.

18. Interview of Howard McClellan, son of Oscar McClellan and nephew of "Bear George" McClellan, by the author, April 1991; interview of Bob Edgar, Cody, Wyoming, January 1993.

19. Grand jury testimony of Sydney Ingram, 6.

20. Grand jury testimony of George Pickett, 1; Charles Runge, 1. Other names mentioned in connection with the Bay State were "Mormon" Jack and John Camel. Grand jury testimony of Sydney Ingram, 7.

21. Grand jury testimony of Charles Runge, 6; W. A. Miller, 1.

22. Rhodes, *The Rest That Came,* 13; Ed Eaton weighed 149 pounds when he entered the penitentiary in 1909. Wyoming Department of Commerce, Archives and Records, Ed Eaton (No. 1439) Penitentiary File, "Description of Convict"; Charles Kurt, "Massacre at Big Horn Basin," *Official Detective Stories* (December 1941), 26, et seq.; *Big Horn County Rustler,* 5/7/09; Ed Eaton tombstone, Ten Sleep Cemetery.

23. Paul Frison, *Under the Ten Sleep Rim* (Worland: Worland Press, 1972).

24. Grand jury testimony of Bounce Helmer, 8.

25. Gage, *Ten Sleep and No Rest,* 110, 194–197; interview of Howard McClellan by author, April 1991; preliminary map showing site of Spring Creek raid, April 2, 1909, based on the notes of a survey on April 26, 1909 by Clyde W. Atherly, by the Northwest Chapter of Professional Land Surveyors of Wyoming, January 1989. This map was prepared from Atherly's survey notes, which were discovered by Clay Gibbons of Worland in the Big Horn County Courthouse.

26. Grand jury testimony of George Pickett, 2. Sutherland came into the country in the early 1880s when he started working for his brother-in-law, Fred Hesse, the foreman of Moreton Frewen's huge Powder River Ranch, the "76." See L. Milton Woods, *Moreton Frewen's Western Adventures* (Boulder: Roberts Rinehart, 1986), 32, 33. Also see Grand jury testimony of Arthur McVay.

27. Pendergraft, *Washakie: A Wyoming County History;* 27; testimony of Fred Greet, *State v. Brink,* 106. A copy of this transcript is available at the Wyoming Department of Commerce, Parks and Cultural Resources, Archives and Records Management Section. See also biography of Fred Greet, 1, Paul Frison papers in the possession of the author. The Greet twins were born in Indiana in 1885.

28. This incident is taken primarily from Pendergraft, *Washakie: A Wyoming County History,* 34, 35, but much of it is corroborated by the biography of Fred Greet.

29. Pendergraft, *Washakie: A Wyoming County History,* 30.

30. Trial testimony of Fred Greet, 106, and Porter Lamb, 139.

31. Pendergraft, *Washakie: A Wyoming County History,* 27.

32. Trial testimony of George Rogers, 282.

33. Pendergraft, *Washakie: A County History,* 142; interview of Howard McClellan, April 1991.

34. Letter of 4/16/09 from Virgil Chabot to the ambassador of France in Washington, Governor B. B. Brooks' Sheep Raid File ( Record Group 0001.17), 1907–1910, Wyoming State Archives, Cheyenne; Wasden, *Beaver to Oil;* Ainsworth, *To The Wilds of Wyoming,* 158, 180.

35. Trial testimony of Ada Allemand, 354.

36. Wasden, *Beaver to Oil,* 142.

37. Ainsworth, *To The Wilds of Wyoming,* 158.

38. Ibid; Gage, *Ten Sleep and No Rest,* 31, 62, 63. "Emge" is pronounced with a hard "g."

39. For example, Rhodes, in *The Rest That Came* discusses this in some detail at pages 15 and 16, though he doesn't offer any direct evidence to support his supposition.

40. Pendergraft, *Washakie: A County History,* 101, 105. Many stories were told of confrontations between Emge and other cattlemen. None are possible to verify, yet all of them must contain a good deal of truth.

41. Stephens and Ehrlich, *The Shell Valley,* Marie Mayer Herren (a sister), 87, 88; Rhodes, *The Rest That Came,* 16.

42. Rhodes, *The Rest That Came,* 11, 15; trial testimony of Pete Cafferal, 160; Pendergraft, *Washakie: A County History,* 106.

43. Records of the Big Horn County Clerk, book 11, p. 173, of mortgages. In 1909, $5,800 was equivalent to more than $100,000 in 1991 dollars. See John W. Davis, *Sadie and Charlie* (Worland: Washakie Publishing, 1989), 52, 62.

44. Interview of Howard McClellan by the author, April 1991. Bounce's age was stated as being seventeen, eighteen, nineteen, or twenty; he probably didn't know his true age himself.

45. Paul Frison notes in the possession of the author, 62.

46. Grand jury testimony of George Coleman, 1; Interview of Howard McClellan by the author, April, 1991.

47. Trial testimony of Charles Faris, 245, 266; interview of Howard McClellan by the author, February 1991.

48. Percy Metz speeches.

49. Trial testimony of Albert Keyes, 205, 227.

50. Pendergraft, _Washakie: A County History_, 31, 39. Trial testimony of John Buckmaster, 287–290.

51. Interview of Howard McClellan by author, April 1991.

52. Notes of Paul Frison in the possession of the author.

53. Wyoming Department of Commerce, Archives and Records, Gov. Joseph M. Carey Petition for Pardon (Alexander) File, 1/9/13 letter of Dr. Walker to Governor Carey. The _Denver Post_ stated on 11/3/09 that he was worth almost $150,000, nearly as much as George Saban. See also Rhodes, _The Rest That Came_, 7; trial testimony of Billy Goodrich, 339.

54. Interview of Howard McClellan by author, April 1991. The 1909 prison records give his weight as 184 pounds. Wyoming Department of Commerce, Archives and Records, Milton Alexander (No. 1442) Penitentiary File, "Description of Convict." See also Kurt, "Massacre at Big Horn Basin," 29; Rhodes, _The Rest That Came_, 12; Governor Carey Petition for Pardon (Alexander) File, 1/9/13 letter of Dr. G. F. Walker to Governor Carey.

55. Interview of Howard McClellan by the author, April 1991. This road can still be made out from the present location of the highway.

56. Pendergraft, _Washakie: A County History_, 31.

57. Frank S. Ainsworth and Frank D. Helmer, 5/15/85. Tabulation of Adjudicated Water Rights of the State of Wyoming, Water Division Number Three (Cheyenne, State Board of Control, 1978), 125.

58. Gage, _Ten Sleep and No Rest_, 38.

59. Notes of Paul Frison in the possession of the author.

60. Trial testimony of Eliza Brown, 307, and Frank H. Brown, 311.

61. Letter of Anna Goodrich to Marlene and Bob Orchard dated 8/9/69, copy in the possession of the author; trial testimony of George McClellan, 381; Grand jury testimony of Mrs. Billy Goodrich, 1.

62. Interview of Kent Orchard, grand-nephew of Billy and Anna, by the author, June 1991; trial testimony of Henry Helms, Frank B. Helmer, George B. McClellan; interview of Howard McClellan by author, April 1991.

63. Rhodes, _The Rest That Came_, 12, 14; _Big Horn County Rustler_, 5/7/09; grand jury testimony of Herbert Brink, 7.

64. Brink was born in Pennsylvania, but his family moved to Colorado when he was four. Wyoming Department of Commerce, Archives and Records, Herbert Brink (No. 1443) Penitentiary File, "Biographical Sketch of Prisoner Eligible to Parole Under Provisions of Law." See also _Sweet Smell of Sagebrush_, 148.

65. Interview of Howard McClellan by author, April 1991; grand jury testimony of Edward Goodale, 1. Brink also got into some minor trouble before a Justice of the Peace when he was accused of stealing a calf. The charges were dismissed, however. Rhodes, _The Rest That Came_, 12.

66. Prison records of Herbert Brink; "Biographical Sketch of Prisoner": trial testimony of Felix Alston, 43.

67. Trial testimony of Mrs. William Goodrich, 326.

68. Wyoming Department of Commerce, Archives and Records, Thomas Dixon (No. 1440) Penitentiary File, "Description of Convict"; Pendergraft, *Washakie: A Wyoming County History*, 109; Rhodes, *The Rest That Came*, 14; *Big Horn County Rustler*, 11/13/09.

69. *Big Horn County Rustler*, 5/7/09; Rhodes, *The Rest That Came*, 12, 14.

70. Oscar attended Ottawa University in Ottawa, Canada. Interview of Howard McClellan by the author, April 1991. Howard McClellan is one of the children of Oscar McClellan. He and his sister, Margaret Chastain, reside in Worland. Pendergraft, *Washakie: A Wyoming County History*, 216.

71. Trial testimony of W. G. Colethorpe, 306.

72. This discussion is taken primarily from Paul Frison, *The Apache Slave — Charles Wells*, (Worland: Worland Press, 1969), 21–23, 33–47.

73. Pendergraft, *Washakie: A Wyoming County History*, 25; Ainsworth, *To the Wilds of Wyoming*, 156–157.

74. Interview of Howard McClellan by the author, April 1991.

75. Pendergraft, *Washakie: A Wyoming County History*, 103, 104.

76. Trial testimony of John Callahan, 294, and Samuel Brant, 190.

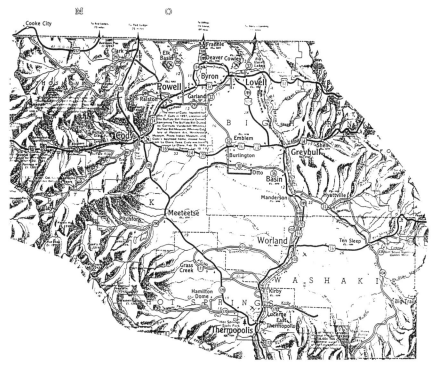

The Big Horn Basin. Copyrighted by the Wyoming Transportation Commission and reprinted by permission.

Roping a Grizzly. Watercolor on paper by C. M. Russell, 1903. Reprinted by permission of the Buffalo Bill Historical Center, Cody, WY.

Waiting for a Chinook. Watercolor on paper by C. M. Russell. Reprinted by permission of the Buffalo Bill Historical Center, Cody, WY.

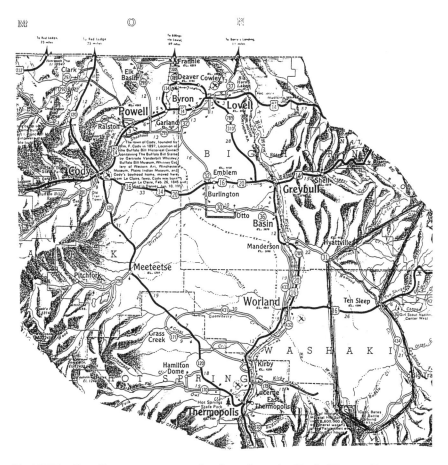

The 1897 Deadline. Sheep were not to cross these lines. Copyrighted by the Wyoming Transportation Commission and reprinted by permission.

PERCY W. METZ,

Percy Metz. This photograph of "the high school kid" was taken during his first year as Big Horn County Attorney. Courtesy Colorado Historical Society.

Felix Alston. Courtesy Colorado Historical Society.

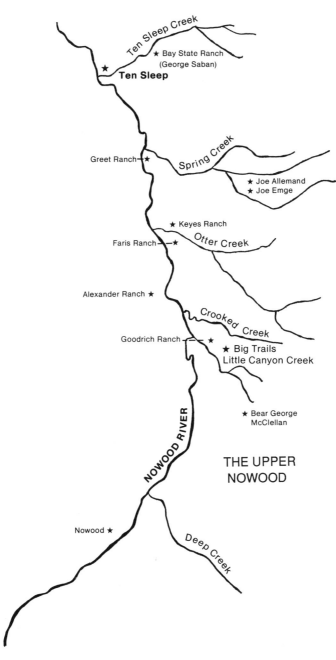

The Upper Nowood. This map shows the principal streams and ranches in the Upper Nowood in 1909.

The Allemand Family. Portrait of Joe and Ada Allemand and their son, 1908. This photograph, as well as several others, was uncovered by Clay Gibbons of Worland, Wyoming. Courtesy Washakie County Museum and Cultural Center.

Joe Emge. Emge was the Allemand's neighbor on Spring Creek. This is another photograph found by Clay Gibbons. Courtesy Washakie County Museum and Cultural Center.

Pete Cafferal and Bounce Helmer. In November 1909, the portraits of several of the principals in the Spring Creek raid were taken. These were also found by the good work of Clay Gibbons. They included the above two — of Pete Cafferal on the left and Bounce Helmer on the right. Courtesy Washakie County Museum and Cultural Center.

Herb Brink. Photograph of Herb Brink, 1909. Courtesy Wyoming State Archives and the Washakie County Museum and Cultural Center.

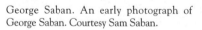

George Saban. An early photograph of George Saban. Courtesy Sam Saban.

"Bear" George McClellan. Here, the Bear was photographed at his desk in the Wyoming State Legislature. Courtesy Washakie County Museum and Cultural Center.

# The Call

## CHAPTER 4

The telephone call came in about 9:50 a.m.; Walter Fiscus, at the hardware store in Ten Sleep, calling Felix Alston. It was Saturday, April 3, 1909, and Fiscus had appalling news: At least three men had been killed south of Ten Sleep, on Spring Creek; wagons had been burned, sheep and dogs killed.

Sheriff Alston immediately contacted his young county attorney, Percy Metz. He then called Al Morton, the deputy in Ten Sleep, telling him to get out to Spring Creek and make sure that people did not disturb the scene. In the meantime, Fiscus called Dr. George Walker in Hyattville and asked him to go to Spring Creek.[1]

Alston, Metz, and Deputy Ed Cusack left Basin about 10:20 a.m. on a buckboard. Dr. Dana Carter, the county coroner, also started to Spring Creek, but he probably drove his own rig; Dr. Carter took great pride in his handsome teams of horses and their ability to quickly respond to a call.[2] The trip from Basin to Spring Creek in 1909 was taken by driving to Manderson and then following the Nowood upstream. It was a very long trip, over fifty miles, and it took all day by buckboard.

This southbound party probably concluded that what had happened was a sheep raid — the event bore all the earmarks of the grim incidents of the last few years. And they probably knew it had occurred Friday night near the Greet Ranch and that one of the Greet brothers had reported it. They could not have known much more, though. It is not even clear whether they had any information about who had been killed.

Al Morton had quickly gone to the scene of the crime, and it was a good thing he had, because during the day a large crowd found its way there. When Fred Greet was later asked who was there that day, he simply said: "Everybody."[3]

The buckboard from Basin arrived at Spring Creek between 6 and 7 p.m.[4] The site of the raid is hidden until a traveler comes over the final divide, and then the whole Spring Creek Valley opens up. Spring Creek stretches to the southeast, and three or four miles upstream (behind the Chatfield Ranch in 1909) sit bluffs peppered with green cedar. Behind these are the Big Horn Mountains, rising there to about 8,000 feet. In early April they still have their winter snow, and toward evening the spring sun hits that snow and paints it yellow and red. In the valley, bright green grass is just starting, meadowlarks are singing and phlox are blooming.

This was the scene greeting Alston, Metz, and Cusack that April 3. But it was blighted by two black and unnatural things. A little over a quarter-mile from their wagon, on the opposite side of Spring Creek, was a large charred area. Not forty-eight hours before, wagons had been sitting here — a sheepwagon, a supply wagon, and a buggy (forever after, collectively known as the "south wagon"). Now there was just a heap of ash and blackened metal. Around these south wagons were dead and maimed sheep and at least two dead dogs, which had been shot.[5]

On the north side of the creek, the same side as the Alston wagon, was another charred area. When the Basin party arrived, about five or six men stood just west of this spot. Here, a sheepwagon had faced south, its door toward Spring Creek. It had burned completely, although a buckboard stood unharmed next to it, except for the tongue, which had been burned off. Lying about fifteen feet in front of the burned sheepwagon was a man. He was on his back with his head toward the north; his right foot was drawn up, and his left hand was on his side.[6]

It was Joe Allemand, and he was dead. Metz and Alston both knew Allemand, and there was no question as to his identity. Allemand had been a private client of Metz's and the county attorney knew him particularly well. Some fifty years later he recalled Allemand as "a very fine gentleman."[7] Close to the stiff body of this very fine gentleman was a shovel, which had been stuck in the ground, and a horse blanket draped over a sagebrush.

Around this burned wagon, the "north wagon," were two dead dogs. One of them evidently had puppies, for lying on Allemand's body was a little woolly puppy, still alive, with another one curled up against it.[8]

The sheepwagon was destroyed; it had burned for hours, since some time Friday night until the light of day on Saturday.[9] Inside the wreckage were two charred bodies. At the trial seven months later, Felix Alston testified about one of them:

> Well that body laying towards the front of the wagon on the right of the stove when you was looking out from the wagon, and almost up to the front, the trunk laying on his stomach, and with its head reared back

straight up, face turned down, chin burned off, and the holes where the eyes were just sunken places, and the top of the head, the skull part of that had frizzled up and gone. You could see the baked brain, baked just whitish like. You could see the seams in them.[10]

Directly under the head of this body Alston found a small lump of gold, resting on part of the stove (the "go to hell" stove). Lying beneath the right side of the body, Alston found a .35 Remington automatic pointed toward what had been the door of the wagon.[11]

The second body lay between the stove and where the bed would have been, facing west. It was not burned as badly as the other but it was still "just a burned body and the trunk," and it assumed the same grotesque posture, with the head "reared straight back and almost standing straight up."[12]

The Greet ranch house was only a thousand feet from the north wagon, and its cellar door was used to carry Allemand's body back to the house. One of the burned bodies, the one under which the gold was found, was put in a box and also taken to the house. It was not hard to fit in the box because the legs and arms were burned off. The remaining body was left that night, but a tarpaulin was placed over the remains of the wagon.[13] By then it was dark, and no more could be done outside, but at the Greet ranch house Alston and Metz got their first chance to interview some witnesses in depth. There were four men — Fred and Frank Greet, Porter Lamb, and John Meredith — who had actually witnessed the attack on the sheep camp.

On Friday, the Greet brothers had been completing the move to their new ranch on the Nowood, the Joe Henry place. In fact, the evening of Friday, April 2, was to be their last night at their old ranch on Spring Creek. During the day, they took a wagonload of their belongings to their new home and then returned to their old one. They arrived back about 6 p.m. and were surprised to find two large bands of sheep just upstream from the ranch house. They also found Porter Lamb, the new owner, and his brother-in-law, John Meredith, at the ranch house, where they had erected a tent in the yard.[14]

The Greets knew the sheepmen, Allemand and Emge, and were on friendly terms with them. Emge came over to the ranch house to ask if he could put some horses in a field, and Greet told him that he would invite him to supper if everything wasn't packed up. On hearing this, Emge invited the Greet brothers over to his sheepwagon for supper. They accepted and had their supper that night with Joe Allemand, Jules Lazier, and Joe Emge at their camp, the site that became known as the "north wagon." Fred Greet had not known Lazier until that night and learned that he was French and Joe Allemand's nephew. He was also told that Bounce Helmer and Pete Cafferal were south of Spring Creek in another camp about a quarter-mile away; he had seen Cafferal when the latter brought over some horses, the ones Greet had earlier discussed with Emge.[15]

After supper, about 8:30, the brothers returned to the ranch house and went to bed. But about 10:30, they were suddenly awakened by gunshots from the north wagon. Shooting continued for about three-quarters of an hour, when the wagon began to burn.[16]

Both Porter Lamb and Fred Greet recalled that when the shooting first started, there was a spate of rapid firing, as if from an automatic.[17] Everybody was awake by that time, and Lamb and John Meredith had come over to the Greet cabin. After the fire started, though, they all moved outside, to the east side of the cabin. Frank Greet then heard a voice say, "throw up your hands, throw up your hands," and heard two shots instantly afterwards. Then they saw two men walk up to the wagon.[18]

Not long after that they heard some horses running, and they all stepped out from the shadow of the house to see the horses. Zing! A bullet came over their heads — Porter Lamb said it came very close to him. With that, the four men retreated to the house; Porter Lamb dragged his bed over to the ranch house, remarking that "a tent didn't afford much protection."[19]

But what of the key evidence? How many raiders? What were they wearing? *Who were they?* To all these questions, there were unsatisfactory responses. The four witnesses did not know how many men — they only saw two of them. They could not tell what the two men were wearing or what their sizes were — they were too far away. They did not know who they were — they could only tell they were men, although it had been a light night.[20]

The shooting had gone on for another hour or so, and then the men in the cabin heard no more. They concluded that they had witnessed a raid and that the sheepmen had all been killed. They still hoped, though, that the sheepmen would show up at the ranch house. Lamb said if they had they would have been protected. None ever did. The four men in the cabin spent an anxious and restless night, getting very little sleep; at least one man was always up, peering out the window. They did not go over to investigate or even try to use the telephone that night, although they discussed it. The men did not want to risk their lives, were afraid that there would be a man around the house, and did not want to be "implicated" any more than necessary.[21]

The next morning, shortly after daybreak, they did go over to the scene. They found Allemand and the two burned bodies in the north wagon, but there was no sign of Bounce Helmer or Pete Cafferal. They did not even know for sure who the two bodies were, although they assumed they were Emge and Lazier. When they tried to place a phone call to report what had happened, they discovered that the telephone wire to Ten Sleep had been cut. They found the cut, repaired it, and about 8:30 Saturday morning finally called Walt Fiscus in Ten Sleep.[22]

That same evening, the evening of April 3, Dr. Walker examined the body of Joe Allemand. He found two wounds; one, entering the body from the left side (where Allemand's hand had been found), was necessarily fatal. It had gone through his body and had struck his right arm, breaking the ulnar bone. Dr. Walker found the bullet embedded in Allemand's arm. There was a second wound along the collar bone, just across the bone's inner ends. There was no puncture but rather a tear the whole length of the wound. The doctor was not sure what had caused this wound, but it was certainly not a fatal injury.[23]

After interviewing the witnesses, all Metz and Alston knew for sure was that there had been a raid in which at least three men were murdered, one by a gunshot through his body. They were not even sure who all the victims were and would not know until Helmer and Cafferal either showed up or were found dead. The one man whose identity they were sure of had suffered a strange wound of unknown origin. And worst of all, they had not the slightest notion who had committed these heinous acts.

The next morning (Sunday, April 4) began with another frustration: It snowed through the night, and Alston could not examine the area until the snow melted off.[24] He was still able to accomplish a few things, though. The body of the third man was removed to the house, and a watch and a small French medal were found under it. Alston and Morton thoroughly dug through the ashes of the north wagon. They found what they believed to be another gold tooth, at the same place the small lump of gold had been found the day before. They discovered two other rifles with all their wooden parts burned off, a .351 automatic and a .30-40. Ten empty shells fired from a gun in the wagon were also found, together with a great many shells that had not been fired but had exploded from the heat of the fire.[25]

Late that morning, even before the snow melted, Bounce Helmer finally showed up. Alston probably was irritated at Helmer: Where had he been? Why hadn't he called? But Bounce had not been able to use the telephone because the line had also been cut south of the Greet place. He and Cafferal had been with Bounce's mother at the Jake Goodrich ranch about seven miles up the Nowood.[26]

The sheriff took Helmer to the Greet ranch house, where Percy Metz talked to him behind closed doors. Metz interviewed a very frightened young man. One of the reasons Bounce did not return to the Greet Ranch until Sunday was surely that he was so badly shaken he needed time to regain some sense of safety. The county attorney learned that Bounce had been working for Emge and Allemand since December, when he tended sheep in the Slick Creek and Sand Creek area east of Worland. Then, in late March, Emge and Allemand started driving two bands of sheep, 4,600 head, from Worland to Ten Sleep. They knew they were going into cattle country and were well armed; Emge told Bounce there was "over $10,000 reward for my scalp."[27]

After five or six days they arrived at Spring Creek, on the evening of April 1. Emge had been relieved that the ordeal of the badlands crossing was finally over and that they had arrived safely at Spring Creek. He had not slept well in the previous few days and looked forward to getting a good night's sleep. Two camps were set up. One was on the south side of Spring Creek, with the camp tender, Pete Cafferal, and Bounce; the sheep were bedded down around that camp. The other was about a quarter-mile north, on the north side of Spring Creek, and Emge, Allemand, and Lazier were there.[28]

On April 2, Bounce went to bed about 8 o'clock, putting his bedroll on the ground west of the buggy. He fell asleep, but later his dog began to bark. Bounce told the dog to shut up and he went back to sleep.[29] But in a little while he was jolted awake by shooting; he blurted out to Pete Cafferal: "Pete, cowboys come." Bounce sprang up and started running down the hill to get away from the shooting. He ran directly into two men with guns, who made him stop and throw up his hands.[30]

The two men took Bounce back to the wagons, where he saw two more men east of the wagons; he was told to put a light in the sheepwagon. When he came out he was asked who else was in the wagon and he told them Pete Cafferal. Then the men asked where Joe Emge was. Nobody questioned him about Allemand.[31]

Cafferall was made to come out of the wagon, and he and Bounce were then told to put their clothes on. Cafferall went back into the wagon for his clothes and was warned to "be careful not to pick up any gun." One of the men then said, "Let us exercise these fellows awhile," and Bounce and Pete were taken down the road toward the other camp. During this time

the men at the south wagon were shooting into the herd of sheep. Helmer
and Cafferal walked down the road, over the bridge across Spring Creek
and under the hill where the north wagon was located, while the raiders
kept telling Pete and Bounce not to look around. They made the two
sheepmen lie down and searched them for weapons. Bounce was asked if
there was any oil over at the south wagon.[32]

The north wagons sat about thirty feet above Spring Creek. The
location has been described as a hill, but it is not so much a hill as a part
of the ridge that defines the valley. There are gravel fingers extending from
this ridge, and the wagon was on one of those fingers. It sat just west of a
small gully. The rise from the valley floor is sharp, and a man below, in the
valley, could not have seen the wagon over the brow of the rise. So Bounce
and Pete, even though they were only forty or fifty paces from the wagon
of their employers, could not see it.[33]

But what Bounce heard was chilling. He heard, and then glimpsed,
two fellows move toward the wagon. Bounce then heard someone say:
"Light that wagon," two or three times. "Put a light on that wagon, or we'll
riddle it with bullets." Then Bounce heard them count to three and start
to shoot rapidly. The two men were shooting into the wagon. Bounce
thought one of the guns was a Remington automatic, because it sounded
much like the Remington automatic that Emge used to shoot a lot.[34]

After the rapid shooting, someone said, "Get them hands up," and
then Bounce heard a couple of shots immediately after. He thought that
this might have been directed at some fellows down in the sagebrush and
away from the wagon, men camped there with lumber wagons who worked
for George McClellan.[35] Bounce and Pete were then taken back across
the creek to the south wagons. The wagons were burning by then, and
Bounce watched one man throwing harnesses and collars into the fire. At
that time he saw six to eight men around these south wagons.[36]

Of course, the key evidence Percy Metz had to uncover was *who* these
raiders were. He had the responsibility, as Big Horn county attorney, to
see that the guilty parties were brought to justice. In all probability, the
raiders were from the immediate area, cowboys determined to keep sheep
out of the Upper Nowood. But Bounce also disappointed Metz; he stated
he didn't know who they were. This seemed unlikely — Bounce had grown
up in the Upper Nowood, knew all the cowboys there, and had gone on
roundups with them. Bounce said, though, that the raiders had on masks
and insisted he had told Metz everything he knew.[37]

Bounce remembered that one of the cowboys had moved to shoot his
dog and that he had told him not to kill his dog. The man relented and

spared Bounce's dog.[38] Bounce had felt threatened, as anyone would in such a situation, but he thought that the men who were in charge of him had protected him.[39]

The raiders decided to turn Bounce and Pete loose after telling them to get away from there, adding, "You better not come around these God damn sheep." Bounce replied: "If you will turn us loose, by God, I won't come back."[40]

Bounce and Pete first walked back toward the Greets, then turned south, down the fence between the Greets and Harvards. Bounce sat down and pulled cactus out of his feet; in his wild flight after the cowboys first started shooting, he had run through cactus in his bare feet. Bounce and Pete kept walking south and arrived at Bounce's mother's between 1 and 1:30 a. m.[41]

It is not clear whether Pete Cafferal appeared at the Greet house with Bounce that Sunday morning, but he probably did. In any event, Pete's version of the events was very similar to Bounce's, although more difficult to understand because of the Frenchman's difficulties with English. On the key point of who the raiders were, Pete supplied no more information than Bounce had. For the time being, additional clues to the identity of these criminals would have to be learned from a more thorough physical examination of the area. So on Sunday afternoon, after the snow had melted, a large group of men returned to the north wagon. Alston led the party, which included Metz, Al Morton, his brother, John Morton, Ed Cusack, Perry Miller, Bill Robinson, and the two Greet brothers.[42]

The area west of the wagon was pretty much tracked up, but on the south and especially the east side, people had been kept away. Alston found eight separate places around the north wagon where men had kneeled down or lay; at least two cartridges were found at each of the places, although single shells were found at other spots.

There were four such sites to the front (that is, south) of the wagon. Most of the shells there had been fired from a .25-35 rifle, but there was one location at which the only cartridges found were five unfired .25-35 rounds. At least one spent .30-30 cartridge was also found at these south locations. At four sites east of the wagon, two .45-caliber pistol shells were found, as well as quite a few more .25-35 shells and at least eight shells from a .35 automatic. All of the sites, east and south, were about forty to seventy feet from the north wagon, but the place where the .35 shells were found was the closest to the wagon.[43]

The party proceeded from spot to spot, and Alston handed the shells he collected to Metz. When they were done, forty-two empty shells had been found. Alston did not mark any of the shells, but Metz marked a few.[44]

On the east side of the north wagon, Alston also found two very plain tracks where a man had walked up to the wagon. The tracks began from a spot where sagebrush had been pulled up, proceeded directly to the wagon, and then returned. Alston could not be sure whether there were tracks of any raiders leading to the wagon from the front, because other people had been toward the front of the wagon. At one of the sites on the east, Alston found a clear track of a cowboy boot that was unusual in that one of the heels was turned over to the inside. He used a piece of paper and traced the pattern of the heel.[45]

The party then proceeded to the south wagon. Alston observed at least twenty-five dead sheep in that area, all of which had been shot. Most important, a clear trail was found from the south wagon back to the east, toward Spring Creek. The party traced these tracks backward for about half a mile, where the tracks came out of Spring Creek, and then another half-mile back along the creek, where they found the place the raiders had tied their horses to some big sagebrush.[46]

The party then broke up into different groups. Alston led one group and followed the trail the raiders had left after the raid. This trail led to the Ten Sleep — Big Trails county road about half a mile above where that road hit Spring Creek; the tracks turned south. Al Morton and Fred Greet followed another trail, the one the raiders made when they first approached Spring Creek. It led from the big sagebrush in a more southerly direction back toward the county road; this trail hit the road about one mile above Spring Creek, and it showed riders coming from the south. In this area, Morton and Cusack also turned up a rifle scabbard, which had apparently been dropped by one of the raiders. Some time was lost when the trail of some range horses was followed.[47]

What all this tracking showed was that eight men, possibly more, had first ridden up from the south on the county road.[48] Then, a mile before the sheep camp, they had cut northeast, across country, down to Spring Creek, where they tied their horses on the large sagebrush. Bounce's dog had probably heard them when he started to bark. They walked to the sheep camps, carried out the raid, and then walked back. From Spring Creek they rode back to the county road by a shorter route and returned to the south.

At the close of April 4, Metz and Alston knew little more about the identity of the raiders than they had the day before. They had learned a great deal more about the crimes, however. There was no doubt that this was a raid, a crime committed to send a message. There were now many clues with which a peace officer could work. Alston knew the raiders had come from the south and had returned to the south; he knew what weapons they had used; and he knew exactly when the raiders had been at Spring Creek. But in order to use these clues, in order to build more evidence from them, it was necessary to follow the raiders, who had flowed back into the Upper Nowood like salmon returning from the ocean. Alston had to remain in the Upper Nowood to investigate.

Percy Metz returned to Basin. At some time during the previous two days, the enormity of the event probably sank in for Metz. Metz knew that in most sheep raids there were no arrests, that when there were arrests there were seldom trials, and that no cowboy in a sheep raid had ever been convicted of a crime in the state of Wyoming. Cattlemen had always supported men charged, supported them financially, politically, and sometimes physically, by intimidating witnesses, juries and lawmen. Just the attempt to prosecute such men could exhaust the treasury of a county. The example of Johnson County and its disastrous effort to prosecute its cattlemen invaders was still a fresh memory.

Percy Metz, the kid prosecutor, must have felt like the loneliest man in Wyoming.

## NOTES

1.  Grand jury testimony of Felix Alston, 1–3, and Fred Greet, 19; Trial testimony of Al Morton, 52, and Dr. Walker, 89. The first report came from Fred Greet to Walter Fiscus at the Ten Sleep hardware store, and he called Morton, who in turn asked him to call the sheriff. The sheriff then called back Morton. As mentioned above, Fiscus also called Dr. Walker. It is not clear why these calls were made in this fashion; today, one would expect the first report to go to the sheriff, with all following calls then coming out of that office. But in 1909, the telephone system to Ten Sleep and the Upper Nowood had just been installed, and long-distance calling was cumbersome at best. Walt Fiscus, who sat at a central switchboard in Ten Sleep, was probably better able to make some of the calls.

2.  Rhodes, *The Rest That Came*, 19; "Massacre at Big Horn Basin," 26–29; *Worland Grit*, 4/8/09; Wyoming State Historical Research and Publications Division, Cheyenne, WPA File # 619, "C. Dana Carter" (an unpublished biography of Dr. Carter), 12; Percy W. Metz speech to Natrona County Historical Society, 11/2/61.

3.  Trial testimony of Al Morton, 52; grand jury testimony of Oscar W. Arnett, 6, and Fred Greet, 19.

4.  In his grand jury testimony, Alston said they "got there just about six o'clock," but at the trial he stated they arrived "about seven o'clock." Grand jury testimony of Felix Alston, 1; trial testimony of Felix Alston, 3.

5.  Trial testimony of Bounce Helmer, 174, 175; Preliminary Map Showing Site of Spring Creek Raid; trial testimony of Felix Alston, 35, and Fred Greet, 119.

6.  This is a description using the trial testimony of several witnesses, including Al Morton at 53, Dr. Walker at 90, Felix Alston at 3, 4, and 34, and Fred Greet at 118. See also grand jury testimony of Felix Alston, 1. The surveyor's map will help the reader follow the ensuing discussion.

7.  Percy W. Metz speech before the Park County Historical Society, 6/9/61.

8.  Trial testimony of Felix Alston, 35, 39, and 45, and Al Morton, 53.

9.  Trial testimony of Fred Greet, 135. It is not clear why the fire burned so long and so completely at the north wagon. There was speculation that oil (kerosene) had been poured on the fire; also, that large quantities of oats had produced an unusually hot fire. But there is no evidence in any of the court records to support these suppositions. If the prosecutors could have proven that oil had been poured on the north wagon fire, they surely would have done so. See *Cheyenne Daily Leader*, 4/7/09, and Percy Metz's Casper speech, 11/2/61. Dr. G. W. Walker, at p. 6 of his grand jury testimony, said: "I know they had not used coal oil there." Oil may have been used at the south wagon.

10. Trial testimony of Felix Alston, 4, 5.

11. Trial testimony of Felix Alston, 5; Gage, *Ten Sleep and No Rest*, 159; grand jury testimony of Felix Alston, 2.

12. Trial testimony of Felix Alston, 5. For a brilliant description of this terrible scene on the morning of April 3, 1909, and a virtuoso writing performance, see Gage, *Ten Sleep and No Rest*, 158, 159.

13. Recollections of the Spring Creek raid as told by Frank Greet to Edna Greet, 4, American Heritage Center Collection of Percy W. Metz, University of Wyoming; Atherly survey map; trial testimony of Al Morton, 53, 54, 55.

14. Frank Greet Recollections, 1–2; trial testimony of Fred Greet, 107.

15. Frank Greet Recollections, 1–2; grand jury testimony of Fred Greet, 20, and Porter Lamb, 9; trial testimony of Fred Greet, 109, 110.

16. Grand jury testimony of Fred Greet, 4; trial testimony of Fred Greet, 135.

17. Trial testimony of Fred Greet, 11; grand jury testimony of Porter Lamb, 3. An "automatic" here is a gun that fires each time the trigger is pulled.

18. Grand jury testimony of Fred Greet, 4–6.

19. Fred Greet Recollections, 3; Grand jury testimony of Porter Lamb, 9, 10.

20. Grand jury testimony of Porter Lamb, 5, 7; trial testimony of Frank Greet, 135.

21. Grand jury testimony of Fred Greet, 6, 14, 19, and Porter Lamb, 3, 6, 9; Frank Greet Recollections, p. 3.

22. Frank Greet Recollections, 3; grand jury testimony of Porter Lamb, 8, 11; grand jury testimony of Fred Greet, 3, 6.

23. Grand jury testimony of Dr. G. W. Walker, 3, 4; trial testimony of Dr. G. W. Walker, 95, 101.

24. Trial testimony of Felix Alston, 32, 36, 37.

25. Letter of 4/9/09 from Percy Metz to Governor Brooks, Sheep Raid File; trial testimony of Felix Alston, 5, 66, and Al Morton, 55. It is not clear when it was found, but an "ugly old automatic pistol" was also discovered in the ashes. Newspaper article from Vertical File (Ten Sleep Raid), Wyoming State Historical Research and Publications Division.

26. Kurt, "Massacre at Big Horn Basin," 3; trial testimony of Bounce Helmer, 199. Kurt indicates that Alston was annoyed at Helmer when he first arrived at the Greet ranch and Kurt's article was probably based on interviews with Alston, albeit thirty years after the event ("Massacre at Big Horn Basin," 28). See also O'Neal, *Cattlemen vs. Sheepherders*, 137.

27. Trial testimony of Bounce Helmer, 190, 196, 203; grand jury testimony of Bounce Helmer, 24; Rhodes, *The Rest That Came*, 17.

28. Grand jury testimony of Bounce Helmer, 4; Rhodes, *The Rest That Came*, 18, 19.

29. Trial testimony of Bounce Helmer, 174, 176.

30. Trial testimony of Pete Cafferal, 160, 176. This is Cafferal's wording of what Bounce said, and it is probably a paraphrase. Pete did not have a solid command of the English language.

31. Ibid, 6, 7. There are indications that the raiders did not expect Allemand to be at the camp. Speech of Percy Metz before the Park County Historical Society, 6/9/61.

32. Trial testimony of Bounce Helmer, 179–181. Bounce's actual description at the trial was: "They drove us over there, took us down the road and drove us to the other camp." See also Pete Cafferal, 163; grand jury testimony of Bounce Helmer, 7.

33. Grand jury testimony of Bounce Helmer, 8; trial testimony of Bounce Helmer, 181.

34. Trial testimony of Bounce Helmer, 182.

35. Grand jury testimony of Bounce Helmer, 10.

36. Ibid, 12, 21.

37. Ibid, 12–13; trial testimony of Bounce Helmer, 197.

38. Grand jury testimony of Bounce Helmer, 9, wherein Bounce said: "I told them not to kill my dog." When Jack Gage interviewed Bounce in the 1950s, Bounce apparently told him a somewhat different version, which appeared in *Ten Sleep and No Rest* at 156. There, Gage quotes Bounce as saying: "Goddamn you, don't you shoot my dog." The man then asked: "Is that your dog, kid?"

39. Bounce didn't know it the night of April 2, 1909, and had good reason to worry about it, but he would live to see old age, almost receiving his biblical allotment of three score and ten years. (Bounce died in the summer of 1956, when he was 66 or 67 — Gage, *Ten Sleep and No Rest*, 222). He would be interviewed many times about that night and he must have enjoyed his status as a minor celebrity. But as the years wore on, Bounce began to embellish the story. When he testified before the grand jury a month later, Bounce didn't mention that he felt threatened that night. In fact, when he was asked whether he wasn't afraid of being killed himself, his reply was: "All I was afraid of was a stray bullet or something like that" (grand jury testimony of Bounce Helmer, 9). Still, at times during that night, Bounce must have feared that the raiders would kill him, and perhaps there was some kind of direct threat. And that is probably the basis for some of what he told many years later. In 1953, Bounce was interviewed

by the *Cody Enterprise* for a story that appeared on January 22, 1953 ("Famous Tensleep Massacre During Sheep Cattle Feud Recalled by Lone Survivor"), and the following appeared in a story based on that interview: "One of the men . . . made an effort toward Helmer and Cafferall, who were lying in the road, but [the man in charge of Bounce] warned him, 'If you lay a hand on the kid [Helmer, then 20] I'll leave your carcass in the sage brush.' Neither were touched. Then the cattlemen burned the wagons and dynamited the sheep."

There was no dynamite involved in the Spring Creek raid, but it is impossible to know whether the source of that reference was an overwrought feature writer or Bounce. A couple of years after Bounce talked to the *Cody Enterprise*, Jack Gage interviewed Bounce. That interview resulted in a passage in Gage's book wherein one of the raiders supposedly said: "I don't give a damn what you say. I'm telling you if we shoot 'em they can't talk." The reply to this (presumably from the man in charge of Bounce), was: "You're going to get so as you give a damn what I say. You shoot them guys and by God I'll kill you soon as you do" (Gage, *Ten Sleep and No Rest*, 154). Gage's book is based upon the trial transcript and interviews of surviving participants, but it is a "fictionalized" history. That is, Gage makes extensive use of quotes that were paraphrased or even created, so some of the apparent embellishment in this version was probably Gage's. For a version that is still more dramatic, but even less accurate, see Bill Judge, "Tensleep Raid," *Frontier Times* (Summer 1962), 17.

40. Trial testimony of Pete Cafferal, 167; trial testimony of Bounce Helmer, 187.

41. Grand jury testimony of Bounce Helmer, 14; trial testimony of Bounce Helmer, 179, 199.

42. Trial testimony of Al Morton, 77; Fred Greet, 131.

43. Grand jury testimony of Felix Alston, 3, 4; trial testimony of Felix Alston, 9, 15, 19, 33; trial testimony of Al Morton, 65. Three to five .30-30 shells were found around the north wagon; total of twenty .25-35 shells were discovered.

44. Grand jury testimony of Felix Alston, 4; trial testimony of Felix Alston, 17; trial testimony of Percy Metz, 86.

45. Grand jury testimony of Felix Alston, 4; trial testimony of Felix Alston, 33, and Al Morton, 68. Charles Kurt reports the use of the paper. This was not mentioned in the transcripts of either the grand jury proceedings or the trial, but perhaps Kurt obtained this information directly from Alston. It is also possible that the statement is not accurate. (See "Massacre at Big Horn Basin," 28).

46. Grand jury testimony of Felix Alston, 5; trial testimony of Al Morton, 58, and Felix Alston, 12.

47. Trial testimony of Felix Alston, 12, 31, and Al Morton, 59, 81, 85; grand jury testimony of Felix Alston, 5.

48. Trial testimony of Billy Goodrich, 337. By the time of the trial, Alston softened this to "at least seven, possibly more" (trial testimony of Felix Alston, 12).

# The Reaction

## CHAPTER 5

A s word of the raid got out, people throughout the Big Horn Basin — indeed, the whole state of Wyoming — reacted with horror and anger. The first brief newspaper article did not appear until Tuesday, April 6, but by then the people closest to Spring Creek — the people of the Upper Nowood, Basin, Worland, and other small towns in the Big Horn Basin — had gathered all the word-of-mouth intelligence they could. The appetite for news was insatiable; people were so anxious for information that someone with an updated report suddenly gained an elevated status. Jack Gage told a tale of one P. P. Paddock, an itinerant preacher, who parleyed apparent knowledge about the raid into numerous free drinks. The story is fictitious but accurately illustrates the thirst for news.[1]

When Percy Metz returned to Basin, he immediately became a major source of information. Peter Enders, the Big Horn county clerk, evidently spoke to Metz, because on April 5 he wrote a letter to Gov. B. B. Brooks containing a detailed and accurate account of the raid. It is an impassioned letter that no doubt expressed the feelings of many people in the Big Horn Basin. Enders wrote:

> This is the Sixth raid made on sheepmen in this section and the Fourth life that has been taken, absolutely nothing has been done heretofore, undoubtedly the miscreants emboldened by the apathy and ineffiecency of the officers in charge together with the deplorable fact that many of our citizens are intimidated from giving criminating information to the authorities, has brought about a state of affairs intolerable beyond imagination. . . .
>
> Many people who would refrain from stealing a horse or a cow have no scruples about burning a sheep wagon and committing murder, it seems it has become fashionable. Upon us rests the responsibility to break up this terrible menace to decent socity. A large reward should be offered at least $5000. . . .

While the eyes of the world are watching the outcome I pray to God that Wyoming justice will be vindicated.[2]

The Big Horn Basin in 1909 was still a frontier society, but the raid offended even *its* rough-and-tumble concepts of civility. Rhodes quotes a Basin citizen who said that it was one thing for a man in the heat of passion to fight his neighbor with a weapon and kill him, but that it was quite another matter to kill him in his sleep and roast him like a Christmas goose.[3]

The first extensive newspaper coverage was carried on April 7 in the *Cheyenne Daily Leader*. The *Leader* devoted much of the front page to the raid, setting out four headlines of descending size:

### RAIDERS ASSASSINATE AND BURN

#### Prominent Sheepmen Atrociously Murdered

EMGE BROTHERS AND JOE LAZIER RIDDLED WITH
BULLETS BY MOUNTED AND MASKED MEN, WHO SPARE
TWO OTHERS

Two Bodies Burned in Oil Saturated Sheep Wagon and Sheep Slain —
Wires Cut to Prevent Alarm — Big Reward Offered

Basin, Wyo., April 6 — In All The Sanguinary History of the Range Dispute in Wyoming has Occurred No More Atrocious and Cowardly Crime than the Assassination of Joseph and Allemand Emge and Joe Lazier, a Brief Report of Which was Sent Out Last Night. The Three Men Were Shot Down in Cold Blood by an Overwhelming Party of Sheep Camp Raiders and the Bodies of Allemand, Emge and Lazier were Burned. Twenty-Five Head of Sheep were Slaughtered and 2,500 Head were Scattered over the Range and left to Fall Prey to Coyotes and Wolves. All Big Horn County is Horrified by the Outrage and Bitter is the Anathematizing of the Murderers.[4]

On April 8, the *Worland Grit* appeared, the first of the local weeklies to be published after the raid.[5] These weeklies, such as the *Grit*, the *Basin Republican*, and the *Big Horn County Rustler*, had the advantage of immediate access to sources, and their articles provide more detail than those of the dailies, as well as more personal observations.

The *Grit* showed that it would not take a back seat to big town papers for lurid headlines. One of its bold print pronouncements read: "**Two Bodies Furnish Food for Flames.**" The *Grit*'s story spoke of the "blackest crime in Wyoming's stirring history," the "hideous and incoherent" rumors that first filtered into Worland, and how those rumors required one to travel to Basin to obtain "authentic news." It reported that "as we go to press this afternoon word comes from a resident of Red Bank that three men supposedly implicated in the affair have been arrested." [6] This last statement was incorrect, but it certainly underlines how difficult it must have been to obtain "authentic news."[7]

On April 9, the Basin papers published their first stories on the raid. They expressed the generally felt outrage and provided information not found elsewhere. The *Big Horn County Rustler*, in its April 9 article, noted that four inches of snow fell Friday night (April 2) and two more Saturday night and concluded that any clue that might have been gained from the trail was eradicated.[8]

During the week of April 4, Sheriff Alston was in the Upper Nowood. If he had been in Basin before the *Rustler* went to press, perhaps he might have corrected this error. Then again, Alston may not have; he proved to be very close mouthed about the investigation. In any event, one wonders if the newspaper's conclusion was read by some of the raiders. They would have taken comfort from the reported "eradication," not knowing that Alston had actually gained a great many clues from the trail. The same article reported that a "bunch of bloody black hair" was found near the creek, and this led to the belief that at least one of the raiders had been wounded.

The *Basin Republican* reported on April 9 that Allemand's wounds included "a gash across the throat, whether from a bullet or shovel." In subsequent days, this story was considerably expanded by other newspapers. It was said, for instance, that Allemand was "hacked to death with a shovel after he had been shot through the abdomen. In the neck was a great gash cut with the edge of a shovel."[9]

The Big Horn County Commission reacted quickly to the raid, and on April 6 the three commissioners petitioned the governor to offer a "suitable award."[10] Sheepmen responded even more vigorously, with the Big Horn County Woolgrowers Association offering a $1,000 reward, the Wyoming Woolgrowers $1,000, and the National Woolgrowers $2,000.[11] J. A. Delfelder and George Walker, the president and secretary-treasurer of the Wyoming Woolgrowers Association, each wrote to Governor Brooks announcing the rewards offered by the state and county associations and urging the governor to offer as large an award as possible.[12]

Delfelder followed this with a letter to members of the executive committee of the woolgrowers in which he solicited contributions. He expressed many of the same views as he had in his letter to the governor, but more strongly. This letter provides insight into the depth of the sheepmen's anger and their commitment to stopping raids:

> I beg to call your attention to the atrocious assasination of Allemand, Lasier and Emge on the night of April 2nd. in Big Horn County by a band of inhuman and muderous raiders. Not satisfied with shooting and beating their victims to death these inhuman fiends deliberately saturated the bodies of Lasier and Emge with oil and burned them beyond recognition.
>
> The time is at hand to call a halt on this willful defiance of the laws; . . . I am confident that there could be no better time or occasion for making a test case than in this Spring Creek raid. It should not be considered a local matter, for if we succeed in bringing these murderers to justice it will have a salutary effect in all parts of the range country for years to come. . . . It is impossible for the local authorities to successfully cope with this matter and therefore we must offer a suitable reward to induce competent men to become interested and conduct the prosecution.[13]

The goal of this plea for contributions was to obtain $20,000, although it is not clear what part of this sum was sought for general reward money and what part to procure skilled attorneys and investigators.

Very early, then, the greatest fears of Percy Metz were assuaged. The general public was apparently going to strongly support prosecution of the case, as were public officials, and the woolgrowers were going to contribute substantial financial support. This assistance would not come without cost, however. The woolgrowers were declaring that Spring Creek was to be a test case. But cattlemen would see it the same way, elevating the case to a symbolic level, increasing not only the importance of the case but also the burden and pressure on officials charged to prosecute it. Percy Metz was fortunate, though, in that there was someone very close to him who could greatly ease that burden.

In the second half of 1908, there were several raids against the S. A. Guthrie Sheep Company in Crook County, Wyoming, that resulted in a great deal of property damage.[14] Guthrie and the Wyoming Woolgrowers were determined to do something about the raids. The woolgrowers sent in their top range detective, Joe LeFors, and Guthrie hired two experienced Sheridan lawyers, E. E. Enterline and William S. Metz (Percy's father), to assist in the prosecution.[15] Primarily because of excellent detective work by LeFors, thirteen different charges were brought against nine cattlemen. They were difficult cases, taking months to put together.

(LeFors was still able, however, to spend time in Basin in February 1909 with his friend Felix Alston.)[16]

The cattlemen of the area committed a great deal to the defense and used threatening tactics. Armed cowboys would arrive in great numbers at Sundance, the county seat, and after hearings, they called over witnesses and tried to dissuade them from testifying.[17] Finally, though, the criminal charges were brought to trial in April 1909. The prosecution and defense examined some 200 prospective jurors but were unable to empanel a jury. The case was resolved through a compromise whereby all criminal charges were dropped but the nine defendants were forced to pay very large civil penalties. They also agreed to forever grant the Guthrie Sheep Company the use of the range without molestation.[18]

Will Metz and E. E. Enterline learned a great deal about the prosecution of sheep raid cases. They were already excellent attorneys, but with this experience in Crook County they were as able to handle a sheep raid case as any attorneys in the state. Percy and his father were very close, and the younger Metz probably contacted his father immediately after returning from that first trip to Spring Creek and alerted him that his assistance would be badly needed.

Metz knew about the public reaction, the promised financial backing, and, of course, the help from his father, but there was still other support of which he was probably not aware.

On April 7, 1909, District Judge C. H. Parmelee wrote Governor Brooks. Parmelee was the presiding judge in the Crook County sheep raid cases and had just heard of the Spring Creek raid. (Parmelee would also preside over the trials arising out of the Spring Creek raid.) In this 1909 letter, Parmelee referred to an earlier letter the governor had written to him. After the Shell Creek raid on Lynn in 1907, Governor Brooks had suggested to Parmelee that a grand jury be convened. Parmelee had not then felt that any good could be accomplished by a grand jury. In Parmelee's 1909 letter, though, he wrote: "It has occurred to me several times since writing you that perhaps I was hasty in my judgment that a grand jury would do no good." Parmelee told Brooks that he was somewhat more alarmed than he had been before and that he was now "very anxious to do anything within my power to reduce the frequency of this class of crime" and that he was very willing to take any suggestions the governor might have.[19]

One comment in the letter was highly significant. Judge Parmelee mentioned deadline arrangements and expressed his disapproval. He wrote that he had always considered these "an unholy arrangement" made "with men who are already in a practical state of outlawry."

The recipient of this letter was an ebullient and active man who was first elected governor in 1904. He was also one of the leading sheepmen in the state of Wyoming.[20]

Brooks had been away from his office but returned on April 10 and immediately fired letters out. He wrote Parmelee and strongly recommended the convening of a grand jury, told the judge not to worry about the expense, and declared that "these murders and acts of lawlessness must be stopped."[21] He made the same declaration in a letter to J. A. Delfelder, and on Monday, April 12, an official proclamation was issued out of the governor's office offering a reward of $500 for the arrest and conviction of the raiders.[22]

The events of the first week after the raid told Percy Metz that he was not going to have to wage a lonely battle without support; a lot of help was coming. But this assistance did not make a case. All of it taken together would only provide the means to eventually present a case to a Big Horn County jury. In order to have a case to present, to obtain a conviction, Metz would need vastly more facts than he had. Gathering facts was Felix Alston's job, what he'd been trying to do for the past week, and Felix was soon to return from the Upper Nowood.

## NOTES

1. Gage, *Ten Sleep and No Rest*, 87–93.

2. Letter of 4/5/09 from Peter Enders to Hon. B. B. Brooks, Governor, Sheep Raid Files.

3. Rhodes, *The Rest That Came*, 19, Note 10.

4. *Cheyenne Daily Leader*, 4/7/09.

5. On April 8, 1909, the *Denver Post* also carried a story about the raid, headlined: "Murderers of 3 Sheep Herders Still at Large."

6. *Worland Grit*, 4/8/09.

7. The reaction of the populace to the raid was not uniform alarm and revulsion. The event also gave rise to a practical joke. On April 22, the *Grit* reported "A Clever Burlesque" whereby a very elaborate hoax was worked upon a Worland barber. The event as reported, seems too pat to be right, but with that caveat it is set out in the Appendix for the reader's amusement.

8. *Big Horn County Rustler*, 4/9/09. The snow did somewhat impair the tracking, but, as stated earlier, it did not "eradicate" the trail. Trial testimony of Felix Alston, 37.

9. *Cheyenne Daily Leader*, 4/13/09.

10. Letter of 4/6/09 letter from Board of County Commissioners, Big Horn County, to Hon. B. B. Brooks, Sheep Raid File.

11. *Cheyenne Daily Leader*, 4/21/09.

12. Letters of 4/7/09 from Mr. Delfelder and George Walker to Governor Brooks, Sheep Raid File.

13. Letter of 4/12/09 letter from the president of the Wyoming Woolgrowers' Association to Governor Brooks, Sheep Raid File.

14. O'Neal, *Cattlemen vs. Sheepherders*, 128, 127.

15. Enterline was born in 1861 in Tanaque, Pennsylvania, and came west in 1886. He had practiced law in Wyoming since 1888, first at Rock Springs and then at Sheridan. The *Lander Clipper*, 10/16/96.

16. O'Neal, *Cattlemen vs. Sheepherders*, 128, 129; Letter of 4/7/09 from Parmelee to Governor Brooks, Sheep Raid File; Joe LeFors, *Wyoming Peace Officer*, 173; 2/25/09 letter from Joe LeFors to Rodney King (American Heritage Center Collection of S. A. Guthrie, University of Wyoming). Interestingly, LeFors, in one of his letters to Rodney King, expressed suspicion of Will Metz's loyalty to the woolgrowers' cause, although LeFors did not repeat this charge in his book (2/4/09 letter from Joe LeFors to Rodney King, chapter 19, *Wyoming Peace Officer*).

17. Letter of 10/29/09 from E. E. Enterline to the Honorable W. E. Mullen, Attorney General, Cheyenne. Metz Collection.

18. LeFors, *Wyoming Peace Officer*, 173.

19. Letter of 4/7/09 from C. H. Parmelee to Hon. B. B. Brooks. Sheep Raid File. Parmelee played a role in the Johnson County War as a captain in the National Guard. See Chapter 30, Smith, *The War on Powder River*.

20. T. A. Larson, History of Wyoming (Lincoln: University of Nebraska Press, 1965), 314.

21. Letter of 4/10/09 from B. B. Brooks to Judge C. H. Parmelee. Sheep Raid File.

22. Letter of 4/10/09 letter from B. B. Brooks to J. A. Delfelder, president, Wyoming Woolgrowers Association. Sheep Raid File.

# Felix Returns CHAPTER 6

Felix Alston returned to Basin on Sunday morning, April 11, after a long week of investigation in the Upper Nowood.[1] When he began this inquiry, he found people who gave him blank looks, shrugged shoulders, and sometimes cold stares of hostility. Felix Alston, however, was not the kind of man to be put off by such receptions. At the time of the Spring Creek raid, Alston had a reputation for doggedness in the pursuit of criminals.[2] Not everyone in Big Horn County shared that assessment, however, as the letter of county clerk Enders shows; many people felt that his diligence toward sheep raids was suspect. Alston had been the sheriff of Big Horn County when the Lynn raid (and others) occurred, and these did not even produce arrests. Perhaps it was unfair, though, to judge Alston's performance by the results in those sheep raids. In the Lynn raid, for example, Felix probably did everything he could to obtain testimony, but he was not able to break the solidarity of that small Shell ranch community. It must have been frustrating, for Alston surely knew who was on that raid. He just couldn't prove it in court.

In the Upper Nowood, though, the sheriff had some advantages. He knew many of these ranch families well. His first deputy was John D. Hopkins, husband of Stella Hopkins (the sister of Billy Goodrich). Hopkins was from the Upper Nowood and had been very well known and well liked. Alston himself had friends in the area; there was hardly a ranch where he had not spent a night. He was an affable after-dinner guest with a good sense of humor who liked to relax with a corncob pipe and draw on his "vast store of reminiscences."[3] So Felix had a reservoir of good will upon which he could draw. Beyond simple good will toward him, there were people with ties to the murdered men, even some who were deeply offended by the crime. Still, it took determination and courage to venture into the heart of the Upper Nowood.[4]

Alston wasted no time. He was told on April 3 (Saturday night, the night he arrived on the scene) about some cowboys who had been in the area on Friday. Porter Lamb reported seeing Herbert Brink and Tommy Dixon between 4:30 and 5 o'clock on Otter Creek.[5] Fred Greet had seen Brink a couple of miles south of Otter Creek and later saw Milton Alexander a couple of miles north of Otter Creek; they were both traveling south.[6] It would have been Monday, however, before Alston had many opportunities to have some quiet conversations with the people he knew well in the Upper Nowood.

On Monday, an inquest was held by Al Morton, and afterward, Felix left the Greet ranch. It is not known where he went, but some of that day was surely spent talking to friends and sympathizers. Much of what he was told was presented carefully, with requests that he conceal the source. But people in the Upper Nowood knew a great deal about what their neighbors did, and even if it was only rumor, it was very helpful in an investigation.

Alston no doubt quickly learned that Allemand and Emge had been the talk of the Upper Nowood for weeks before the raid. When Emge sold out his cattle operation and became partners with Allemand, all of his lands on Spring Creek were given over to sheep grazing. In addition, when Allemand and Emge bought the Shaw place near Ten Sleep in late February, it meant sheep would be intruding into another area. Their whole course of conduct represented a major penetration of this cattle country. When the men of the Upper Nowood learned that Allemand and Emge were crossing the deadline and bringing sheep from Worland, they saw it as the culmination of a threat which had been building and building.

The anger of the cattlemen had been especially directed at Emge, whom they viewed as a turncoat. It was observed that when Emge was a member of the cattlemen's association and one man allowed sheep to run over Emge's range, he wanted to kill that man for trespassing.[7] There was a lot of talk about dry-gulching Emge as he crossed the badlands and about sheep raids in general.[8]

The sheriff probably was told where the raiders had met on April 2 and was given a pretty good idea of who was in the raid. Metz claimed that Alston knew within an hour just who was involved in the raid. "Within an hour" was an exaggeration (on another occasion, Metz said that it was forty-eight hours), but Alston certainly knew very early to whom he should speak and where he should go.[9] That Monday evening he went to the ranch of Bill Keyes.

The ladies of the Upper Nowood had been using their telephones and were talking about Bill Keyes and his neighbor Charlie Faris. Keyes and Faris were said to have stomach trouble, of the kind we would now attribute to ulcers. When Felix arrived at Keyes' ranch house on Otter

Creek, he learned that the ladies were right, but Keyes supposedly said that he was "just a little bilious."[10] The sheriff's appearance could hardly have eased this condition. From his investigation at Spring Creek, Alston had a few key questions: Where were you on the evening of Friday, April 2? What kind of a gun do you use? Who did you see Friday and can they vouch for your whereabouts? Felix was not so unsubtle as to directly ask these questions — he preferred to engage people in more general conversation — but one way or another he meant to have the answers.[11]

Keyes' story was that he had been at his ranch on April 2, that in the morning Ed Eaton and George Saban had been there, as well as his hired men, Farney Cole and Clyde Harvard.[12] Saban was on his way to see Joe Henry further up on the Nowood. Eaton just showed up and helped Keyes turn out his cattle; Keyes didn't even know he was coming.

Keyes sent Farney Cole to Hyattville (thirty-five miles away) for supplies during the noon hour. Just before Cole left, Brink and Dixon came to Keyes' ranch, to get some of Dixon's cattle, which had become mixed with Keyes' herd. Keyes thought that Brink came along just to help out Dixon. He went out to take care of his cattle and took Harvard with him; when he returned close to sundown, Dixon, Brink, and Eaton had left, but Saban and Milton Alexander were at his place; Alexander had appeared that afternoon. Saban and Alexander had dinner at Keyes' and then went on to Alexander's ranch. Charlie Faris came down to see Keyes and then returned to his house. Keyes spent the night of April 2 at his home by himself.

Alston no doubt nodded politely as he listened to Keyes and kept the conversation going in a friendly way, but he only believed a small part of what Keyes was telling him. The one overwhelming reality in Keyes' story was that there had been eight men in and around his ranch during the late afternoon and evening of Friday, April 2 — only an hour's ride from Spring Creek. Five of them were away from their homes, and none of these five had a compelling reason to be at Keyes'. All the rest was window dressing.

From that time, the eight men mentioned by Keyes — Ed Eaton, George Saban, Clyde Harvard, Herbert Brink, Tommy Dixon, Milton Alexander, Charles Faris, and Keyes himself— were the primary suspects. Given this, the next action by Alston was astounding: He spent the night at Bill Keyes' house.

Felix Alston was not considered a foolhardy man, but this action makes a person wonder if he was not trying to get himself killed. Still, Alston seemed to have insight into men's characters; he may have felt that however Keyes was involved in the raid, he was not a killer. Or perhaps Alston just wanted to have his adversary close at hand so he could watch him. Whatever Alston's thinking, the effect on Keyes of having the sheriff under his roof overnight makes for interesting conjecture. How well did Keyes sleep that night?

The next morning Alston pursued questions relating to guns. He had probably learned the night before that Keyes had a .30-30. A .30-30 was a common rifle, but Alston also learned something more significant: Farney Cole had a .35 automatic. Alston likely spoke to Cole about the rifle. (Cole returned from Hyattville Monday afternoon.) It is not clear exactly what he told Alston, but Alston understood that Cole had left that rifle at Keyes' house before he departed for Hyattville and that when he returned it was gone.[13]

The existence of a .35 automatic around Keyes' place was a further tie to the raid. It must have been one that Felix was reluctant to make, for the tie was to his friend George Saban, a man who did not carry a gun and would have used someone else's. Perhaps for that reason Alston investigated further into .35 automatics. Besides, Felix did not have Cole's gun in hand, and some other .35 automatic might have been used. So Alston inquired about other .35 automatics under the guise that he was interested in buying such a gun.[14]

For the next three or four days Alston traveled up and down the valley talking to people and checking out leads. He surely moved in a cautious way, carefully watching the people he talked to and avoiding riding into areas where he might have been ambushed, but he did not avoid the suspects. During this time, Alston spent one night at Billy Goodrich's and another at Keyes'. He talked to Billy Goodrich and all the men at Goodrich's place, Herbert Brink, Bill Garrison, and Tommy Dixon. Among other things, he learned that Brink's gun was a .25-35 and Dixon's a .45 pistol. He spoke to Sam Brant, the stage driver, and to people along Otter Creek and in Big Trails. Alston was told of a .35 automatic that Bill Garrison owned, but in Hyattville he determined that this weapon could not have been involved in the raid because it had an old, defective firing pin. (In Hyattville he also learned that Farney Cole really had gone there.)[15]

John Callahan, the trapper, told Alston something very important. About 5:20 on the afternoon of April 2, Callahan had seen Herbert Brink headed north, toward the ranch of Bill Keyes'. This was contrary to the story Brink had told.[16] Brink told Alston that he had gone *south* from Keyes' ranch beginning about 3 o'clock, had arrived at Joe Henry's place about 5 (Henry's ranch was three or four miles further south from where Callahan had seen Brink), ate supper at Henry's, and then continued south to Goodrich's.[17]

During the investigation Alston probably tried to find a match to that boot track he had found at the scene. He at least suspected that the track was from a boot worn by Herbert Brink, but could never make a solid connection. However, numerous writers about the raid have declared that the boot track was a major piece of evidence that helped crack the case.[18] One even said that Alston noticed the boot track at Greet's ranch house the second day after the raid and immediately arrested Brink.[19] None of that is correct. There was no evidence developed in the subsequent grand jury proceedings linking Brink to a boot or a boot track. At the trial *nothing* about boots was raised by the prosecution.

The funerals of the three murdered sheepmen took place Tuesday, April 6, at the Allemand ranch on Spring Creek. It was a Masonic ceremony presided over by Marvin Rhodes, who later wrote about the event. The funeral was well attended, with a large delegation of Masons from Basin, as well as many people from Ten Sleep and Big Trails, including Milton Alexander. The three men were buried together close to Spring Creek behind the Allemand home. Felix Alston was a member of the Mason's lodge, but no one saw him at the ceremony. He later told Rhodes, however, that, "I heard everything you said that day."[20]

Late that night, after all the guests at the funeral had left, a rider appeared on an "abrupt steep" hill about a hundred yards southeast of the Allemand ranch house. He sat on a white horse, clearly visible to those in the house, stayed until almost dawn, and left just before the coming light would have revealed his identity. Mrs. Allemand believed this ghostly rider was there to frighten her into leaving the country. If so, he was unsuccessful, because Mrs. Allemand stayed on Spring Creek until after the trial.[21]

At some point in the investigation, Alston decided that Clyde Harvard probably was not involved in the raid, but he still felt there might be others beside the seven remaining suspects. The sheriff was also unable to find any confirmation of Bounce Helmer's statement that two men with the McClellan lumber wagon were at the scene of the crime.

During that week Felix learned of a threat to Bounce. On Monday, April 5, two riders approached the ranch of Jake Goodrich. One was Frank Helmer, the other Bill Garrison. Helmer wanted to talk to his son Bounce. He wanted to tell him, the elder Helmer later testified, to relate "just what he knew and nothing else."[22] More likely, Helmer knew Bounce was in danger and wanted to warn him. In the actual event, Bounce was not home, so Garrison went into the house and spoke to Bounce's mother. Frank Helmer stayed outside, probably wanting to avoid an unnecessary meeting with his ex-wife. Years later, Percy Metz spoke to the Natrona County Historical Society about the encounter and said that Bill Garrison told Mrs. Goodrich she had better tell Bounce to keep his mouth shut or he'd get dry-gulched — someone was going to kill him.[23]

Mrs. Goodrich no doubt conveyed this information to Alston; she would have known he was in the area. For obvious reasons, Felix decided to get Bounce out of the Upper Nowood to some place of safety. So, when Felix returned to Basin on April 11, he brought Bounce Helmer with him.[24]

There are other versions of this incident, but none have been verified. According to one, Tommy Dixon told the stepson of deputy Al Morton that someone was going to kill Bounce and that the sheriff should get to the Jake Goodrich place right away. Alston did so and found Herbert Brink hovering over Bounce, so he took Bounce back to Basin, arriving there just ahead of two riders who tailed him all the way from the Upper Nowood.[25] Aside from the fact that this version is not corroborated, it is improbable. Why would Dixon call attention to himself in this way at a time when no arrests had been made and, for all anyone knew, the authorities had no idea who was involved in the raid? It made more sense that the message, whether friendly warning or threat, be conveyed by someone such as Garrison, who was not involved in the raid. Further, if Brink had been hanging around Bounce in a threatening manner, he would have been confronted with that in his grand jury examination, and he was not. (This is not to say that Brink did not have evil intentions toward Bounce, only that he had not menaced him directly.) As to the supposed riders seen "far in the distance," such an ominous event is easy to imagine and almost impossible to disprove. Alston had deputies in Ten Sleep and Basin, and if he felt any real danger, he could have stopped at one of the ranches along the Nowood and simply telephoned for help.

Regardless of the exact circumstances, Alston did start back to Basin, probably on Friday, April 9. In one sense, the last few days had been a great success. Felix had solid suspects who he knew, to a moral certainty, were guilty of the crimes committed the night of April 2. But "moral certainty" is not the same as "beyond a reasonable doubt." Alston had no evidence to put any one of the seven at the scene, no evidence showing any one of them to have burned or killed. And in that sense the investigation was a failure. It was just like the Lynn case.

But then there came a break: Bounce admitted to Alston that he had recognized one of the raiders. When he and Cafferal were taken back to the south wagon, Bounce watched a man untying a wagon. The fire was burning brightly, and the man leaned into his work. The mask on the man's face was not tied at the bottom, and it fell forward as the man leaned over. At that moment, Bounce recognized Ed Eaton, a man he had known most of his life and with whom he had been on roundups. And after he recognized Eaton's face, he also identified his distinctive build.[26]

Bounce had first denied that he recognized any of the raiders, thinking that if that leaked out, someone would kill him.[27] Apparently, though, at least one of the raiders wanted to kill him anyway.

When Bounce testified at the trial in November, he said that the first time he divulged that he'd recognized Eaton was at the grand jury.[28] This statement doesn't wash. For one thing, after April 9, he was in the protective custody of the sheriff (and would be for the next seven months). There would be no reason to wait until the grand jury was convened. Also, Bounce's testimony before the grand jury does not show a witness surprising the questioning attorney but rather a smooth presentation by a lawyer who was drawing out what he already knew was there.[29] Most significant, as soon as Alston returned to Basin, he swore out a warrant for the arrest of Ed Eaton and only Ed Eaton. Other than Bounce's statements, there would have been nothing to distinguish Eaton from the other six suspects. But with it, the prosecution had a case, at least against Eaton.

On Monday the 12th, Felix met with Percy Metz and various members of the Allemand family. Jacques Allemand, Joe's brother from Buffalo, had offered a reward of $1,000, bringing the total reward money to $5,500.[30] That was a huge sum in 1909, worth something over $100,000 by 1991 values. On Tuesday the 13th, a warrant was issued for Ed Eaton's arrest, and the same day Felix left again for the Upper Nowood. In the day and a half he was in Basin, however, someone made it clear to Alston that they thought he had been more than diligent in pursuing this sheep raid and that continuing to do so might be harmful to his health. That unknown person slipped an anonymous note into Alston's coat pocket warning him "not to look too far into this affair." Alston ignored the threat.[31]

Al Lattig and Ed Cusack made the arrest of Eaton on Thursday at the head of Lake Creek, north of Black Mountain. Lattig and Eaton were old friends, having ridden the range together. Eaton is supposed to have said: "Al, I would have killed anyone but you." Whether it was because of the presence of Lattig or not, Eaton surrendered peacefully.[32]

The sheriff returned to Basin Thursday evening. He had probably learned additional information about Herbert Brink. Both before and after the raid, Brink had talked. Before the raid, he told one man that if Allemand and Emge brought over their sheep, he would "go out with my rifle and mob the sons of bitches and drive them back."[33] A few days after the raid, Brink was in a conversation with several people, including F. P. and Eliza Brown of Big Trails. Brink said that Joe Allemand "came out of the wagon and stood like he was listening and was shot and he fell and staggered out to where he laid." It was as if Brink had been there, but then he added: "That was the supposition."[34]

The additional evidence did not add a great deal to what Alston already knew, but it was enough to file charges against Brink. There may have been other considerations, too. Alston may have been worried about what Brink might do to witnesses. A warrant was issued, and Brink was arrested in Worland by deputy Abe Kent. On Saturday evening (April 17), Kent brought him to the Basin jail.[35] Alston would tell the press little about the charges against Eaton and Brink, but Percy Metz indicated that the cases were very strong.[36]

Somewhere around this time, probably during the week of April 18, Percy's father, W. S. Metz, and E. E. Enterline became active in the case. They were not officially hired by the county until later in the week but had surely been involved before then. From that time, the prosecution was under the control of these senior lawyers. Even had W. S. Metz not been Percy's father (and legal mentor), such experienced and competent older lawyers would have assumed control. A lengthy apprenticeship is required before a graduate of law school becomes able to handle a complex case. Percy Metz candidly admitted that he was not competent to handle a case such as this one, and he asked the Big Horn County Commissioners to appoint special counsel.[37] The commissioners acceded to Metz's request and let him select the attorneys he wanted. Will Metz and Enterline were obvious choices, but it was also desirable to have a local attorney participate. By this time, however, cattlemen had retained every lawyer in the Big Horn Basin except William Simpson of Cody. Simpson was the attorney for a number of woolgrowers on the western side of the Basin, though, and so was a natural choice in any event.[38]

Enterline, Simpson, and Will and Percy Metz convened, and the first thing they addressed was what the prosecution's position should be regarding the calling of a grand jury. In Big Horn County, the calling of a grand jury was an unusual event; it had only been done twice before. But public sentiment had already been expressed in favor of a grand jury, and Judge

Parmelee had made it clear that he thought one ought to be called. [39] It should not have taken these four attorneys long to conclude that a grand jury was not only desirable but essential. As things then stood, more evidence had to be developed.

The case against Brink, if presented on April 19, would probably have been dismissed immediately after the prosecution finished presenting its side. They could show that Brink had made some threatening statements before Allemand and Emge brought their sheep over from Worland, but a number of men had been guilty of that, men who were quietly sleeping in their beds the evening of April 2. They could show that Brink had been in the general area on April 2, that he had really gone back toward that area in the late afternoon (contrary to his statement that he was going away from it), and that he had made statements that seemed to show more knowledge than simple supposition. But this evidence was not nearly enough to establish, beyond a reasonable doubt, that Herbert Brink had committed murder and arson on Spring Creek the evening of April 2.

The case against Eaton appeared stronger, but it depended almost entirely on a scared, sometimes confused boy who had at first insisted he had not recognized anyone. A skilled defense attorney could probably make a shambles of all the prosecution's bright theories. Moreover this was a sheep raid case, and there was a good chance that a jury would require more than just proof beyond a reasonable doubt.

As to the remaining suspects, there was not even enough evidence to justify their arrests. It was not likely, either, that Felix was going to develop more evidence. The Upper Nowood was a very small society; most of its members were united in their determination not to help Alston, and they inhibited the remainder of the citizens. If a further investigation was to develop usable information, it would have to be an investigation with teeth.

So when the county commissioners met in special session on Friday evening, April 23, there was unanimity that a grand jury should be called. The commissioners formally approved Percy Metz's choice of special counsel, E. E. Enterline and W. S. Metz (to be paid $2,500 each), and William Simpson (to be paid $1,000). The pledge of woolgrowers' money no doubt affected their generosity. [40]

The commissioners also approved the appointment of William Harnden, an attorney from Lander. The prosecution team felt there would be a lot of lying before the grand jury and wanted a record of it. [41] Only prosecuting attorneys were supposed to be present in a grand jury proceeding, but Mr. Harnden, in addition to being an attorney, was a stenographer and could make a stenographic record of the testimony. If they could not make a case for murder or arson, maybe they could get some perjury convictions.

## NOTES

1. *Big Horn County Rustler*, 4/16/09.
2. See Rhodes, *The Rest That Came*, 26, Note 17.
3. Rhodes, *The Rest That Came*, 26, Note 17. Hopkins was apparently what we now call an undersheriff, the chief deputy of a sheriff. He died in 1908.
4. Ed Cusack also spent at least part of the week of April 4 in the Upper Norwood, but all of the available information relates to Felix Alston. *Worland Grit*, 4/8/09.
5. Grand jury testimony of Porter Lamb, 1.
6. Grand jury testimony of Fred Greet, 7–9.
7. Grand jury testimony of Samuel W. Richie, 3, 4.
8. Andre Nelson, "The Last Sheepman-Cattleman War," *True West* (May 1988), 15. The exact event reported is questionable, but it cannot be doubted that there was talk of isolating Emge and killing him; grand jury testimony of Oscar Arnett, 14.
9. Percy Metz speech before Park County Historical Society, 6/9/61, speech before Natrona County Historical Society, 11/2/61; see Rhodes, *The Rest That Came*, 25–29.
10. Rhodes, *The Rest That Came*, 25, 26; Kurt, "Massacre at Big Horn Basin," 29. This quote is taken from Kurt's article and is a plausible statement, but it is unlikely that Keyes actually used those words.
11. For an idea of Alston's investigative techniques, see Rhodes, *The Rest That Came*, 25–29.
12. All of the following discussion is taken from pages 1–9 of Keyes' grand jury testimony, which would have been almost identical to what Keyes earlier told Alston.
13. Grand jury testimony of Farney Cole, 3, 12.
14. Rhodes, *The Rest That Came*, 27.
15. Rhodes, *The Rest That Came*, 27–28.
16. Trial testimony of John Callahan, 295.
17. Grand jury testimony of Herbert Brink, 4, 5.
18. For example, Kurt, "Massacre at Big Horn Basin," Rhodes, *The Rest That Came*, at 22, and Wentworth, *America's Sheep Trails*, at 542.
19. Arlene G. Robinson, "Ten Sleep Raid," available in the Miscellaneous Files (WPA #1307), Wyoming State Archives, Cheyenne, 4.
20. Rhodes, *The Rest That Came*, 24.
21. This incident is fully described by Gage in *Ten Sleep and No Rest* at 180.
22. Trial testimony of Frank Helmer, 373.

23. Percy Metz speech before the Natrona County Historical Society, 11/2/61. See also 12/11/61 letter of Percy Metz to Bill Judge, Metz Collection.

24. Rhodes, *The Rest That Came*, 30; Pendergraft, *Washakie: A Wyoming County History*, 110; trial testimony of Bounce Helmer, 194, 195.

25. Pendergraft, *Washakie: A Wyoming County History*, 109, 110.

26. All of this paragraph is taken from the grand jury and trial testimony of Bounce Helmer. Grand jury testimony, 12, 13; trial testimony, 186.

27. Trial testimony of Bounce Helmer, 201.

28. Ibid, 194–196

29. See grand jury testimony of Bounce Helmer, 12–13.

30. *Big Horn County Rustler*, 4/16/09.

31. Rhodes, *The Rest That Came*, 29; *Cheyenne Daily Leader*, 4/20/09.

32. *Greybull Standard*, 6/4/59; *Big Horn County Rustler*, 4/16/09. Black Mountain is a promontory which rises about 1,500 feet; it sits in the southern part of the Basin, about twenty miles due east of Lucerne.

33. Trial testimony of W. G. Colethorpe, 305.

34. Trial testimony of Eliza Brown, 308; trial testimony of F. P. Brown, 315.

35. *Basin Republican*, 4/23/09.

36. See, for example, the *Denver Post*, 4/21/09, p. 6, col. 5.

37. Speech of Percy Metz to the Park County Historical Society, 6/9/61.

38. Including H. S. Ridgely, R. B. West, W. S. Collins, T. M. Hyde, C. F. Robertson, J. J. Jones, W. L. Walls, C. A. Zaring, and C. H. Harkins. J. L. Stotts, known as "Judge" Stotts, of Sheridan, was also retained. Index to the testimony, transcript of *State v. Brink*.

39. *Big Horn County Rustler*, 4/30/09. A rape case from Shell was the reason for the first; the second was called after the 1902 attack on the jail. See also *Cheyenne Daily Leader*, 4/20/09.

40. *Big Horn County Rustler*, 4/30; *Basin Republican*, 5/14/09.

41. Percy Metz speech before the Park County Historical Society, 6/9/61.

# The Grand Jury

## CHAPTER 7

T
he grand jury is an ancient and honorable institution. At its best, a grand jury can be a superb investigative device. A prosecutor can take a group of people, individuals smug and secure in their combined strength, and strip them of that mutual support. Singly, each is taken from friends and family and brought alone into a room. In that room, they face a grim jury and a prosecuting attorney who is hostile and implacable. The witness cannot bring an attorney or a family member into that room. He will know nothing of how other witnesses have testified, and all of his statements will be scrutinized for perjury. A grand jury will intimidate the boldest of witnesses. And for those who secretly wish to provide information, an appearance before a grand jury provides a first-rate excuse: "I didn't want to tell them, but I knew I'd be in terrible trouble if I didn't tell the truth."[1]

Enterline and Simpson were conducting the grand jury proceeding and they were going to do it right; they sent out over a hundred subpoenas.[2] Percy Metz said: "We were going to put every man, woman and child of age to be a witness on record as to where they were that night, who they saw, had they seen any of these people, everybody on the east side of the Big Horn County."[3] This was something of an exaggeration, but the prosecution put out enough subpoenas to create an effect like that of a bomb in a chicken coop — it was going to rain feathers for a long time.

The subpoenas commanded appearance beginning Thursday, April 29, and when that time came the road from the Upper Nowood to the county seat had a veritable traffic jam. Every time two buggies or horses got close, people would pull over and talk and wonder and conjecture about the grand jury.[4]

The grand jury convened in Basin at 2 p.m. on the 29th, and Judge Parmelee began the proceedings by giving the jury a stirring charge. He stressed the need for absolute secrecy and pointed out that matters other than the Spring Creek affair might come before them. The bulk of his remarks, though, were directed toward a condemnation of mob rule, emphasizing that under no circumstances should a body of men be allowed to redress grievances outside the forms of the law: "All acts of a mob give occasion for reprisal. The spirit of lawlessness grows by what it feeds on." He concluded by telling the jurors to "pursue your investigation thoroughly and demonstrate that law and not violence is the ruling principle in Big Horn County."[5]

The fundamental job of a prosecutor before a grand jury is to persuade the jurors that they should return indictments. That burden may have been lightened because the foreman of the jury, George Taylor of Meeteetse, was a prominent sheepman.[6] The first two witnesses were Al Morton and Felix Alston, friendly witnesses called to show what was already known.[7] They testified to the results of their investigation at Spring Creek, what they learned at the scene. Their testimony was assisted by a map drawn by the county surveyor, Clyde Atherly. On Tuesday the 26th, Atherly and William Simpson had gone to Spring Creek along with Alston and Morton. Atherly had undertaken a survey, with his survey instrument set over the spot where Joe Emge's body was found. This map, which established unassailable information about the site of the crime, proved particularly helpful at the trial.[8]

Bounce Helmer was the third witness called. After being brought back to Basin, he had been taken by Alston to Sheridan, where he stayed for only two days. Then he went to Dietz (near Sheridan) and worked for a sheepman, Bill Wagner, until he was called for the grand jury.[9] Bounce repeated his tale but added some additional information for the grand jury. He testified that as they were driving the sheep from Worland, he had met Jake Frison in a buggy, and Allemand and Emge met Harry Johnson. He also said that the fellows in the lumber wagons who were at the site included Walter Nelson.[10]

Bounce testified that at one time during the raid he thought he recognized Jake Frison's voice, but he wouldn't swear to it. The questioner (probably Enterline, but the grand jury transcripts do not usually identify the questioning attorney) picked up on this and led Bounce through a series of questions about Frison. By the time they were completed, Bounce was saying that he had definitely heard Jake Frison's voice.[11] In response to other questions, Bounce seemed to deny that he had heard an automatic, but then the questioner got him to admit to the grand jury that he heard rapid shooting. Bounce also related that important identification of Ed Eaton.[12]

The fourth witness was Pete Cafferal. He testified much as did Bounce but added some helpful details. He remembered that one of the raiders was wearing corduroy pants and that when he and Bounce were lying below the north wagon, he heard groaning after one shot.[13]

Porter Lamb was the fifth witness, to be followed by Fred Greet. Lamb repeated what he'd told Alston of coming to his new place on Spring Creek on April 2; of seeing Sam Brant, the stage driver, and Herbert Brink and Tommy Dixon; and, of course, about the events of that evening. He quite readily asserted that he had seen the blaze of two shots fired toward where Allemand was found. Lamb didn't see any camp of the McClellan lumber wagons, though, and the first time he observed these wagons was an hour after he'd gone to the site; they were then trying to climb a hill just north of Spring Creek. The interrogating attorney went over these points time and again, obviously because of Bounce Helmer's previous testimony, but Lamb was quite sure there had been no lumber wagons camped at the site of the crime.[14]

Fred Greet also testified that there were no lumber wagons camped on the site, saying that it was a mistake if anyone testified otherwise. He recalled seeing Milton Alexander the afternoon of April 2 and Herbert Brink riding a sorrel horse, "just leaping along." The attorney conducting the examination pressed Greet as to why he hadn't gone to the rescue of the besieged sheepmen or at least tried to telephone the authorities that Friday night. Greet responded, apparently with some heat, that, "If I reported it, those raiders could not kill me could they?" The questioner moved away from this subject but returned to it to close the examination:

Q. You seemed to be scared of these raiders?
A. Yes sir. to a certain extent I am, and there are others.
Q. You hesitate to tell anything you know?
A. I told everything I know and I told the truth too.[15]

From a distance of over eighty years, it is easy to be critical of Fred Greet and others for their failure to act the night of April 2. But a whole valley was "scared of these raiders," and most of them did much less than Greet. It took quite a bit of courage for anyone in the Upper Nowood simply to stand up and tell the truth, and Fred Greet did that throughout the life of the case.

The next witness, Samuel Walter Richie, was evidently quite willing. This is surprising, because Walt Richie was a ranch hand who worked for George and Oscar McClellan, both staunch cattlemen.[16] Richie had been at the Buckmasters' the afternoon of April 2. He had seen Brink and Dixon between 3 and 4 o'clock heading south and also observed five horsemen coming out of Bill Keyes' field. He saw another man pass by that day on a grey horse and thought he was Milt Alexander.[17]

Richie also related a conversation he'd heard a few months before the raid. Tom Dixon and a man named Blackledge were discussing Emge and Allemand. They thought that the Ten Sleepers should wake up and do something. They recalled that when Emge was in the cattlemen's association, a man had run sheep over Emge's range and Emge had wanted to kill this man for trespassing. They agreed that Emge knew the penalty for trespassing on cattle range with sheep.[18]

W. G. Colethorpe was witness number eight. About two weeks before the raid, Colethorpe was working for Goodall and Whitmeyer on the Nowood. He was getting breakfast when he overheard a conversation about Emge and Allemand. This was the conversation in which Brink said they never would get through with their sheep, that he was ready to go out with his rifle and drive them back. There was no mystery why Colethorpe, Joe Allemand's brother-in-law, was willing to come forward and tell about this conversation.19

The next witness was George Rogers, a ranch hand who worked at the Chatfield place. He was also at the Buckmasters' the afternoon of April 2, and he testified that about 2:30 or 3 o'clock he'd seen Brink, riding a sorrel horse, with Dixon, and they were headed south. He also remembered seeing four or five riders around Keyes' place a little later.[20]

Lizzie Lamb was the tenth witness, and her interrogation is a good example of the kind of detail the prosecuting attorneys were trying to elicit from the witnesses. Mrs. Lamb was a fastidious lady, and her answers reflect a care for accuracy. She stated who was there when she and her husband arrived at the Goodrich place on April 1 (Mr. and Mrs. Goodrich and Tommy Dixon) and who she saw the next day (Mrs. Goodrich, Herbert Brink, Dixon, and Bill Garrison). She was asked where she went the next morning (Helmer ranch), with whom (Mrs. Goodrich), the exact time they left (9:30), and who remained at the Goodrich ranch (Brink and Dixon).[21] She told of returning to the Goodrich ranch at 5 o'clock, finding only Garrison there, and hearing nothing of Brink and Dixon, even though she went to bed at 10 o'clock with her upstairs bedroom "right west" of the bunkhouse, which was in plain view.[22]

She saw Brink, Dixon, and Garrison early the next morning and thought they were all at the dinner table on the 3rd; she was sure they were all at supper. On Sunday the 4th they were all there except Dixon, who went to Worland. That morning, about 11 o'clock, Mrs. Goodrich received a call from Mrs. Crowley at the Helmer ranch that three men had been killed in a raid at Spring Creek. They could not call the Greet ranch directly because the line had been cut, and Mrs. Lamb became worried about her husband, who had gone to the Greet place. Mr. Goodrich and Mr. Brink volunteered to go to Spring Creek and see what the situation was.[23]

Bringing out such detail was probably tedious at times, but it was crucial to counter the suspects' alibis.

Charles Mann, Joe Emge's brother-in-law, was the eleventh witness. He had no direct knowledge of the raid but did know the value of the property burned, important in cases of arson.[24]

Anna Goodrich is listed in the Metz notes as witness number twelve. Her testimony is particularly interesting because it indicates that the prosecutors were already aware of some startling evidence of which her husband, Billy, had possession. This evidence was probably the biggest break of the whole investigation, the one development that finally made the prosecution's case.

What remains unclear is just when and how the prosecutors got this information. Billy Goodrich is listed as witness number twenty in the Metz notes, suggesting that he testified *after* his wife did. However, the order of the witnesses is made confusing by the fact that a number of men — Goodrich, Brink, Dixon, and Garrison — were called back to the stand on May 1 to clarify earlier testimony.[25] It may be that Billy Goodrich was counted as witness number twenty on his *second* appearance on the stand and that his initial appearance came at some point before his wife's but was left out of the Metz notes.

If this initial testimony was left out of the notes, there was ample justification for doing so — it was wholly inaccurate. When Billy first testified, he denied knowing anything about the raid and was excused. [26] But then, presumably somewhere in Basin, Joe LeFors had a talk with Billy.

In the movie *Butch Cassidy and the Sundance Kid*, Paul Newman repeatedly looks at Robert Redford and asks: "Who *are* those guys?" "Those guys" were a posse led by Joe LeFors, tracking down our heroes after a train robbery. In real life, Joe LeFors did lead such a posse — he was an amazingly skilled and indefatigable tracker — and he was probably responsible for pushing the Hole in the Wall gang out of Wyoming. Later, LeFors got Tom Horn drunk and induced him to confess to the murder of Willy Nickels, a tactic that is still controversial. LeFors was a remarkable combination of ice-cold daring, skill of the highest order with weapons, and a doggedness bordering on obsession. He was that rarest of western men — a legendary character whose life really does read like a TV script.[27] LeFors had only been in Basin for a few days (he had been brought there by the woolgrowers), although it is hard to know at any given time where LeFors was. He was a man who quite deliberately chose a very low profile.

Billy Goodrich was no match for Joe LeFors. Somehow, LeFors had deduced that Goodrich knew more than he told the grand jury, and he persuaded Billy to return and tell the true story. The details of this encounter are very sketchy; the only evidence that it happened at all is in a letter written by E. E. Enterline some nine months later in which Enterline told how the "exceedingly valuable" testimony of William Goodrich had been secured through the "influence" of Mr. LeFors.[28] Judging from LeFors' techniques in other cases, we might surmise that he sat down with Billy and talked about how the prosecutors were looking to charge people for perjury, how there was no question Billy had committed perjury, and how miserable the state penitentiary was. Then he could have hinted broadly that Billy would receive a large share of that big amount of reward money. Whatever LeFors said, Billy did return to the grand jury, and what he told them was a blockbuster.

Both Brink and Dixon had talked to Billy after the raid. Brink did so first, on the Sunday night after he and Billy left the Greet place. At Greet's, Felix Alston had told Brink and Goodrich that eight men had been in on the raid. Brink said to Goodrich, however: "Felix was mistaken, there was only seven." Alston had also said that the wagon was surrounded, but Brink told Billy that only two men took the wagon. Goodrich then said to Brink: "You must have been there." Brink replied, "I was."[29]

From his conversation with Brink, Goodrich determined the names of four of the men: Brink, Saban, Dixon, and Alexander.[30] Brink gave Goodrich a number of other details about the raid. He told him that he had shot the first shot right through the door of the sheepwagon, that they had "turned loose" when there was no light lit in the wagon, that he (Brink) had set the wagon on fire with sagebrush, and that when Allemand came out of the wagon, he thought it was Emge. Brink also mentioned John Callahan. In a chilling remark, Brink said that Callahan was the only one who had seen him go back to Keyes', and if necessary he would take care of him.[31]

Later, when Dixon talked to him, Billy learned that Farris, Keyes, and Eaton also had participated. Dixon told him that Allemand did not come out until after the wagon was burning, that he said something such as, "For God's sake, don't kill my sheep," and that somebody hollered, "Throw up your hands." Dixon said Allemand might not have understood, because he didn't throw up his hands and then he was shot; he thought it was either Brink or Saban that had shot Allemand. Dixon said Allemand had sunk down after the first shot and had fallen after the second; he heard groaning after that. Goodrich learned that Dixon had been the primary guard of Cafferal and Helmer.[32]

The state of Wyoming had a case — finally! With the testimony of Billy Goodrich, the prosecution could put all seven of the suspects dead center on the scene. Suddenly, all those odds and ends and bits and pieces of evidence, all circumstantial and none determinative (except for the identification of Eaton), became simply corroboration — evidence supporting what Billy Goodrich said. And as corroboration they became highly persuasive. Now the thrust of the investigation would be to find additional corroborating evidence and to cut off alibis. The core case was made.

The prosecutors knew as much by the time Anna Goodrich took the stand, judging by the questions she was asked. Her testimony in large part paralleled that of Lizzie Lamb, but she also testified about Brink and Dixon's admissions to her husband. Because of his inquisitiveness about the case, she suspected Brink even before Billy and Brink went to Spring Creek, and she told her husband of her suspicion. When Billy returned, he confirmed her suspicions by telling her what Brink had said. She spoke with Brink later, and he said something about money matters. He said he didn't know whether he and Tommy Dixon would get their money or not. Then he started talking about the killing and asked Mrs. Goodrich if she knew anything about it. She said she didn't want to know anything about it. Brink "hushed up then" and didn't say anything more about the subject.[33]

Mrs. Goodrich also testified that George Saban had been at their house on Thursday, April 1. She didn't know why he was there; it was the first time he had been there for three years. She testified further that neither Dixon nor Brink attended to the chores, that Brink had boots and wore them, and that she had not seen Brink or Dixon return to the ranch the evening of April 2.[34]

The thirteenth witness was Clyde Harvard, Keyes' hired man, and he testified to the various men coming and going around Bill Keyes' ranch on Thursday night and Friday, before he left the place between 1 and 2 p.m. Unfortunately, the actual transcript of Harvard's testimony is missing, but there is a summary prepared by the prosecution. It was a relatively long examination, and the summary reflects a large gap, in which pages 4 through 16 are not referred to. It is entirely possible that the prosecutors still thought Clyde might have been involved in the raid and spent a long time thoroughly examining his story as to his whereabouts.[35]

In fact, Clyde Harvard may have been much more closely associated with the raid than anyone knew. Sometime in the late 1950s, Clyde Harvard, who was then elderly, appeared at the home of Jack Seaman, a young man who happened to be one of George Saban's grandsons. Harvard had ridden over twenty miles that afternoon, by horseback, and his appearance was uninvited and unexpected. What he wanted to talk about was the raid. He arrived in the evening and spent the entire night talking with Seaman; he told Seaman things he said he had not even told his family.

Harvard said that on April 2, 1909, the men at the Keyes place sent him away, supposedly to find a bull, which Harvard suspected didn't exist. But young Harvard felt that something big was up, wanted to be part of it, and found an excuse to return to the ranch (he claimed that he'd forgotten his coat). When the men found him, however, they literally kicked him in the buttocks, put him on his horse, and told him to "get the hell out of here." He did leave but still hung around the ranch headquarters, although at a more discreet distance. Harvard saw the men leave and followed right behind them, all the way to Spring Creek. There he was supposedly close enough to watch and hear all the burning, the shooting, and an argument over the captured men. Harvard finally realized why the raiders had not wanted him around and decided he'd better leave and make the best alibi he could.[36]

This tale, if true, would explain why Felix Alston concluded there were eight riders and why the authorities may have continued to believe Clyde Harvard was involved in the raid.

Fred Whitmeyer, witness number fourteen, testified that Brink had said that if Allemand and Emge crossed the cattle range with their sheep, "there is liable to be something doing."[37] Sam Brant, the stage driver, testified that he saw Milton Alexander riding west a mile or a mile and a half above Spring Creek about 4:15 on April 2.[38]

Farney Cole, the sixteenth witness, was particularly important, for he provided a solid connection between George Saban and the raid. Saban did not normally carry a gun; therefore, if he went on the raid, he would have had to use someone else's. The ready availability of Cole's gun the evening of April 2, the subsequent use of a gun of that type in the raid, and the fact that the other suspects used other calibers, all raised a reasonable inference that Saban had taken Cole's automatic, used it in the raid, and then discarded it somewhere.

At first Cole seemed a cooperative witness. He told the grand jury that just before the raid Keyes wanted to know where Allemand and Emge's sheep were, and he told about the men at Keyes place (including Saban) before he left for Hyattville. But as the questioner, again probably Enterline, began asking Cole about the .35 automatic, things took an alarming turn. Cole testified that he had lost that rifle south of Otter Creek a few days before the raid. He was then asked a series of questions about how that happened, but he stuck to his story.[39] This was a bad development for the prosecution. If Cole lost the gun several days before the raid, it could hardly have been available to Saban.

What happened next is not captured well in the transcript. A typewritten transcript can be a lifeless thing. It doesn't catch the inflections or volume of a voice, nor the pauses between questions and answers, not to mention all the visual drama. Still, what happened next was one of the most dramatic moments in the grand jury's proceedings. With the help of some plausible stage direction, perhaps some of that drama can be recaptured:

> Enterline (sternly, while looking directly into the eyes of the young witness): Don't you know it to be a fact, on the day you left Keyes ranch, that gun was at Keyes' house? (long pause)
> Cole (softly): Yes.
> Enterline (firmly): Why is it you told us that you lost that gun and now you say that that automatic gun was at Keyes ranch on the day of this killing? (another long pause) Will you answer my question?
> Cole (softly again): Yes if I know how to do it. (pause) I was afraid it would get me into trouble.[40]

The rest of the testimony went much more smoothly. Cole had heard that automatic shells were found at the scene and that made him afraid of getting into trouble. He *had* lost his gun *before the raid* but had found it within about fifteen minutes.[41]

He kept the automatic rifle standing up in a corner of the kitchen, where everybody could see it. It was there when he left for Hyattville, along with eight or ten shells, with perhaps five more in the magazine. When he returned from Hyattville both the shells and the gun were gone. Cole admitted that Keyes had talked to him about the gun. Keyes said something about hating to have Cole's gun in that mess and suggested that "the best way to get out of it" was to say he'd lost the gun off his saddle.[42]

The next three witnesses were John and Mary Buckmaster and the trapper John Callahan. Like Walt Richie and George Rogers, the Buckmasters told whom they saw Friday afternoon, April 2. Callahan told the grand jury of that important sighting of Brink going north rather than south, as he had claimed. Callahan said Brink was on the county road, stopped briefly for a talk, and then continued north, proceeding toward Keyes' ranch.[43]

It is not certain who witness number twenty-one was, but it was probably Dixon or Garrison. The exact order wasn't that significant, though, because of the recalling of witnesses.

Witness number twenty-two was Herbert Brink. At this stage, the grand jurors probably had a strong and abiding belief of the guilt of Brink, and they must have found his testimony fascinating. Brink was already represented by an attorney — indeed, he could have had his pick of almost any attorney in the Big Horn Basin. The attorney probably working with him was H. S. Ridgeley.[44] Ridgeley was a competent lawyer, and he would have instructed Brink before his grand jury appearance. He no doubt told Brink to answer *only* the questions put to him. *Don't volunteer!* was then and is now a cardinal rule for witnesses. A defense counsel's nightmare and a prosecutor's dream is a witness who rattles on at great length.

At first, Brink was fairly succinct in his answers. But then he became so anxious to tell his story that he blurted it all out. He was asked: "So you wish us to understand that you found Tommy Dixon at Keyes'?" Then followed testimony that fills more than two legal-sized pages. In response to this thirteen-word question, Brink said, among other things, that he and Tommy left the Goodrich place together and that Tommy turned out some cattle at Ainsworths, that he had been riding for four or five days and came down to Billy's, that Billy wanted to sell him his ranch, that on Thursday evening he went to the Rebideaux's and stayed all night, that the next morning he rode to Goodrich's where he met Tommy, that he and Tommy went through some Ainsworth land, where Tommy stopped to talk to some fellow and Brink went on to Keyes', that he was going down to Keyes' for cattle, that he had dinner at Keyes' (Tommy arrived about this time), that he and Tommy then left and went by Buckmaster's, that Tommy split off to look for cattle in mudholes, that he then went to Joe Henry's and ate supper, that Joe wanted him to stay the night but that he decided to go on to Goodrich's because he didn't know if anyone would be there to do the chores, that he arrived after dark and saw the chores had been done, that he went to the bunkhouse, where after a while Dixon and Garrison showed up, that they talked a while and then he went to bed, that the next morning he, Tommy, and Garrison went to Joe Henry's to turn out some cattle, that they ate dinner at Henry's but then returned to Goodrich's, that Mrs. Goodrich called that afternoon about Emge and two others being killed, that he then called Mrs. Brown about the raid, that Mrs. Lamb was worried about her husband, that Billy offered to go to Greets and told Brink he wanted him to go, too, that they did, that they talked to a number of people, looked at the corpse, and ate supper there, that when they started back it started to storm, that they stopped at Shaw's place, and that the next morning they went home.[45]

What a gift! After this answer, the prosecutors knew exactly what Herbert Brink's defense was; all they had to do was fill in a few details.

Brink was asked about the horses he had ridden on April 2, and he told the grand jury that he had changed to a dark bay horse at Joe Henry's, had borrowed a saddle of Henry's, and had arrived back at the Goodrich ranch between 8 and 9 o'clock that evening. Brink admitted that it was possible he was wearing corduroy pants on April 2, but he asserted that he had never heard of anybody being against Emge and Allemand. He repeatedly denied that he had met John Callahan on April 2, saying at one point: "I am positive I did not." When asked about automatic rifles, Brink said, "I never saw an automatic rifle in this country." He must have anticipated questions about his boots, because he said that on April 2 he was wearing not boots but dancing shoes, and he declared he had no boots.[46]

There were a few other interesting odds and ends. He was asked why he hadn't settled a cattle transaction with Joe Henry and, in the course of his answer, said: "Mr. Henry is like a father to me." He testified that Bill Garrison had been with him all day on Saturday, April 3.[47]

It is unlikely that Brink's testimony was believed by a single juror. After what they had learned, such testimony could only convince the jury that Brink had committed wholesale perjury. But it had a drastic effect on the importance of Bill Garrison as a witness, and this, in turn, led to another tragedy.

Even before Brink's testimony, Garrison was going to receive a lot of attention. It was Garrison who had spoken to Bounce Helmer's mother about the peril to Bounce. The prosecution was inclined to see Garrison's message as a threat, but this view is inconsistent with the fact that Bounce's father accompanied Garrison to the Jake Goodrich ranch. Frank Helmer would not have been part of a threat to his son.

A more charitable interpretation is that Dixon and Garrison did not want Brink to hurt any more people. Whatever Tommy Dixon's faults, there is no evidence that he expected to kill three men on this raid (the men Dixon had charge of, Bounce Helmer and Pete Cafferal, were released unharmed, despite the menacing of Brink[48]) and both Dixon and Garrison may have been alarmed at the slack-jawed beast into which their wide-eyed friend had turned. As freely as Brink talked about the raid to other people, he no doubt bragged to his bunkmate Garrison about his part in the killings and made threats, such as the one he made toward Callahan when talking to Billy Goodrich. Bounce Helmer was an obvious target of such threats, so Dixon and Garrison probably decided that Bounce should be warned. Perhaps Garrison approached Frank Helmer, and Frank suggested they go talk to Bounce's mother, Mrs. Jake Goodrich. The logical one to convey a warning to Mrs. Goodrich would have been Garrison, because he wasn't in on the raid.

But in so doing he opened himself to terrible questions before the grand jury. Why did you think Bounce's life was in danger? By whom was Bounce threatened? And how? And when? And *why*? The grand jury had already learned of Brink's loose-lipped propensities, and the members were surely convinced that Brink had told his bunkmate everything.

Garrison probably had the opportunity to participate in the raid and declined to become involved. But with Brink's testimony, he became deeply involved as a critical support for the alibis of both Brink and Dixon. It was still another reason to turn the heat up on Garrison.

The grand jury testimony of Tommy Dixon is not available. Given Brink's testimony, however, Tommy's story is quite predictable. The crucial time was Friday afternoon and evening, and Tommy's story was certainly that after he and Brink left the Buckmaster's, he split off to look for cattle in mudholes. He did this for several hours and then returned after dark to Goodrich's, where he found Brink and Garrison. Of course, some hard questions were no doubt directed to Dixon, but he wasn't as vulnerable as Garrison. Besides, Tommy seemed to be made of sturdier stuff than Bill Garrison.

The grand jury testimony of Garrison is also not available. This is a greater loss, both because his testimony is not so predictable and because of its very sad aftermath.

## NOTES

1.  This paragraph is based in part on an interview of John Speight of Cheyenne, Wyoming, a former assistant U.S. attorney (in the federal court system grand juries are used extensively), and in part on the author's own experience.

2.  Letter of 3/22/20 from W. F. Simpson accompanying trial transcript. W. S. Metz had other court hearings he had to attend (*Basin Republican*, 4/30/09). Even a partial list of the people subpoenaed is very long. Such a list is set out in the Appendix.

3.  Speech of Percy Metz to the Park County Historical Society, 6/9/61.

4.  Grand jury testimony of Arthur McVay, 3; See Gage, *Ten Sleep and No Rest*, 182–184.

5.  *Big Horn County Rustler*, 4/30.

6.  Trial testimony of Bounce Helmer, 189; *Big Horn County Rustler*, 5/3/09. Other members of the grand jury were F. Thayer of Meeteetse, G. C. Beal of Meeteetse, W. O. Harvey of Basin, Jens Peterson of Byron, C. C. Ellis of Basin, G. Herrick of Basin, C. E. Musgrave of Basin, George Baker of Burlington, and H. A. Tucker of Lovell.

7.  American Heritage Center Collection of Lola Homsher, University of Wyoming.

8.  Grand jury testimony of Felix Alston, 3; see trial testimony of Clyde Atherly, beginning at 47. Atherly survey map, which is set out at p. herein. This map was re-created by the Northwest Chapter of Professional Land Surveyor's of Wyoming from the original survey notes of Atherly. See Bibliography.

9.  Trial testimony of Bounce Helmer, 195.

10. Grand Jury testimony of Bounce Helmer, 2, 10, 16.

11. Ibid, 14, 15, 19, 20.

12. Ibid, 17, 19, 23.

13. Summary of evidence before the grand jury; grand jury testimony of Pete Cafferal, at 7, 9, 10, 13, Homsher Collection.

14. This paragraph is based upon the grand jury testimony of Porter Lamb, 3, 4, 10–14.

15. Grand Jury Testimony of Fred Greet, 2, 8, 14–20.

16. Interview of Howard McClellan by the author, April 1991.

17. Summary of evidence before grand jury; grand jury testimony of Walt Richie, 4–6, Homsher Collection.

18. Ibid, 3, 4.

19. Summary of grand jury testimony; grand jury testimony of W. G. Colethorpe, Homsher Collection; trial testimony of Colethorpe, 304–306.

20. Grand jury testimony of George Rogers, 2, 3.

21. Grand jury testimony of Lizzie Lamb, 1. Mrs. Lamb actually testified that she believed it was Mrs. Horton who was visited. Despite her concern for accuracy, though, Mrs. Lamb was incorrect here. From the context of this and other testimony, it is obvious they visited the Double H, the Helmer place. Grand jury testimony of Anna Goodrich, 4.

22. Grand jury testimony of Lizzie Lamb, 1–4.

23. Ibid, 6, 7. The line between the Helmer and Goodrich ranches was a separate line, what was known as the "Red Bank Telephone line."

24. Grand jury testimony of Charles A. Mann, 1.

25. Rhodes, *The Rest That Came*, 32, 33. As noted previously, we know that Garrison testified Saturday night. See Note 21, infra, this chapter.

26. Trial testimony of Porter Lamb, 378.

27. LeFors left an autobiography, *Wyoming Peace Officer, An Autobiography* (Laramie: Laramie Printing Company, 1953). LeFors was hardly a braggart, and what he describes seems authentic, if sometimes astonishing. See also Dick J. Nelson, *The Big Horn Basin* (San Diego: Dick J. Nelson, 1957), 68–70.

28. LeFors says nothing in his autobiography about his work on the Spring Creek raid. Letter of 2/7/10 from E. E. Enterline to B. B. Brooks, Sheep Raid Files.

29. Summary of grand jury testimony, Homsher Collection; trial testimony of Billy Goodrich, 337.

30. Summary of grand jury testimony, Homsher Collection; grand jury testimony of Anna Goodrich, 7.

31. Trial testimony of Billy Goodrich, 338–340; summary of grand jury testimony, Homsher Collection.

32. Summary of grand jury testimony, Homsher Collection.

33. Grand jury testimony of Anna Goodrich, 6, 7, 9.

34. Ibid, 1, 3, 4, 7.

35. Summary of grand jury testimony, Homsher Collection.

36. Interview of Jack Seaman, Worland, Wyoming, by the author, November, 1991. Seaman has had a lifelong interest in the Spring Creek raid. The apparent motivation for Harvard's conversation was that Harvard had just read *Ten Sleep and No Rest* by Jack Gage and wanted to talk to Seaman about it. Seaman feels that Harvard was an unusually honest person with an excellent memory.

37. Homsher Collection; grand jury testimony of Fred Whitmeyer, 1.

38. Grand jury testimony of Sam Brant, 1, 2.

39. Grand jury testimony of Farney Cole, 2, 3, 8.

40. Grand jury testimony of Farney Cole, 10.

41. Ibid, 10, 11.

42. Ibid, 11–13.

43. Summary of grand jury testimony, Homsher Collection.

44. Ridgeley was the chief defense counsel for Brink at the trial and was evidently the primary defense attorney very early in the proceedings; he appeared for Ed Eaton at a bond hearing on Thursday, April 22. See trial transcript; also *Big Horn County Rustler*, 4/23/09.

45. Grand jury testimony of Herb Brink, 4–6.

46. Ibid, 10–13, 16–22, 26–31.

47. Ibid, 5, 20.

48. See discussion of Herbert Brink in Chapter Three, infra. As noted previously, given Bounce Helmer's varying statements, it is hard to know exactly what did happen, but it is interesting to note that in these stories, Brink is usually mentioned as the threatening one.

# Another Sacrifice to Spring Creek

## CHAPTER 8

Poor Bill Garrison; he was filled with fatal knowledge. And the prosecution knew it. What happened inside that grand jury room will forever remain a tantalizing mystery, but it must have been a grueling ordeal for Garrison. Whatever happened, Bill Garrison left his grand jury testimony dazed and depressed. It was Saturday evening, May 1, when he was excused, but he was told to be available for still more questions.[1]

Basin was full of people, and Garrison must have wandered through loud and rowdy crowds; he is supposed to have visited the Basin red light district that Saturday night. Sometime during the evening he found Billy Goodrich and paid him a debt of $6.50. He asked Billy if he had brought his gun with him and was told that the gun had been left at Joe Henry's.[2]

The next morning Garrison met Joe Henry on the street. He was apparently still disturbed, because Henry suggested that he go over to his house and lie down, as he seemed to need rest. Garrison did so, but he also obtained Goodrich's gun and returned downtown, where he was seen at various places until 11 o'clock that night.[3]

It is not clear exactly what Garrison then did, although it is known that he left the saddle horse he had ridden to Basin and, about 8 o'clock the next morning (Monday), appeared at the Voss Ranch near Manderson.[4] He evidently took a tormented journey, walking south through the night, following the railroad tracks until he arrived at the Voss place.

Garrison ate breakfast and dinner at the ranch and then returned to a haystack about a hundred yards from the ranch house; he was said to have "acted queerly." At the ranch he asked for and was given writing paper, an envelope, and a pencil. Mr. Voss saw him about 4 p.m., but then he was not seen for a while and, as the *Big Horn County Rustler* reported: "A traveling man for a grocery house stopped at the house for the night, and when the queer actions of the man were referred to he suggested that the men see if he could be found." A search was then undertaken, and about 7 o'clock Garrison's dead body was found lying near the haystack. The authorities were contacted as soon as possible, and they left Basin about 10 p.m.[5] When word was received of Garrison's death, the story was also told that Garrison had left a trunk with a statement telling all about the raid.[6]

Percy Metz wanted to get to the scene quickly to make sure cattlemen did not obtain these papers first. Metz, Alston, LeFors, and Ira Waters got in Waters' automobile and headed toward Manderson. Ira Waters was a county commissioner, and he had bought the car that year, one of the few in the area; Metz referred to it as a "one-lung Oldsmobile." When they were a short distance out of Basin, they caught up with Dr. Carter. Carter was the county coroner and had a legitimate reason to go to the Voss ranch. Even at this early stage, though, people who were neither cowmen nor sheepmen were choosing sides, and Carter was already identified as a cattleman sympathizer. In fact, he was traveling with one of the defense attorneys, and Metz felt they had one primary purpose — to get those Garrison papers. There was a race in the night, Dr. Carter with his fine team of horses and Metz and company in that primitive Oldsmobile. As Metz tells it, they were neck and neck, when they both hit a wire fence. It had just been put up by a farmer, and nobody expected it to be there.[7]

Dr. Carter stopped to see if his horses were cut, but the automobile kept going and thereby won the race to Manderson. When Metz arrived at the Voss ranch, however, the only papers found were a note to inform John Garrison (Bill's brother) of his death and an order to the First National Bank of Buffalo to turn over all his credits to his brother. Despite this disappointment, Metz wasn't going to completely lose an opportunity. Just to give the defense something to worry about, he put out the word that the prosecution had found some very damaging evidence.[8] This disinformation found its way to the newspapers. In the *Rustler,* for example, it took the following form: "There were other papers on the body, but the authorities decline to disclose the nature of their contents."[9]

Garrison was found lying on his side, with a .38 pistol in his left hand; the gun contained two empty shells. One bullet had been fired into his chest, leaving his back near his backbone, and a second was fired through his head, entering behind his left ear and extending upward to a point above the right ear. There is conflict as to whether powder burns were found on the body. Garrison's boots, hat, and gloves had been taken off and laid carefully to one side.[10]

The body was returned to Basin that night, with the party returning about 3 a.m. The county coroner, Dr. Carter, held an inquest on Tuesday, May 4, before a coroner's jury consisting of Ira Waters, Joe Henry, and Billy Goodrich. This odd collection of jurors came to the conclusion that Garrison had committed suicide, first firing into his chest and then, when that did not produce the desired result, firing into his head.[11]

Garrison's death was a sensational event, and all of the newspapers covering the raid carried stories about it. There was much conjecture about why Garrison committed suicide and, for that matter, whether he had at all.

The *Worland Grit* said the most plausible theory was that "he was obliged to tell some truths before the grand jury that were damaging to his friends, and this had caused him to be so remorseful that he courted death rather than face them."[12] The *Cheyenne Daily Leader* wrote, "it now appears that Garrison was hounded to death by fear of vengeance from these men."[13] Some months later the *Denver Post* gave a bit more thoughtful analysis when it said: "Fearing that he would again be called before the jury, and not caring to do anything further against the defendants, (he committed suicide)."[14] Garrison was probably pulled by strong conflicting feelings — remorse because of what he had testified to and fear of a perjury charge because of what he had *not*.

More insight into Garrison's state of mind was given when the *Thermopolis Record* published on May 8. The day before his death, Garrison had written his brother in Thermopolis, and according to the *Record,* "he plainly indicated his intention." He wrote of his broken health, indicating that he didn't have long to live in any case, and stated that he was gradually losing his mind. Cryptically, Garrison began the letter to his brother with: "I am charged with what I am innocent of." The *Record* observed that he seemed to feel that the grand jury suspected him. More likely, the grand jury did not suspect him but the prosecutors were accusatory, hoping he would try to exculpate himself by accusing his friends.[15]

Perhaps, though, the Thermopolis newspaper missed the point of Garrison's letter. To say that "I am charged with what I am innocent of" may be equivalent to saying, "I am not charged with what I am guilty of." Garrison must have felt guilt, for what could explain his suicide more than an overwhelming feeling of guilt? It was true that he was innocent of the crimes being investigated, but he must have felt guilt over the terrible things his friends had done, over his help in covering up after the raid, and over the things he said or did that might have incriminated his friends.

Most people seemed to accept the verdict of the coroner's jury, but the *Denver Post* at first questioned it, and the *Sheridan Post* flatly did not accept it, stating that Garrison was waylaid and killed and his assailants were unknown. The *Worland Grit* took the *Post* to task for these statements, saying that they were "absolutely without the slightest foundation in fact."[16] But even today, questions remain about Garrison's death. Ray Pendergraft, a former police chief of the city of Worland, plausibly maintains that the official theory is flawed.[17] Pendergraft's position, however, is based on the assumption that there were no powder burns on the body, and at least one source says there were.[18]

But though there are questions, the verdict of suicide was very probably correct. The most persuasive point in its favor is that the law enforcement people in Big Horn County accepted it. If they had felt the verdict was questionable, they surely would have challenged it. Neither Felix Alston nor any of the special county attorneys objected to the conclusion of suicide. Percy Metz, after fifty years of silence, started giving talks about the raid, and in them he fully accepted that Bill Garrison had committed suicide. These men all had intimate knowledge of the circumstances leading to Garrison's death. They knew his frame of mind before the grand jury and as he left the grand jury. They also probably knew the whereabouts of all the suspected raiders and their strongest supporters. It appears they were all in Basin, including Brink, who was in jail, and at no time was there any indication that any of these men (or any other men for that matter) were around that haystack on the Voss place on Monday, May 3.

One thing that was not subject to controversy was how widely liked Garrison had been. The *Worland Grit* used this point to argue that it was inconceivable anyone had murdered him.[19] Of course, it is commonplace for a man to be praised upon his death, all threat and menace having been removed. But the comments about Garrison seemed to express feelings transcending the invariable cliches. A good example is found at the close of a *Basin Republican* article:

> The deceased was one of nature's noblemen, honest, humble and upright in all his dealings with his fellowmen. He was well known all over northern Wyoming, having been prominently identified with the cattle industry for many years. The news of his sudden and tragic death comes as a great shock to his friends, who are legion.
> Peace to the dust of big-hearted, whole-souled Wm. Garrison.[20]

The funeral was held on Thursday morning and a special casket had to be built for Garrison because of his height. Out of respect for him, the grand jury adjourned during his funeral.[21] But that brief Thursday morning adjournment was the only delay Garrison's death caused the grand jury. During Tuesday and Wednesday, while the sensational events about Garrison's death were being reported, the grand jury plunged on. Percy Metz was the attorney making late-night excursions to recover bodies (and not Enterline or Simpson) because he was not directly involved in the grand jury proceedings; the attorneys who were had quite enough to occupy their attention.

The material available only provides the order of witnesses through Herbert Brink, witness number twenty-two. Those first twenty-two witnesses were the most important to the case, but there were still many loose ends, including alibis to counter, and almost eighty witnesses from which to obtain additional information. A lot of the questioning would be very general, the prosecutors hoping something would turn up. But some witnesses still had some very specific and helpful information to supply.

Mr. J. W. Cook was called. On April 2, he was staying at Emge's ranch; he and Emge and Allemand were good friends. He had been asked to assist in a horse roundup at Frank Helmer's ranch and went to the ranch that day, finding Helmer and Billy Goodrich there. (Afterward, he wondered if all this was an effort to get him out of the locality of the Emge ranch.) The next morning, he and some other men started out from Joe Henry's place and went to a place several miles up Bud Kimball Draw; Cook referred to it as a dugout or cabin. He saw Eaton at the cabin about 11 a.m., and Eaton's horse looked like it had been ridden hard, being "pretty racked." Eaton just stayed at the cabin that day, and Cook did not learn why Eaton didn't help with the work.[22]

Cook then supplied some startling information. Two brothers peddling groceries had told him about finding "plunder" under a flume, only 300 or 400 yards from the scene of the killing. Cook testified: "Two men told me they found two gunny sacks that were tied up with a string at the top and the bottom was cut open, two holes cut in the sacks and the sacks were situated with other plunder and a pair of overalls of medium size a part of which was all bloody, was all saturated with blood and the overalls were cut off about half way between the bottom and the knee." This statement, if true, supported rumors that one of the raiders had been shot. The problem with it was that the two brothers were apparently not available, nor was the "plunder." The statement was pure hearsay, and so it was impossible to test the accuracy of this testimony.[23]

But Cook had other, more reliable information. Only a week or so before the grand jury was convened, while at the scene of the killing, he heard Alexander say that "if the truth was ever known that Allemand was shot just as he was coming out of the wagon, that they did not intend to kill him." Alexander said he did not know of anyone who had a grudge against Allemand, but as for himself, he had no tears to shed for Emge. Furthermore, Bill Keyes had made a statement to Cook around the middle of March. Cook was telling Keyes about Emge and Allemand buying the Shaw place and using Shaw's range. Keyes blurted out, "The people of the country won't allow that S of a B. to go upon that range with sheep."[24]

Cook concluded his testimony by telling the grand jury about the atmosphere in the Upper Nowood. He agreed that many people felt that if a man was for the sheepmen in this controversy he was in danger of personal violence. He told how one Mr. Abplanalp had recently stated that "if a man knows anything he had better keep his mouth shut (or) it would not be safe for him." Cook did not think Abplanalp was part of the raid; he was just taking sides with the cattlemen.[25]

It is not clear when Dr. Walker testified about his examination of the bodies, but he was an important witness, and the prosecution probably put him on the stand as soon as he was available. Dr. Walker recounted his medical findings, of course, but he had more to offer.[26] He had had conversations with cattlemen, including Milton Alexander. Before the raid, just after the annual stock meeting of the Paintrock Land and Cattle Association (to which almost all the cattlemen belonged), Milton Alexander had dinner at Dr. Walker's house. There had been talk at the stock meeting about sheep, and the doctor asked Alexander what he thought the probable outcome of that dispute would be. Alexander said they can't run sheep in here, but the doctor rejoined that you couldn't keep them out, and he used the example of Lynn going through with sheriff's deputies. Alexander replied that next time they would not stop at killing sheep. The doctor must have been taken aback, and he asserted that you can't kill deputy sheriffs going along with a sheep outfit. According to Walker, Alexander responded: "Deputy sheriffs all look alike to me."[27]

Two days after the funeral of the three sheepmen, there was another conversation with Alexander. The doctor's wife, out of curiosity, wondered why Allemand had been killed, saying he was an inoffensive man. Alexander said: "Well, probably they had ordered them to light the lamps, come out without guns, that Allemand had started out and that someone in the gulch to the left of him had fired, had gotten excited and for some reason fired and killed Allemand, and probably did not know him." Then the doctor asked Alexander how the wagon was set afire. Alexander suggested that they pulled up sagebrush, set it afire and then piled that on the tongue back of the doubletrees and set the wagon afire.[28]

Dr. Walker also had a conversation with Oscar Arnett shortly after Emge and Allemand bought the Shaw place (in late February 1909). The doctor testified that as Arnett talked about it his temper rose and he finally said that they ought to be raided. Arnett especially directed his anger at Emge, remarking that Emge would eat the cattlemen out of house and home and that he ought to be raided, the matter should be seen to.[29]

The questioning attorney asked the doctor about the wound to Allemand's neck, suggesting that it was caused by something at the scene (presumably the shovel). Dr. Walker ignored this suggestion, however, stating: "I found nothing to satisfy me as to what made that wound." The attorney asserted to the doctor that blood-soaked sacks and overalls were found, showing that a person had been wounded there. Dr. Walker denied any knowledge of such things, though, and said he had neither treated anyone for gunshot wounds nor furnished anything for the treatment of such wounds.[30]

With the testimony of J. W. Cook and Dr. Walker, the case against Milton Alexander was strengthened. Alexander's observations, like Brink's, sounded remarkably like he had been there. Likewise, Bill Keyes' statement to Cook would be helpful in any case against Keyes. (Keyes also testified before the grand jury, repeating the alibi he had already given the sheriff.[31])

The doctor's testimony made it appropriate to call Oscar Arnett. The prosecuting attorneys had another reason for calling him: They had information that Arthur McVay had ridden to the Arnett ranch shortly before the raid and asked after Arnett (one of his employers). McVay learned that Arnett was not there but still excitedly told Mrs. Arnett that the sheep were coming in and "we are going to smoke them up." Mrs. Arnett is supposed to have said that she was glad her husband wasn't there and that even if he was he couldn't go with McVay that night or any other night.[32]

Oscar Arnett proved to be considerably more restrained in his testimony than he had been in his conversation with Dr. Walker. He testified that he was friendly to sheepmen and never had trouble with them. When pushed, though, he admitted that he didn't want sheep there and said that Allemand and Emge had not respected the agreement between sheepmen and cattlemen (apparently referring to the deadline).[33]

Arnett did not openly confront the prosecutors but was certainly not a cooperative witness. After much pulling, he admitted his wife had told him that McVay had come to his house before the raid saying something about sheep and something about "smoking out" but denied everything else about the incident. He also denied he'd been called up Friday night to participate in the raid. He was asked about contacts with some of the suspects after the raid and testified that he had talked to Saban and Alexander and they had expressed great disgust about the killings and were "mortified." He couldn't tell the grand jury whom he suspected of being in the raid, could not even guess at it.

Arnett did testify to one thing of interest: He said that Art McVay always rode a white horse.[34]

Of course, McVay was called to testify. He had a good alibi for Friday night, April 2: He was at the ranch of Jim Richardson, one of his three employers. His approach to the questioner was very similar to Arnett's. For instance, with respect to the discussion with Mrs. Arnett, he admitted one had occurred but indicated his statement about sheep was only incidental to his purpose for being there and denied all other aspects of the conversation. He closed his testimony with the statement that he had heard people talk about the sheep coming into the country but nobody had objected to it.[35]

This was the pattern encountered with most of the remaining witnesses. Yes, they always got along with sheepmen, and they had occasionally heard people talk about sheep, but no one really had a problem with sheep. And, of course, no one had any idea who might have committed this raid, but it was certainly a terrible thing. On other points, all was evasion and obfuscation, and the only specific information elicited was done so after direct confrontation.[36]

The only things that came easily were matters the witness did not feel were significant. That is apparently what McVay felt about the kind of horse he rode, because he quickly admitted that he rode white horses.[37] Of all the many witnesses who testified about the horses they rode, Arthur McVay was the sole man shown to ride only white horses.[38] Although McVay didn't participate in the raid, he was a very good candidate for the man on the white horse, that reprehensible rider determined to torment Ada Allemand. Perhaps McVay knew that his actions after the funeral did not amount to a crime, only a moral lapse.

The prosecution tried to develop additional evidence tying the individual suspects to the crime. A good example of this process involved the rifle scabbard found at Spring Creek in the initial investigation. The .35

automatic had tied Saban to the raid. In addition, given the fact that he carried no weapon, it would have been handy for Saban to borrow a scabbard for the rifle he had borrowed. Perhaps the scabbard could provide a further connection to Saban.

The key witness here was William Robinson, a young man who worked for Jake Goodrich. Robinson went down to Spring Creek the day after the raid and was there when the rifle scabbard was found. He told Al Morton that he knew whose it was, but he wouldn't tell for $500. The prosecutor, though, forced Robinson to divulge where he had seen the scabbard. Robinson admitted he had seen it in the possession of Harry Johnson two months before, when he and Johnson had been hunting. He had ridden with Johnson off and on for two years, and whenever Johnson used a scabbard, that was the one. Robinson was shown the scabbard and identified its distinctive characteristics: It was long and had been cut off, with holes punched in it that were sewed up with buckskin.[39]

Harry Johnson was a young cowboy who lived on Ten Sleep. Robinson testified that he understood that Johnson was at a dance at Bonanza the evening of April 2 and other witnesses confirmed that.[40] One of the men associated with the Bay State, Sydney Ingram, was called and testified that George Saban had no scabbard.[41]

So the stage was set for the testimony of Harry Johnson. Johnson lived fairly close to Saban, and step one was to determine how that scabbard got from Johnson to Saban. The only trouble was that Johnson refused to let the prosecution reach step one. He denied the scabbard was his. He denied he *ever* owned a rifle scabbard. He denied that he'd ever gone hunting with Bill Robinson.[42] No doubt frustrated, the prosecution re-called Robinson. He did acknowledge he didn't know that Johnson *owned* the scabbard, but it was certainly the scabbard he had seen in Johnson's possession, and he strongly reaffirmed everything to which he had earlier testified.[43]

Johnson was recalled. The prosecutor put pressure on him, reminding him he was under oath, handing him the scabbard and asking (no doubt in véry grim tones) whether he had ever had this scabbard. Johnson denied it: He denied he had ever owned the scabbard, had it in his possession, borrowed it, or used it prior to April 2, 1909. There was nothing more the prosecution could do. They had no way to link the scabbard to Saban other than through Johnson. And unlike Farney Cole, Johnson would not break.

Not all the lines of inquiry led to such frustrating dead ends. Indeed, from some of the cowboys close to the suspects, the prosecution was able to develop a surprising number of very helpful facts. For example, Clyde

Harvard's brother, Louis, who worked for Milton Alexander, testified that on April 2 his boss was home at noon, but Louis did not see him until the next morning. Harvard read in the bunkhouse that evening until about half past nine, and Alexander had not returned home by then, at least that Harvard saw. The bunkhouse was only about forty feet from the house, and Louis had not heard any horses or horsemen. Mr. and Mrs. Alexander made a point of telling Harvard where they claimed Alexander had been on Friday, April 2 — as if the Alexanders thought it would be well if Harvard knew where Mr. Alexander was. Harvard said he had heard Alexander express regret over the killing of Allemand but not of Emge. He further testified that Alexander carried a .30-30 when he went out.[44]

The importance of Harvard's testimony was primarily defensive. The alibis of both Saban and Alexander were that they had left Keyes' place around 8 p.m. and traveled to Alexander's ranch, about five miles away.[45] Alexander's ranch hand could have been a very important witness for them. Saban and Alexander, however, would get precious little help from Harvard's testimony.

Sydney Ingram worked at the Bay State, and he testified that Saban had asked him to return Farney Cole's horse; he did so about ten days after the killing.[46] Saban had used more than Farney Cole's rifle; he also rode one of his horses, supposedly because his own had "played out."[47] The significance of this revelation was that Saban was doing a lot of riding around April 2. Saban had been at the Bay State until the morning of Wednesday, March 31, but then he left and was gone for three or four days, returning Saturday evening. Wes Harvey also confirmed that Saban had not returned until after the killing.[48]

W. W. Early was called as a witness, and his principal distinction seemed to be that he was one rancher who did not deny the trouble between sheepmen and cattlemen. He testified: "Of course, all the sheep men have been threatened for years, it's an old sore in that country.[49] There was another witness who wasn't afraid to speak some obvious truths. Charles Runge had been working for George Saban before April 2, more as a farmhand than as a cowboy. Before the raid he had heard talk about Emge, because Emge bought the Shaw ranch and "that put a bitter feeling in all of them." He never heard anything from Saban, however, but Saban was a very quiet man.[50]

Runge had left Saban's shortly before the raid to have an injured finger attended to and didn't return to the area until a week or two after the raid. He spent a night at Billy (W. A.) Miller's, when he and Miller had a conversation about the raid. Miller told Runge, "It's a good job and it's well done." But Runge expressed his strong disapproval and said he "would like to see some of them sinched." Miller responded that "it was cool heads that performed it and that they would not be captured." Runge then left Miller's place and stopped at Saban's. Saban tried to rehire him, but Runge refused because he was offended by the raid. While Runge was at Saban's, Alexander rode up. Someone hollered out: "How is the sheep business?" Alexander's reply was similar to Miller's statement: "It's a good job and well done." Runge then told Saban that he would like to see "every one of them sinched"; he said that Saban did not like that very well.[51]

Runge overheard a conversation in which Jake Frison was critical of the murdered sheepmen.[52] Jake Frison was over at the Bay State quite a lot, and Runge obviously counted him as one with an attitude similar to others around the Bay State. Indeed, there came a time in the grand jury proceedings when Jake Frison was in trouble. Bounce Helmer had earlier testified that he heard Frison's voice during the raid. After Runge, still another witness was called who was not helpful to Frison. Frank Tully worked for Frison, and he testified that Frison was gone the evening of April 2 and that he didn't see his employer until the next morning. Tully was very vague about the ranch to which Frison was supposed to have gone that Friday. Tully had also ridden horses back and forth from Frison's to McClellan's, which sounded a lot like what Syd Ingram had done for Saban.[53] It seemed more and more that a case could be built against Frison. But then Frison himself was called, and the shaky structure of the case collapsed.

Frison testified directly and candidly. It soon became clear why Frank Tully had been so vague about where Frison had gone on April 2. Frison had left the ranch early in the morning and had gone to several places north of Ten Sleep, including Mr. Jones' ranch (eighteen or twenty miles from the Frison ranch), Dr. Walker's ranch, and the ranch of the Bakers (about twelve miles from the Frison place and twenty-two to twenty-four miles from the scene of the crime). He left the Baker place about 9 p.m. and returned home about 11 p.m.[54] All this could be easily confirmed, and presumably the prosecution did so.

Frison was asked whose names he had heard in connection with the raid, and he said a Mr. Linn had accused George Saban of being in the raid. Frison testified, though, that he had discussed the raid with Saban, and Saban said he thought it was awful and that he did not know Allemand had an enemy in the world. Frison declared that in no way, shape, or form was Saban a participant in the killing. The prosecution pressed him to give more names, but he avoided doing so. It was unlike his other testimony, which seemed so straightforward, but Frison explained: "The first man arrested was the best friend I have, Ed Eaton has been the best friend I have in Big Horn County."[55]

The grand jury proceeding was winding down, and there were only a few more witnesses to hear. One of its last chores was to finally and completely set to rest Bounce Helmer's assertion that a lumber wagon was camped at the scene of the raid on April 2. Both of the men on that wagon, Walter Nelson and Rufus Barrington, were called as witnesses. They both testified that the night of April 2 they had made a dry camp about two miles south of Spring Creek, heard nothing that night, and only passed the scene the next morning between 9 and 10 a.m. It is clear that Bounce was simply confused, but it is hard to understand what might have been the source of his confusion. The two men did provide some helpful information when they testified that on April 2 Alexander had ridden by them about two miles north of Otter Creek. He was headed south, it was about 3 p.m., and he was riding a bay horse.[56]

Charles Shaw testified, and his appearance was brief and poignant. He felt remorse over his part in the events leading to the raid: "It has been one of the hardest things in the world to me — now understand — here is Allemand and Emge who I sold to at the mouth of Tensleep — they went in there — and this thing occurred, I presume they blame me, for selling them the ranch, you understand I would be very much worried from that fact." But Shaw had very little sympathy for the men who committed the crime, "a man that would burn a man up like that."[57]

One of the last witnesses was Dr. J. R. Richards. It had been reported that Dr. Richards had purchased some gauze for the treatment of wounds and had desired to conceal that fact. But Dr. Richards explained that a druggist had been "jobbing" (teasing) a customer when the druggist said that, and he (Dr. Richards) had not purchased any bandages or gauze of any kind.[58]

The prosecution was still chasing that will-o'-the-wisp, the wounded raider. Dr. Richards was their last chance, however, and nothing was developed. Indeed, nothing was ever developed to show that a raider had been shot. It is difficult to evaluate this theory, because the information about it was all secondhand. Even if the existence of blood-soaked articles had been established, though, there were several possible sources of blood, including dogs and sheep.

The last witness was heard either late Wednesday (May 5) or early Thursday, and the rest of the day was given over to the voting of indictments.

## NOTES

1.  Rhodes, *The Rest That Came*, 33. It is not clear how long Garrison testified on Saturday or even whether he was recalled. More than one source indicates he was, but the one definite statement as to the time of his testimony only mentions Saturday evening testimony. See Note 33, Chapter 8 infra.

2.  Gage, *Ten Sleep and No Rest*, 190; *Big Horn County Rustler*, 5/7/09. Gage claims that this gun was owned by Herb Brink. Gage, Ten Sleep and No Rest, 190.

3.  *Big Horn County Rustler*, 5/7/09.

4.  *Basin Republican*, 5/7/09.

5.  *Big Horn County Rustler*, 5/7/09.

6.  Speech of Percy W. Metz before the Big Horn County Historical Society (Lovell), 3/1/62.

7.  *Big Horn County Rustler*, 5/7/09; Speeches of Percy W. Metz before the Natrona County Historical Society, 11/2/61, and the Big Horn County Historical Society, 3/1/62.

8.  Ibid.

9.  *Big Horn County Rustler*, 5/7/09. As late as 1941, Marvin Rhodes was discussing the controversy over whether incriminating letters were found. See Rhodes, 34, Note 23.

10. *Big Horn County Rustler* and *Basin Republican*, 5/7/09. The only two references to powder burns the author was able to find are from articles in the *Denver Post*. One, an article with many errors of fact, published on May 11, refers to a general allegation that there were no powder burns. But a later *Post* article specifically states that powder burns were on Garrison's head (*Denver Post*, 10/31/09). Pendergraft says that were no powder burns, but provides no source for this information (*Washakie: A Wyoming County History*, 111).

11. *Basin Republican*, 5/7/09.

12. *Worland Grit*, 5/6/09.

13. *Cheyenne Daily Leader*, 5/11/09.

14. *Denver Post*, 10/31/09.

15. *Thermopolis Record*, 5/8/09. Regarding Garrison's reference to his health, this is apparently an example of hypochondria; there is nothing else in the historical record showing that Bill Garrison suffered serious health problems.

16. *Denver Post*, 5/11/09; *Worland Grit*, 5/13/09.

17. Pendergraft, *Washakie: A Wyoming County History*, 111, 112.

18. Denver Post, 10/31/09; See Note 10, this chapter.

19. *Worland Grit*, 5/13/09.

20. *Basin Republican*, 5/7/09.

21. Rhodes, *The Rest That Came*, 34; *Cheyenne Daily Leader*, 5/11/09; *Big Horn County Rustler*, 5/7/09.

22. William (J. W.) Cook's Grand Jury testimony, 1–5.

23. Ibid, 6.

24. Ibid, 7–9.

25. Ibid, 10. Mr. Abplanalp would have been Silas P. Abplanalp, a rancher associated with an area above Big Trails known as the "Dry Farms." See the records of the Washakie county clerk, regarding NW1/4NE1/4, Section 33, T. 44 West, R. 86 North of the Sixth Principal Meridian.

26. Jack Speight indicates that when witnesses are friendly, a grand jury proceeding is an excellent means to just have a gossip session about a case. See Note 1, Chapter 7.

27. Grand jury testimony of Dr. G. W. Walker, 7, 8.

28. Ibid, 6. Percy Metz believed that the raid would not have occurred but for the erroneous conclusion that Joe Allemand was not present at the range site. He stated that one of the raiders overheard Ada Allemand's March 30 conversation with her husband on one of those all-party lines and understood that Joe Allemand was telling his wife he would be staying in Worland. Speech of Percy W. Metz before the Big Horn County Historical Society, 3/1/62.

29. Ibid, 6.

30. Ibid, 4, 6.

31. Grand jury testimony of Albert Keyes.

32. Grand jury testimony of Oscar Arnett, 14.

33. Ibid, 4, 10.

34. Ibid, 7, 11, 15.

35. Ibid, 2–4, 10. Surprisingly, McVay was not confronted by another statement he was supposed to have made, that "there was one son of a bitch in that outfit that would give it away" and "they would have to kill him." Presumably, he was speaking of the raiders when he referred to "that outfit." Grand jury testimony of Mike Lynch, 6.

36. Included within this category would be Mike Lynch, George Sutherland, Clarence Gardner, Nick Carstensen, J. O. Fish, Mark Warner, and W. A. Miller. The testimony of some of the most outspoken of the cattlemen is not available; it was probably not transcribed because it was of no use to the prosecution.

37. Grand jury testimony of Arthur McVay, 2.

38. Saban occasionally rode a light-colored horse, but his actions after the raid were extremely discreet. See grand jury testimony of Charles Runge, 2, 5. He would not have done such a nervy thing as did the horseman on the hill.

39. Grand jury testimony of William Robinson, 1–5.

40. Grand jury testimony of William Robinson, 6; Edward Ilg, 3; Harry Johnson, 2.

41. Grand jury testimony of Sydney Ingram, 12.

42. Grand jury testimony of Harry Johnson, 2.

43. Grand jury testimony of William Robinson, 10.

44. Grand jury testimony of Louis Harvard, 1–8.

45. Grand jury testimony of Albert Keyes, 7–9.

46. Grand jury testimony of Sydney Ingram, 1, 2.

47. Grand jury testimony of Farney Cole, 5.

48.  Grand jury testimony of Sydney Ingram, 4; grand jury testimony of Wes Harvey, 3. Harvey was asked a lot of questions about the 1,000 rounds of ammunition he ordered on April 2. He testified that he was just going to use it for practice shooting, and the prosecution, after some sharp questioning, accepted this.

49.  Grand jury testimony of W. W. Early, 4.

50.  Grand jury testimony of Charles Runge, 1, 2.

51.  Ibid, 2–4. Miller denied all this in his grand jury testimony.

52.  Ibid, 5.

53.  Grand jury testimony of Frank Tully, 1. Apparently, the reference was to *George* McClellan rather than Oscar. Frank Tully mentioned that his brother worked for McClellan. That would have been Henry Tully, who was foreman for the 1/4.

54.  Grand jury testimony of Jake Frison, 2–4.

55.  Ibid, 5–7. It is very hard to tell from a typewritten transcript, but Frison seemed to be sincere in the defense of his friend.

56.  Grand jury testimony of Walter Nelson, 1–5; Rufus Barrington, 1–3.

57.  Grand jury testimony of Charles E. Shaw, 2, 3.

58.  Grand jury testimony of Dr. J. R. Richards, 1.

# The Indictments

## CHAPTER 9

The arson charges were easy. There was not much doubt that seven men had engaged in a joint undertaking that resulted in the burning of a great deal of valuable property. All of them, the men at the south wagon and the men at the north wagon, contributed to the burning in one way or another. So when the prosecution asked the grand jury to return seven arson indictments, it probably did so very quickly.

Ed Eaton's indictment was typical. It read:

> That Ed Eaton late of the County aforesaid, on the 2d day of April, A.D. 1909 at and in the County of Big Horn, in the State of Wyoming, two sheep wagons, each of the value of two hundred dollars, and each the property of Joseph Allemand, unlawfully, feloniously, wilfully and maliciously did burn . . . contrary to the form of the statute in such case made and provided and against the peace and dignity of the State of Wyoming.
>
> Percy W. Metz
> County and Prosecuting Attorney
> of the County of Big Horn, in
> the State of Wyoming.[1]

The murder charges must have been harder, in part because they were so much more serious. Who could say which man had killed Emge and Lazier? They were apparently killed in that first hail of bullets from Brink and Saban, but one could not be sure of that. Tommy Dixon had fired two shells from his .45 pistol from a place east of the north wagon, and they may have been fired into the wagon and hit and killed Emge or Lazier. The same held true for the raiders firing a .25-35 or .30-30 south of the wagon. As for Allemand, it was probably Brink or Saban who shot him, but the evidence did not even firmly establish that.

But the law does not always require proof beyond a reasonable doubt of who pulled the trigger and which bullet killed the victim. The clearest instance of this principle is felony murder. A "felony murder" is a murder committed during the perpetration of a felony, and such an offense constitutes first-degree murder. This is the law today, and it was the law in 1909.[2] It also was well established in Wyoming that if two persons were committing a felony and one of them shot and killed another person, then *both* were guilty of murder in the first degree.[3]

The prosecuting attorneys no doubt carefully explained all these points to the grand jury. What it meant, of course, was that because one or more of the raiders had killed the three sheepmen during the commission of arson, all seven of the raiders were guilty of three counts of first-degree murder. Therefore, the murder indictments probably did not take that long to come back, either; the jury returned three indictments of murder in the first degree against Milton Alexander, Herbert Brink, Tommy Dixon, Ed Eaton, Charles Faris, Albert Keyes, and George Saban.

The wording in all the murder indictments was virtually the same; one of Herbert Brink's reads as follows:

> That Herbert Brink late of the County aforesaid, on the 2d day of April, A.D. 1909, at and in the county of Big Horn, in the State of Wyoming, unlawfully, feloniously, purposely and with premeditated malice did kill and murder one Joseph Allemand . . . contrary to the form of the statute in such case made and provided and against the peace and dignity of the State of Wyoming.
>
> Percy W. Metz<br>County and Prosecuting Attorney<br>of the County of Big Horn, in<br>the State of Wyoming.[4]

What happened after the indictments were voted is best told in an article in the *Big Horn County Rustler:*

> The scene on the streets of Basin last evening was a dramatic one. Scores of men from the Tensleep and Big Trails country have been before the grand jury during the present session. The streets were lined with people last evening when Sheriff Alston and Deputy Cusack walked up to Alexander, who was standing on the sidewalk in front of the postoffice, and placed him under arrest. Alexander smiled and walked with the officers to jail.
>
> A few moments later the same officers found Dixon in the Luxus, and he was placed in jail.
>
> Officers Cusack and Lefors arrested Saban a little later in front of the Rogers House.

These same officers arrested Keyes a few minutes later, and he, like all the rest, surrendered without a word of protest.

Sheriff Alston arrested Farris in front of the court house as he was passing along the road which leads across the square.

There will be astonishment among their friends when some of these names are read. The lives of some of these men have been above reproach. They have been good neighbors and in every way they have led lives of honor and integrity. Nevertheless, after a thorough and searching investigation by the grand jury they stand today charged with one of the most heinous crimes on the calendar.[5]

Surprisingly, the newspapers did not react to the indictments with blaring headlines. There was "general satisfaction," reported the *Cheyenne Daily Leader*.[6] Perhaps the big town newspapers were disappointed that the grand jury hadn't listed any really big names. Still, for the local people, the men indicted, especially Saban and Alexander, were important enough to create a real stir. The *Thermopolis Record* observed: "As was predicted, the charges implicate some of the prominent men in their neighborhood and have caused a great sensation."[7]

The timing of the indictments was fortunate for a reason that the authorities of Big Horn County would not have expected — the French government had taken an interest in the case. In late April, the consul for France in Chicago, Monsieur St, Laurent, wrote Governor Brooks and asked for information about the raid.[8] And on April 24, the French ambassador to the United States wrote from the embassy in Washington, D.C. to P. C. Knox, the U.S. secretary of state.[9] He told of having received two letters from French residents of the United States, including one from Virgile Chabot that provided "very clear and precise information." (It was not, however, wholly accurate. Chabot wrote that the murderers had "put him [Allemand] to death with a shovel" and asserted that kerosene was poured on the wagon and the bodies of Emge and Lazier.)[10]

The French ambassador referred to men "massacred" and to "murders committed under peculiarly atrocious circumstances upon the persons of Jules Lagier [*sic*], a Frenchman, Joe Emgee, an American, and Joseph Allemand, a naturalized American of French birth." It was noted that this crime was "not an uncommon or solitary instance and impunity could not but cause further crimes; Americans and Frenchmen alike are, as shown by this occurrence, interested in having such cruelty brought to an end."[11]

This was not a pro forma letter to placate a constituent. Huntington Wilson, the acting secretary of state, promptly sent a translated copy of the ambassador's letter to Governor Brooks with a request for a "detailed report concerning the facts in the case."[12] Brooks immediately replied to Acting Secretary Wilson, telling him: "The State and local authorities will use every possible effort to bring the perpetrators of this outrage to justice." Governor Brooks told of the rewards, the arrests that had been made, and the great expectations from the grand jury proceedings. He concluded by stating that "we confidently hope, despite the difficulties surrounding raids of this character, to secure a number of convictions and wipe out for all time this sort of thing in Wyoming."[13]

Brooks' letter was written on May 7. On the same day he passed on to Judge Parmelee the correspondence he had received, with the comment: "The whole state is deeply interested in the proceedings of the Grand Jury."[14]

Coincidentally, also on May 7, Felix Alston wrote what must have been a very satisfying letter. He addressed the governor: "I take pleasure in informing you of the fact that I have under arrest seven men all have three charges of murder and I know that I have the guilty ones and all that was in the affair there may be some that were into it as strong as these but I have all that actualy participated in the murder."[15] Governor Brooks responded to Sheriff Alston's letter on May 11:

> I see by the newspapers confirmation of the information contained in your letter as to arrests made and the excellent progress you are making in endeavoring to bring the guilty ones to justice. It is a very difficult case, and is bound to be a long, hard, uphill pull, but I have every confidence in your staying qualities."[16]

Quite soon after the French ambassador's inquiry, there were very positive things to report to him. Indeed, the case quickly turned even more positive. Only two days after Felix Alston's May 7 letter to the governor, the prosecution gained two more witnesses, a pair of men who would be among the state's best witnesses at the trial.

Either Saturday, May 8, or Sunday morning, May 9, Sheriff Alston reported to the county attorney that two of the prisoners wanted to talk to him. There was apparently a time of negotiation, during which the two men, Charlie Faris and Bill Keyes, bickered over what they had to do to avoid the murder charges. The prosecution insisted that they turn state's evidence and tell everything. Faris and Keyes were hardly in a strong bargaining position, and they soon capitulated.[17]

The two men were brought out of the jail. Metz describes them as not only scared but also mad. They were scared because they had no idea they would be facing capital charges. They had gone along for something of a lark, to kill a few sheep and put the fear of God into some sheepherders, and now they were suddenly facing the hangman. And they were mad because they had been promised there would not be any killing.[18]

To the peace officers of Big Horn County and the prosecuting attorneys, the confessions of Keyes and Faris were a deeply gratifying culmination of their investigation. The confessions confirmed and corroborated the entire case of the prosecution. More than that, they added details that only the raiders could have known.

Bill Keyes understood that in return for his testimony he would be indicted and put in jail but not prosecuted.[19] He told of all the men gathering about his place on April 1 and 2 — Saban and Eaton, Brink and Dixon, and Alexander. During the day of April 2, they sent away the two hands, Cole and Harvard. When Keyes returned to his ranch, at about 5 p.m., all the players were there except Faris. The leaders were Saban and Alexander, and a plan was formulated to go down and "do up" the sheep outfit at Spring Creek. Keyes understood that they would kill sheep and burn wagons, but there "was no killing to be done." Saban and Alexander then asked Keyes to get Faris, and he did so. Saban took Farney Cole's automatic rifle and some shells Cole had left, and Faris brought along a pair of pliers with which to cut the telephone wires; all seven of the men then saddled up and left Keyes' place about 8 p.m. The moon was "shining considerable," and it was warm, so the men did not wear overcoats. Brink did wear cowboy boots, however, and Keyes wore high-topped gum rubbers.[20]

The men followed the public road for five or six miles, then cut across "over the hills," going directly to Spring Creek at a point about a quarter-mile upstream from the camp. They dismounted, tied their horses to large sagebrush and started walking toward the sheep camp. They were wearing masks, mostly handkerchiefs, but one had a gunnysack mask. Keyes expected to find Emge and his herders at the camp.[21]

It was about 10 p.m., and when they got in sight of a wagon, the raiders sat down on a bank and made plans. They broke into two groups, which were to take the men out of wagons and bring them down to the creek. Then they would run the sheep over the bank and burn the wagons. Keyes said that Saban was in general command of the expedition but that Alexander gave the orders for the five men who went to the south wagon; Saban and Brink went to the north wagon. The latter two were to fire a signal shot so the men at the south wagon would know when to start in. That signal shot was fired, and Helmer and Cafferal were taken prisoner;

Faris and Dixon, who were their guards, then took them down to the creek.[22]

Keyes told how several men pushed the sheep toward the creek and how he joined them; he admitted that "we fired some shots" into the flock. Saban then came and took Keyes, Eaton, and Alexander across the creek, where Saban caught the telephone wire with a rope and pulled it down so that Keyes could reach up with his pliers and cut the wire. Their purpose was to stop all telephone communication. Saban then took Keyes up near the north wagon. The wagon had just started to burn, and Keyes stayed there until it was about "two-thirds burnt," at which time he headed back to the south wagon. Keyes said he did not see Allemand at all. He also said that he did not fire any shots at the wagon, nor at any person, and that no shots came from the wagon.[23]

When Keyes returned to the vicinity of the south wagon he saw Bounce and Pete Cafferal, and he noticed Ed Eaton throwing "plunder" into the fire, which was blazing when Keyes arrived there.[24]

Keyes related that the group headed back after turning Bounce and Cafferal loose and heading them west. The raiders rode right up the road and didn't separate until they arrived at Otter Creek. There, Faris and Keyes went to Faris' house, and the other parties continued up the main road. It was about 12:30 a.m. and, ironically, Brink turned around and cautioned everyone not to say anything about the raid.[25]

Saban gave the automatic to Keyes, who first put it inside his granary and then moved it into the house. But on Monday afternoon, Saban came to Keyes' house and advised him to throw the gun in Otter Creek, which he did. Afterwards Keyes was advised to take it out of the creek and clean it up, which he also did. He then put it into a gunny sack and set up a box in front of it in the chicken house.[26]

Remarkably, Keyes didn't know that anyone had been killed, and it was the next evening before he learned that fact.[27] Given where Keyes was during the raid, though, this was not implausible. But Charlie Faris knew that men had been killed that night, and he had a much sharper eye for detail than Keyes. Because of this combination, Faris was to become the most devastating witness against the raiders.

Faris said that Keyes came to his place about 7 p.m. on April 2. Keyes asked Faris how his courage was that evening, explaining that they were going down to give the sheepmen a scare, to "ditch those sheep" and burn the wagons of Emge and Allemand. Faris replied that if there was any killing to be done he didn't want any part of it, but Keyes assured him that they didn't intend to do any killing.[28]

Faris remembered the guns of all the participants. He had a .30-30 Winchester, and Brink had a .25-35, as did Alexander. Dixon had a .45 Colt, Eaton and Keyes .30-30s, and Saban had the automatic he took from the Keyes' ranch. Faris described the route from Keyes' ranch to Spring Creek differently than had Keyes, saying: "We went through Keyes ranch to the main road, and we followed the foothills as near as I can remember about with the telephone line, and we came down near the school house and from there we followed the road until we came on top of the bench again, and cut across the bench to Spring Creek."[29]

As the raiders neared Spring Creek, they found a gulch, which they "cut down right by the side." Earlier that day, Saban, Alexander, and Eaton had been to Spring Creek and had located the sheep camp. Faris said that all seven of the men remained together until they were about 250 yards from the first wagon, where they separated. Their purpose was to hold the sheepherders and if they were willing to come out, to take them. Most of the men were wearing masks which were folded handkerchiefs tied across the nose, but Dixon had a gunnysack mask and Faris wore a dark mask of mosquito bar doubled several times.[30]

Faris described the initial shooting. He said that at the south wagon he fired four or five shots into the air before they captured Cafferal and Helmer. Faris noticed that Saban took Keyes, Eaton, and Alexander over to the north wagon but that Keyes soon returned to the south wagon. Faris and Dixon took charge of Helmer and Cafferal and took them toward the north wagon. Saban then came over to where Dixon and Faris were holding their prisoners and led Faris to the north wagon. Faris asked him where his men were. Saban's answer was that he didn't know, but he thought they were all dead. Faris remembered seeing Eaton, Saban, Alexander, and Brink at the north wagon. Saban told Faris to go start a fire under the south wagon, but he refused, so Saban told Eaton to go start a fire, and Eaton left to do that.[31]

Soon after Faris arrived at the north wagon. Brink started a fire under the wagon using sagebrush. Faris said there were no shots being fired at the wagon when he was there and that he did not personally fire any shots. After the wagon "got to burning pretty well," a man came out of it. When Faris first saw him he was twelve or fourteen feet in the front of the wagon. Faris heard someone commanding: "Halt there, halt, throw up your hands." The man coming out of the wagon was stooped, but he was holding up his hands. Faris then heard a shot and saw the man fall.[32]

It was Herbert Brink who fired the shot, and right after doing so he said: "It's a hell of time of night to come out with your hands up."

Milton Alexander walked up to the body, and when he came back he said it was Allemand. Saban then announced: "That is enough, we will leave." The group went to the south wagon, where Faris saw Eaton throwing harnesses and saddles into the fire. He also noted that Dixon had control of Helmer and Cafferal until they were finally turned loose. The raiders rode back to Otter Creek; from there, Eaton was to go to a camp in the badlands, Saban and Alexander to Alexander's place, and Brink and Dixon to Billy Goodrich's.[33]

It is not known exactly where the scene of Faris' confession was played out, but it was probably a room filled with lawmen. They would have been gathered around Faris, some standing, some sitting, all intent on the words of the seated figure.

From those frustrating first few days, in which it seemed that no case at all could be made, the prosecution had slowly built a powerful body of evidence, and the scene on Spring Creek the evening of April 2 had come into sharper and sharper focus. Now it was up to the prosecution to hold that sharp definition, not to allow their witnesses to suffer the fate of Johnson County's witnesses or those in the Sundance cases. The strength of the Spring Creek witnesses was in their mutual support. Bounce and Goodrich became that much more convincing because of the testimony of Faris and Keyes. In turn, it was essential that the testimony of the two raiders be supported by others. Faris and Keyes, seemingly the most potent of witnesses, were actually quite vulnerable because of a rule of law stating that the testimony of accomplices must be corroborated by other evidence. If it was not, it could be disregarded entirely.[34]

The first witnesses to protect were Faris and Keyes themselves. As Percy Metz observed fifty years later, the jail wasn't very big, and one could just imagine what might have happened if the other five learned that Faris and Keyes were turning state's evidence.[35] On Sunday, May 9, therefore, Faris and Keyes were moved from the county jail to the Basin city jail. The defense attorneys quickly perceived that something might be amiss and the same day went to see the two men. The local newspapers were on top of this story, and the *Rustler* related what happened next: "They were told that the men did not want to see them. Astonished at this information, the attorneys wanted to know why. They were simply told that they would have to figure it out for themselves."[36]

The next morning Faris and Keyes presented an application to the district court formally asking to be moved to some other jail. The request was quickly granted by Judge Parmelee, and that same day LeFors took them to the Sheridan County jail.[37] Even after they arrived at Sheridan, an attorney retained by the remaining defendants tried to talk to Faris and Keyes, but the two men would not see him.[38] The defendants and their lawyers could have had little doubt what this all meant, as the newspapers printed remarkably accurate stories about the confessions and the circumstances under which they were acquired.[39]

With Faris and Keyes safely tucked away in Sheridan, the prosecution found a safe place for another important witness: Bounce was sent to the state of Washington, and his location was carefully concealed.[40] The Goodriches ended up in Washington, too, although at first they stayed in the Upper Nowood.[41]

In the middle of all this excitement over the grand jury, the indictments, and Faris and Keyes turning state's evidence, how was the young county attorney holding up? Was the responsibility for the Spring Creek case bearing so heavily on Percy Metz that the weight of it was becoming overwhelming? A letter from Mamie Metz, Percy's wife, to his parents in Sheridan provides some insight. The primary subject of the letter was Will Metz's new car. Percy had just been in Sheridan before returning to Basin on Saturday, May 8, and had been trying out the car. Mamie Metz wrote: "Percy can talk of scarcely anything but the new car, and how he can use it better than his Father (?) and what a feather bed it is — etc. He wondered what made his arm so stiff after he came home and only a short time ago decided it must be from cranking the machine."

The letter was dated Sunday, May 9, the very day Faris and Keyes confessed. But the letter contains not one mention of Faris, or Keyes, or indictments, or anything else about the Spring Creek case. It appears, then, that young Percy was not feeling at all oppressed by the weight of his responsibility.

There was some thought that the raiders might be tried that summer, in July, but then it was decided to set off the trials until the fall.[42] The five defendants in Basin sought bail, but because these were capital charges, bail was set at a very high level, $10,000 *per murder charge*, making release impossible.[43]

In most criminal cases, there is an initial flurry of publicity, with the indictments and appearances of the defendants, but then the case goes out of the spotlight until the trial approaches. There is activity — attorneys gathering and evaluating evidence, preparing legal arguments, deciding tactics, and working up their presentations — but these are not the sorts of things to interest headline writers. This was not the ordinary case, however; it was the Spring Creek raid. Soon there were more headlines.

## NOTES

1.  *State of Wyoming v. Ed Eaton*, Case No. 420, Records of the Big Horn County Clerk of Court.

2.  §4950, Wyoming R. S. 1899, 6-2-101, W. S. 1977.

3.  Clay v. State, 15 Wyo. 42, 86 Pac. 17. (1906)

4.  *State of Wyoming v. Herbert Brink*, Case No. 419, Records of the Big Horn County Clerk of Court.

5.  *Big Horn County Rustler*, 5/7/09.

6.  *Cheyenne Daily Leader*, 5/6/09.

7.  *Thermopolis Record*, 5/8/09.

8.  Letter of 4/24/09 from St. Laurent to Gov. B. B. Brooks; this letter was immediately referred to Felix Alston. Letter of 4/26/09 to Sheriff Felix Alston from Governor Brooks, Sheep Raid File.

9.  Letter of 4/24/09 from the Embassy of the French Republic to the United States to the Honorable P. C. Knox, Secretary of State, Sheep Raid File.

10. Letter of 4/16/09 from Virgile Chabot to the Ambassador of France at Washington; Sheep Raid File. Chabot also provided some additional information about Lazier. He said that Lazier was twenty-two years old, had only been in Big Horn County for ten days, and was about to leave for France to perform his military services after bidding goodbye to his friends.

11. Letter of 4/24/09 from French Embassy to Knox, Sheep Raid File.

12. Letter of 5/4/09 letter from Huntington Wilson to His Excellency, the Governor of Wyoming, Sheep Raid File.

13. Letter of 5/7/09 to the Honorable Huntington Wilson from Gov. B. B. Brooks, Sheep Raid File.

14. Letter of 5/7/09 from Governor Brooks to Judge C. H. Parmelee, Sheep Raid File.

15. Letter of 5/7/09 from Felix Alston to Gov. B. B. Brooks, Sheep Raid File.

16. Letter of 5/11/09 from Governor Brooks to Mr. Felix Alston, Sheep Raid File.

17. Speech of Percy W. Metz before the Natrona County Historical Society, 11/2/61. Percy Metz told this story as if he had been the primary player for the prosecution, when it was probably one of the older attorneys who was calling the shots. Letter of 5/9/09 from Mamie Metz, Metz Collection.

18. Speeches of Percy W. Metz before the Park County Historical Society, 6/9/61, and the Big Horn County Historical Society in Lovell, 3/1/62.

19. He made this agreement with Enterline and the sheriff. In his trial testimony, Keyes seemed to indicate that the agreement was made before he testified to the grand jury. In Keyes' testimony before the grand jury, however, he admitted nothing, supporting the alibis of the other men. More than that, such an assertion would be inconsistent with a number of circumstances, including the reports of the newspapers and many statements of Percy Metz.

20. Trial testimony of Albert M. Keyes, 207–210, 214, 219–221, 225–226, 232–234.

21. Ibid, 209, 210, 219, 243.

22. Ibid, 210–212, 234.
23. Ibid, 213–217, 236.
24. Ibid, 217, 218, 222.
25. Ibid, 222, 223.
26. Ibid, 223, 224.
27. Ibid, 225.
28. Trial testimony of Charles Faris, 247.
29. Ibid, 248.
30. Ibid, 249, 250, 263.
31. Ibid, 252–256, 263.
32. Ibid, 258, 259.
33. Ibid, 260–264.
34. *Clay v. State*; see Note 3, this Chapter.
35. Speech of Percy W. Metz before the Big Horn County Historical Society, 3/1/62.
36. *Big Horn County Rustler*, 5/14/09.
37. *State of Wyoming v. Albert F. Keyes and Charles Faris*, Big Horn County Case Number 411; *Big Horn County Rustler*, 5/14/09.
38. Speech of Percy W. Metz before the Big Horn County Historical Society, 3/1/62.
39. In addition to the *Rustler* article on 5/14/09, see the *Billings Gazette*, 5/12/09, *Thermopolis Record*, 5/15/09, and *Cheyenne Daily Leader*, 5/11/09.
40. Trial testimony of Bounce Helmer, 188.
41. Trial testimony of Anna Goodrich, 329, 330.
42. *Worland Grit*, 5/20/09.
43. *Big Horn County Rustler*, 4/23/09. The newspapers only reported the bail set for Ed Eaton, but because each of the defendants faced three-first degree murder charges, their bail amounts were probably identical. A later story in the *Basin Republican*, on 5/14/09, just indicates that "an effort was made to have the entire seven released on bond, but Judge Parmelee refused the application."

# The Counterattack

## CHAPTER 10

A disinterested observer in May 1909 might have concluded that there was strong and uniform public support for the prosecution. With the exception of a few members of the general population and, of course, the Upper Nowood community, it seemed that the vast majority of people in Big Horn County was committed to the zealous prosecution of the raiders. Such an impression would have been mistaken.

Cattle ranchers throughout the Big Horn Basin, not just from the Upper Nowood but also from Shell Creek and Paintrock Creek and Owl Creek and the Stinking Water, had contributed to the defense. They had built a huge war chest, which they used to retain almost every lawyer in the Basin.[1] The figures given vary from $20,000 to $200,000 (which seems fancifully high), but in any event the amount was substantial. Even in 1909, it was a very expensive proposition to retain ten or twelve lawyers.

Many of the cattlemen were highly influential members of their society; men such as Milo Burke, John Luman, and George McClellan were going to be heard. Their lawyers were also highly influential, including C. F. Robertson and W. S. Collins, who not only were founders of their communities (Worland and Basin, respectively), but also were presently the mayors of their towns. Out of this network came other allies — certain banks were cattlemen's banks, and some newspapers sympathized with the cattlemen's point of view. It was not apparent at first, but one of the newspapers in Basin, the *Republican,* became strongly identified as a cattlemen's newspaper, the other, the *Rustler,* as a sheepman's.

In the early stages of the case, there was very little room for opposition. Even those with a deep antipathy for the prosecution could hardly complain out loud about the indictment of men who were responsible for three murders. Their opportunity would come on a collateral issue: the attorney fees of Will Metz. (In 1909, Metz, a former district judge, was always referred to as "Judge Metz.")[2] The *Basin Republican*, as the loyal opposition to Percy Metz, a Democratic officeholder, reminded voters of Judge Metz's pledge to assist his son without charge to the county. It was a legitimate political issue, although, given Metz's high qualifications to prosecute a sheep raid case and the extreme gravity of the Spring Creek cases, it might be expected that any controversy over his fee would be muted. It was not.

The first story to appear, in the *Basin Republican* on May 14, gave small hint of the furor to follow. It was only two paragraphs long. The first referred to the $3,300 received by Metz, $2,500 for the prosecution of the raid and $800 for opposing county division, and stated: "A universal roar of protest is coming from all sections of Big Horn County over the excessive fees paid from the county funds to special counsel employed to assist the prosecuting attorney." The second paragraph referred to the pledge of Judge Metz: "They (the taxpayers) are also wondering what was the true meaning of that pledge so widely and persistently distributed during the campaign last fall."[3]

It was surely not a pleasant article for the Metz family to read, but it must have seemed like routine political carping. Indeed, Will Metz, writing a May 18, 1909, letter from Sheridan to his wife in California, made no mention of this critical story. He did note that "Percy dropped in on us this morning" and was looking fine. With pardonable pride, he said of their son: "He is *It* in the Basin country now."[4]

But the May 21 issue of the *Republican* removed any illusions that the matter would be quickly forgotten. The opening sentence in its lead editorial was savage: "The people of this sadly buncoed county are learning much to their chagrin and disgust that ante-election promises like egg shells are easily broken, especially when made by 'tinhorn' politicians." Then the descriptions descended to "greed for graft," "unscrupulous politicians," and "dirty politics" — all within the first two paragraphs. Thereafter, the editorial settled into a denunciation of Will and Percy Metz that stretched to two page-long columns.[5]

The same day the *Republican* presented this vitriolic opinion, the Big Horn County commissioners probably also received a letter from the Wyoming state examiner, Harry B. Henderson. Citizens of Big Horn County had obviously been writing him. The purpose of his letter was to call the county commissioners to task because "in the heat of excitement you seemingly have gone wild as to the employing of counsel and the fees to be paid therefor." He declared that the personnel of the board were liable on their official bonds for this "hasty action," that they had absolutely no right to award the amount of fees they had, and that they must "advise this office why the Board permitted these conditions to obtain."[6]

The letter from the state examiner was a more serious matter than the criticisms of the Republican; it struck at the core of the prosecution. Percy Metz could not prosecute the Spring Creek raid cases, and lawyers experienced and competent enough to take on the array of legal talent retained by the cattlemen were going to be expensive. In fact, the fees of Enterline and Metz were considerably less than those charged by the lead counsel for the defendants.[7] Still, no public official could ignore a letter such as Henderson's, with its threat of liability and call to officially account. Harry Henderson was a curmudgeon of a bureaucrat who had clung tenaciously to his office since 1892, even in the face of a determined effort by at least one governor to remove him, and no doubt had a very expansive idea as to the power of his office. But here he was going considerably beyond his authority. Under no circumstances does a state examiner have the right to dictate what shall be the policy of a governmental body. If such a body deems it appropriate to undertake a vigorous prosecution, spending great sums for competent lawyers to do it, and the money is available, its actions are not illegal.

It is not clear how this challenge by the state examiner was finally resolved; it simply disappears from the historical record. The commissioners probably received assistance from that old sheepman, B. B. Brooks. An examiner may resist a governor's influence but is certainly not immune from it: In 1909 (as well as today), the state examiner was appointed by the governor to a four-year term. In one way or another, Harry Henderson's seemingly very serious challenge was turned away.

Irrespective of the efficacy of the examiner's threat, though, this fee problem could no longer be ignored. On May 27, 1909, Will Metz wrote the Big Horn County commissioners an explanatory letter. What he said, essentially, was that he had already assisted his son on many matters but that no one could have anticipated that a matter of the magnitude of the Spring Creek raid would arise. It would have been unfair to require him to shoulder without fee a task that might take all his time for an indefinite period. Besides, there was all this sheep money available, as well as money from other outside sources, so the fees would not have to be borne by Big Horn County citizens. Metz went further and announced that he was placing the warrant issued to him with the Basin State Bank until the completion of the cases. Then, if the board decided he had not earned his compensation, he would return the warrant for cancellation. But if the Board felt that he should, "in justice and fairness," receive compensation, he would retain the warrant.[8]

The *Big Horn County Rustler* felt that this explanation by Metz should more than satisfy the complaints of the *Republican*. It pointed out that the fees were being awarded on a matter of great importance, convicting the perpetrators of "the Spring Creek outrage. . . . The cost was a matter too trivial to be considered — they must be brought to justice, no matter what the cost. We all felt the same way, didn't we?" The *Rustler* thought that part of this attack on Judge Metz and his son came from "saloon men and gamblers" who had been charged by the "kid" prosecuting attorney for keeping saloons open on Sundays, selling liquor in brothels, and running gambling houses. It referred to the violation of Republican pledges and spoke of "the taunt of unfaithfulness coming from men who never knew what faithfulness meant when they were being tested."[9]

Not surprisingly, the *Republican* didn't find Judge Metz's letter at all satisfactory. In its June 4, 1909, issue, it said: "The 'explanation' was made! Wasn't it a bummer?" Another long, critical column followed.[10]

In another place on the front page, the *Republican* printed a satire, "The Story of Percival the Young." This was about "Percival, son of William," who was "young and not versed in the wicked ways of the world." "The three wise men who disburse the revenues of the province" paid William gold (worth $3,300) for assisting Percival. But when the people of the province heard this, they were "exceeding angry" because of William's earlier pledge not to take money for assisting his son, and they decided that "the younger a counselor may be the larger are his grafts." The final paragraph of this article was exceeding unkind: "When Percival heard this he laughed and mocked the people and William, the father of Percival, turned his head toward the side as does the dog who steals another dog's dinner."[11]

After June 4, the *Republican* finally moved away from this matter. But citizens had learned how deeply divided their community was. What the whole dispute came down to was that the *Rustler* and its allies felt that in such a great work as the prosecution of the Spring Creek raiders, this matter of lawyers' compensation was of little moment. The *Republican* and its allies, however, only accepted the prosecution through gritted teeth, an apparent but very distasteful requirement of the law. To them lawyers making too much money on this prosecution, and perhaps pursuing it too zealously, were also very distasteful.

Another distasteful matter soon arose. As early as May 7, Felix Alston had mentioned to the governor the possibility of stationing some militiamen in Basin.[12] Alston was worried about the condition of the jail, which had been condemned by the grand jury, and felt he needed more men to protect his prisoners and prevent an escape. After the indictments, much talk had been circulating in Basin about a jailbreak (then referred to as a "delivery"). Too, there had been threats against the prosecuting attorneys, and cowboys would call out insults in the street when they met the state's lawyers. The attorneys felt intimidated enough that they all carried guns.[13]Governor Brooks replied to Alston: "It is generally better, . . . not to call on the local militia, if it can be avoided as in some instances it is liable to create an adverse public sentiment, but take no chances. You are on the ground and are better able to judge as to the urgency of these matters, than I am at this distance."[14]

The *Republican* must have caught wind of the prosecution's intentions, because on May 21 it ran a preemptive article. It was headed: "No Fears of A Jail Delivery":

> Several times, we understand, fears have been expressed that an attempt would be made by a mob composed of their friends to liberate the five men now in the county jail on the charge of the murder of Allemand, Emge and Lazier. These fears are absolutely groundless. There is a pronounced disposition in all sections to let the law deal with these men. The day of resorting to mob violence to liberate prisoners belongs to the lawless past, when small respect was felt for the laws and little effort made to enforce them."[15]

Sheriff Alston, however, was not convinced that the "lawless past" had suddenly fled Big Horn County. In late May, Alston traveled to Cheyenne, where he personally requested Governor Brooks to assign a squad of militia to Basin. On June 10, seven men from Cody arrived and took up stations around the courthouse.[16] The *Republican* editor was very upset.The paper asked by headline, "Why has Militia Been Employed?" and wrote:

> The citizens of Basin were dumfounded yesterday when the three o'clock train came in with a squad of state militia, with its camp equipments and accouterments and at once took up its position at the county jail and it was learned that they had been brought here to guard that institution. . . . It has the appearance of simply being a move to arouse prejudice against the men accused of the murder of Allemand, Emge and Lazier.[17]

The *Republican* predicted that there would be a protest circulated to remove the militia and that 90 percent of the population would sign it. It demanded an explanation of why it was necessary to take this action, which "casts a reflection upon the entire county, leaving the impression on the people in the outside world that we are a lawless class, beyond the control of the civil authorities."[18]

Despite the prediction of the *Republican* and the continued expectation of Felix Alston, B. B. Brooks never received a petition in the summer of 1909 complaining of the stationing of militia in Basin. There was obviously agitation along those lines, though; Governor Brooks received several letters speaking of it. On July 1, Felix Alston wrote to say he had been informed that "the defense has a movement on foot to have you order the militia away from here" and that the Governor should wait until Alston could talk to him about that. Alston also mentioned that the defense had purchased "one of our leading newspapers" in order to support its cause.[19]

Alston need not have worried about a hasty move by the governor to remove the militia, not after the remarkable letter Brooks had just received. It is written in an ungainly scrawl by a man who obviously was unaccustomed to writing letters to governors, and it violates every rule of punctuation. But this letter must have had a stunning impact upon the Governor:

> Ten Sleep Wyo    June 26 1909
> Hon Bryant B Brooks Governor of
> Wyo    Dear Sir there is a jail delivery
> of the Seven men in Jail at Basin for the murder of Allemand Emge and Lazier being planed by sympathizers of the murderers W S Collins Mayor of Basin is in the Deal the plan is to get the Militia removed if possible if not at the proper time they are to be overpower and the men released the wires are to be cut — both Telegraph and Telephone leading from the City it is to be pulled off when the jailor takes the Supper to the prisoners there will be men in the court house in all the offices doing business guards will be Stationed in all the streets — to keep up a fire and keep people off the Street — it will not be pulled of before the first of aug unless something unusual happens I have been on the roundup and am on to the Deal then I was in Basin and found the thing is working I wont give my name for my Life wouldnt be worth a 22 cartridge if they even guessed I had squealed I dont notify the officers in basin because I don't think they could place guards enough to prevent it — what is needed is at least 100 Soldiers to prevent one of the worst Slaughters of human life in the history of Wyoming you Should confer with the Attorney General and if possible Send in at least 100 Soldiers and be sure and have them there before Aug first and place a watch on the movements of W S Collins Mayor also on the Basin State Bank as that

is to be an important point if any thing new develops I will communicate with you but whatever you do keep this out of the papers as it would precipetate a crisis at once now this is no guesswork I am sure of my ground I am in the confidence of the leaders and know whereof I speak hoping that no more crimes may be committed to further blot the fair name of Wyo I am yours for good government"[20]

Most likely this was a letter from a cowboy who had overheard some loose talk from other cowboys, probably after excessive drink, and none of it should have been taken seriously. But then again there was the possibility that some very desperate characters were actually planning the described delivery. At the least, the letter showed the strength of the anger and frustration in the cattlemen's camp. With this letter in his files, Governor Brooks was going to be very hesitant to withdraw the militia. But neither was he going to send a hundred soldiers. During the summer, though, a few soldiers were added to the detail, and Brooks wrote Sheriff Alston immediately and sent him a copy of the letter.

Alston replied that he was "not surprised one particle" because Mayor Collins was one of the strongest supporters of the defendants and the Basin State Bank "one of the next." He said that one of the bank's principal shareholders "sent his boy over the country soliciting signatures to a petition to you asking you to remove the militia from here and gave for an excuse to have them removed that it was cheaper to the county." Alston warned the governor that the supporters of the defendants would, if possible, bring political pressure to bear on him. He said that he had it on fairly good authority that Ridgely (H. S. Ridgely, the chief defense counsel) and Collins were controlling the four papers that were "howling," although he could not absolutely vouch for this.[21]

On July 23, 1909, Alston again wrote Brooks, telling him that he had heard nothing from "the fellows who propose to liberate these fellows." Alston thought that "the man who wrote the letter knows what he is talking of" but did not think that there would be any action while the soldiers were there. He spoke highly of the soldiers and said that if anyone came after the imprisoned men, it wouldn't be necessary to call a grand jury to "ascertain who some of them were," because the next morning some of them would still be lying there on the public square.[22]

One more letter was written by Alston to Brooks during the summer of 1909. Alston told the governor that he felt the chances of an attempted delivery by the cattlemen were much less "as they are taking new tactics now." He went on to discuss some recent actions by George McClellan:

Our friend G. B. McClellan is here and made the trip to assist them if possible and he is attempting to coerce witnesses, and I am much surprised for I have always considered him one of our best citizens and a very honorable man, till now and from now on in the future I certainly will have a very different opinion of him, and seems to me if the proper man (W. A. Richards) would approach him he would be glad to quit, but some here seem to think that he is not right in this matter, but I can not think that, have too high opinion of him to think he would tolerate such murderous crimes, and by such disreputable men as some of them are who are charged with this crime."[23]

The most serious charge in the letter is that McClellan was attempting to coerce witnesses. What Alston was probably referring to were discussions between Billy Goodrich and McClellan. Goodrich had consulted McClellan and asked him what he should do; he was in a difficult position because the men in the raid were friends of his. McClellan told Billy that if he were in his place, he'd leave the country.[24]

Felix Alston was as partial to his side of the case as the cattlemen were to theirs, and it is at least an exaggeration to characterize McClellan's remarks as "coercing" a witness. McClellan was a strong partisan, however, and his remarks, as well as those of other people, probably convinced Billy Goodrich that feelings against him were so strong it would not be healthy for him to stay in the area. About August 23, the Goodriches left the Upper Nowood and went to North Yakima, Washington.[25]

Bounce Helmer was also in that part of the country, but only Felix Alston knew that. Bounce's location was a topic of much discussion in the summer of 1909. The defense knew he had been sent somewhere, had no idea where, and very badly wanted to know his whereabouts. Their intentions may have been simply to learn his intended testimony, or they may have been much more malevolent.

In the early 1960s, when Percy Metz started to talk about the Spring Creek raid, he told a wonderful tale of how he tricked the defense. Metz was a master storyteller. He spoke quickly, in a clipped manner, like a man with a New England accent (except he didn't add or delete "r"s). There are many tapes extant of Metz's speeches in 1961 and 1962, and it is fascinating to listen to him tell this story, playing his audience like a musical instrument. Percy Metz, though, sometimes did not let facts get in the way of telling a good story, so the following quote should be taken with a grain of salt:

So Felix leaves one night with Bounce, he comes back in a few days and the word gets around: "You seen Bounce?" Everybody was looking for Bounce and nobody had seen him, he has disappeared. The word got around that, God, he got scared and left the country, and all kinds of tales.

Felix understood that he was the only one who knew where Bounce was. I didn't want to know, and it wasn't anyone else's business. We told the mother and father, they had to trust us that Bounce was being taken care of, to protect him, but we didn't even tell them where he was. We had to be cold about this. We knew Frank Helmer, the father, was a cowman sympathizer, and would try to talk Bounce out of testifying. Felix took Bounce to some friends in Vancouver, Washington, the friends took Bounce over to Victoria Island, a British possession, and he had a pretty good time, didn't have to work.

To make a long story short, Ridge (H. S. Ridgeley) got to messing around the Sheriff's office. He would go to the county clerk's office, then come back into the sheriff's office, and would sort of be looking around on the desk; Alston caught him at it.

"Percy," he says, "that damn Ridge, he is an inquisitive cuss. I'm getting fed up on him frisking my mail, what do you think we should do?" "Well," I said, "let's job him, there's no use putting up with this, what's he after?" Felix said: "I think he's trying to find where Bounce Helmer is. I'm scared of this telegraph operator down here, I know he tipped off when we left, he don't know where Bounce is now, as there have been no telegrams." I said: "I tell you what we will do. You go back over and write a nice letter to Bounce. Oh hell," I said, "let's send it to him in Fort Lauderdale, Florida."

So Felix gets out this Oliver typewriter that he had, and pecks away "Dear Bounce" at some place, with a street either to St. Augustine or Fort Lauderdale, I forget which, and he picks out some street out of his head, with a number, and writes Bounce the news, his mother and father are fine, Bobbi is all right, etc., and the general news, you know what to do if you need money or if you are sick, how to contact us. He leaves the letter in the typewriter, leaves the office and pretty soon, here comes Ridge to the courthouse.

In those days, we had big, high sagebrush all over the courthouse square, but there was a trail through it. Ridge had sort of a little catch as he walked. Alston meets Ridge on the trail. Ridge goes to the county clerk's office and back through the door to the sheriff's office. Pretty soon, he came high-tailing it back, hippity hip to Main Street. Felix was sitting on the steps in front of the bank so he could watch Ridge when he came back; he knew he could tell by the way he was acting if he had seen the letter.

We had up in the Ten Sleep country some old-time cowmen, fine fellows, honest as the day is long. They didn't like this murder business, but burning sheepwagons and killing sheep, they weren't going to complain much about that. . . . One of these fellows, I don't need to mention his name, all of a sudden, by gosh, the word got around that so and so had a heart attack, and Doc Carter prescribed that he had to go to a lower altitude right away. So, in about a couple of days, down to the bank came this individual and got several hundred dollars and headed for Florida.

The word got around that the old gentleman was pretty bad, he was wobbly. When he came to town, feeling bad, Doc Carter gave him not too long to live and all this. Of course, Felix and I at this time were the only ones who knew the story and we got a great kick out of it. We told Enterline and my father about it.

This chap is down to Florida quite a while before anyone got any word back; finally got word back that the old man was getting along pretty well, and didn't know if he would be there much longer. After about two weeks, word came that the old man was coming home, by gosh, he hadn't had a heart attack since he had been there and back to Basin he came. The word then got around (we didn't have an FBI but were pretty well posted on what the other side knew, secret service men of our own type).

What happened was, the old man got to Florida and started hunting this place. He found a street sort of like the one Felix had on the letter, but not spelled the same, but there was no such number as was on the letter, and they kept searching, but couldn't find sign of Charles Helmer. Word got around that they were discouraged as it cost several hundred dollars, which I presume the cow men had put up.[26]

Meanwhile, what of the five defendants in jail in Basin? We know a great deal about their time in jail because of the fortunate writings of another prisoner, a man who was placed in the jail a few weeks before the trial. This writer, whose identity is unknown, had a long criminal history and through it all kept a diary. He wrote at length of what he found when Felix Alston brought him to Basin.[27]

The five defendants were there, and the anonymous diarist said they were in the best of spirits, being absolutely sure of acquittal. "They were all goodnatured and full of fun and as far as I could tell they had but one enemy in the world." That enemy was Felix Alston; they saw him as having betrayed them. The writer explained that all five of his cellmates were in the cattle business, and two were prominent cattlemen who had been staunch supporters of Alston when he ran for sheriff. They blamed Alston for the fact that their bail was set at a level they could not meet.[28]

This prison writer remembered Herbert Brink very distinctly. Brink had a perpetual golden smile (like Joe Emge, Brink's mouth was full of gold fillings) and a very bald head. On one occasion, though, Brink did not smile. Tommy Dixon, whom the writer referred to as "Bowlegs," had fashioned a noose out of a small rope Brink was using to make hackamores (Brink was remarkably able at such close work). Dixon went so far as to arrange "the hangmans knot in the popular position, which he ajusted to be in the vicinity of his left ear." This very much upset Brink and he told Dixon to undo the arrangement immediately and not to do it again; Brink "sat there muttering to himself for an hour afterwards."[29]

Brink talked about Dixon and said that he was "plumb powder shy." The writer felt, on the other hand, that Brink "was suffering from an overdose of powder smoke, . . . always talking about shooting of some kind." He gave his opinion that as far as he could tell, "Bowlegs" was not troubled with a weak heart, and if he had to choose men for a dangerous expedition, he would have to leave Brink behind.[30]

Among the men, Saban was clearly in command, a "born leader" who fully appreciated his position. He was very popular and had a host of friends, including "some of the best citizens of the county and state." Saban regarded the coming murder trial as a farce and spoke of the big dance and great celebration being planned when they got out. But the writer was skeptical, noting that there were "just as many good men trying to get [Saban] hanged as he had working to get him turned loose."[31]

Once, a large group of men approached the jail, and it appeared it might be a mob unfriendly to the defendants. For just a moment Saban showed apprehension: "i thought that i seen Sabin cast a furtive glance at a deep dent in the iron wall of the cell, which had been made [some time before] by a bullet after it had passed through the head of a prisoner who had been killed by the vigilantes and of whom Sabin was a member." It turned out to be a false alarm, though, and Saban quickly recovered, turning the whole thing into a joke.[32]

One man whom the writer particularly liked was Milton Alexander: "he was a good old fellow and i felt for him for he had a wife and several children." The writer made a statement about Alexander that could well summarize the whole event:

[H]e had wantonly slain one or more of his fellow man but to one of his primitave ideas, of what was the proper way to settle the dispute as to who should control the cow range, he no doubt thought that he had done right, and while he had lived the greater part of his life in a day, when each man was a law unto himself, that day had passed by unnoticed by the old cow man.[33]

At that time, several weeks before the trial, no such sober thoughts troubled the defendants. They were visited by many people, who showered them with gifts such as fruitcakes and boxes of cigars; the soldiers even set up a phonograph just outside the jail window.[34]

The defense lawyers visited their clients every day, but the writer found their conduct "queer." The attorneys firmly believed the case would never even be called for trial and in their daily consultations did not spend time discussing and preparing for the coming trial. Rather, each day they brought "a new joke to spring on the lambs, that was all that i could see that they were doing."[35] By-mid October, though, the jokes and laughter must have been wearing very thin indeed, as the trial suddenly loomed before the defendants, emerging with terrifying reality from the fog of their fantasies.

## NOTES

1. O'Neal, *Cattlemen vs. Sheepherders*, 143; *Denver Post*, 10/31/09.

2. *Basin Republican*, 5/14/09; Rhodes, *The Rest That Came*, 32.

3. *Basin Republican*, 5/14/09; *Worland Grit*, 5/27/09, quoting the *Meeteetse News*.

4. Letter of 5/18/09 from Will Metz to his wife Jennie, Metz Collection.

5. *Basin Republican*, 5/21/09.

6. Letter of 5/20/09 from Harry B. Henderson, State Examiner to Honorable Board of County Commissioners, Sheep Raid File.

7. See *Stotts v. Saban*, et al, Big Horn County Civil No. 1007, wherein Joseph L. Stotts ("Judge" Stotts) sought to obtain the balance of his $4,500 fee. Stotts was not the principal trial attorney, but did give the primary final argument.

8. *Big Horn County Rustler*, 5/28/09.

9. Ibid.

10. *Basin Republican*, 6/4/09.

11. Ibid.

12. Letter of 5/7/09 from Felix Alston to Gov. B. B. Brooks, Sheep Raid File.

13. Letters to B. B. Brooks from Felix Alston, 5/7/09 and 5/11/09, Sheep Raid File; *Worland Grit*, 5/13/09; speeches of Percy Metz before the Big Horn County Historical Society, 3/2/62, and the Natrona County Historical Society, 11/2/61.

14. Letter of 5/11/09 from B. B. Brooks to Felix Alston, Sheep Raid File.

15. *Basin Republican*, 5/21/09.

16. Letter of 5/5/09 from P. A. Gatchell (Adjutant General) to B. B. Brooks, 5/5/09, Sheep Raid File; 1909–1910 Biennial Report of the Adjutant General, Wyoming State Archives, Cheyenne. Rhodes says there were eight men, but Gatchell is a more authoritative source; Rhodes, *The Rest That Came*, 37. Other references are to a "squad" of men.

17. *Basin Republican*, 6/11/09.

18. Ibid.

19. Letter of 7/1/09 from Felix Alston to Gov. B.B. Brooks, Sheep Raid File.

20. Letter of 6/26/09 to Hon. Bryant B. Brooks, Sheep Raid File.

21. See letter of 7/8/09 from Felix Alston to Gov. B. B. Brooks, Sheep Raid File, and the 1909–1910 Biennial Report of the Adjutant General.

22. Letter of 7/23/09 from Felix Alston to Gov. B. B. Brooks, Sheep Raid File.

23. Letter of 8/2/09 from Felix Alston to B. B. Brooks, Sheep Raid File.

24. Trial testimony of George B. McClellan, 382–384.

25. Trial testimony of Anna Goodrich, 329, 330. On August 23, Billy Goodrich was served with a summons for the trial. He probably accepted the summons just as he was leaving town. *State v. Brink*, Big Horn County District Court File No. 443.

26. Percy Metz speech to the Natrona County Historical Society, 11/2/61.

27. *Sweet Smell of Sagebrush, a Prisoner's Diary, 1903–1912* (Rawlins: Friends of the Old Pen, 1990). The writer was anonymous, although the publishers of the diary believe he was a man named William Stanley Hudson.

28. Ibid, 90, 91.

29. Ibid, 94.

30. Ibid, 94, 99.

31. Ibid, 92, 94, 95.

32. Ibid, 95.

33. Ibid, 93.

34. Ibid, 94.

35. Ibid, 92.

Trials for the raiders were to start in the first few days of the October term, which began on October 18, 1909.[1] Normally a jury panel would then have been selected from the list of eligible jurors in the county. But on this first day of the term, the defense attorneys filed a plea in abatement, a document sworn to by George Saban, and this pleading had to be addressed before the process of obtaining jurors could begin. Saban sought to have all the indictments against him set aside on several grounds. Through his attorneys, he said that there had been no proper county jury list for the year 1909; the existing list had been improperly made up by Alex Linton, the chairman of the County Commission, and by Felix Alston, not by the proper officers. These would have been the county treasurer, C. E. Shaw, and the county clerk, Peter Enders, in addition to Linton. Saban further said that the "purported jury list" contained only 731 names when in fact there were 1,746 qualified jurors. The plea asserted that Alston acted "clandestinely, unlawfully, illegally, improperly and fraudulently" when he assisted in making up this jury list. Finally, the charge was made that "there was not one member of the grand jury that was engaged in the cattle business, while upon said jury were some of the leading and largest sheepmen in the County, the foreman of said jury being one of the largest sheepmen in the state of Wyoming and of Big Horn County; consequently the personnel of the grand jury showed it to be a biased and prejudiced jury against the cattle industry and those engaged in it, and against this defendant." Because of all of this, it was asserted that the purported jury list was "void and invalid."[2]

If Saban succeeded in having his indictments thrown out, all the indictments against the other defendants would, of course, also be thrown out. Perhaps George Saban's knowledge that his attorneys would be firing the first salvo before the trial, that this plea in abatement would be directed toward the heart of the prosecution's case, contributed to his confidence while in jail. Certainly the defendants must have relished this attack on Felix Alston, the man they identified as their chief tormentor.

Subpoenas were issued for several men, including George Russell, the Big Horn County clerk of court; Charles Shaw, the county treasurer; Alex Linton; and Peter Enders, the county clerk. The very day after the plea was filed, Judge Parmelee heard evidence relating to it.[3]

What emerged was that the jury list had been prepared in the latter part of January and the first of February (well *before* the raid) and that several people were involved in its preparation.[4] Enders and Shaw testified that Sheriff Alston's involvement was to write down the names of jurors as Alex Linton took them from the assessment roles.[5] As the names were read out, some of them were struck, as one participant or the other would note such things as the death of a voter or his having moved from the county. When the list was finally completed and placed in a jury box, however, far more names had been removed than any of the witnesses remembered as having been deleted during the preparation of the jury list. It was never established who had removed the additional names or how it was done. What was sure, though, was that those who prepared the jury list had worked off old lists that were very incomplete, not naming, for example, most of those new voters who had come in with the big new irrigation projects.[6]

The evidence was presented intermittently through the week of October 18 and had not been completed when the Basin papers went to press on Friday, October 22. The two papers treated the story quite differently. The *Rustler* printed a relatively short piece in which the plea in abatement was discussed in a matter-of-fact manner. It was noted that even if the court decided that the list was illegal, the accused would not go free; informations (essentially, declarations by a county attorney that someone has committed a crime) would simply be filed, the charges would be reinstated, and the cases would proceed to trial the week of October 25.[7] Filing an information is by far the most common procedure for bringing criminal charges; the notoriety of the Spring Creek raid had resulted in the unusual circumstance of charging by indictment.

The *Republican* felt the subject deserved much more attention, and its story was three times as long. Excerpts show that the *Republican* had some difficulty maintaining the appearance of impartiality:

> The attorneys for the defense showed at the out set that they have not been idle during the long months that have elapsed since the arrest and indictment of the defendants. In a motion to quash the indictment

George Saban under oath makes allegations of a most grave and serious character.

The defense have prepared their case with great care and no detail, however unimportant, apparently, has been overlooked. . . . That the trial will be conducted with great brilliance, and become one of the celebrated cases of Wyoming and Big Horn County goes without saying."[8]

As might be inferred from the article in the *Rustler,* the prosecution did not take the plea in abatement very seriously. In letters to his wife, Will Metz indicated the trials would begin the week of October 25, and he clearly anticipated no delay. He did express irritation that the plea had wasted "one whole week," and he was anxious to get started.[9]

But though the prosecution did not take the plea seriously, other people did, and not just the defense and its closest allies. The *Thermopolis Record* published on Saturday, October 23, and it was closely watching the progress of the plea. Its article indicated that if the plea was granted, "the whole proceedings will have to be gone over from the start."[10] This is an overstatement of the legal effect the plea could have, but it does show that if the indictments were thrown out, many people in Big Horn County would view the prosecution's case as requiring correction because of a fundamental taint, even if the charges were immediately reinstated. Whether jurors will admit it or not, there is a presumption that the criminal charges of a grand jury are right. But if indictments are declared invalid, that presumption is lost, and the prosecution's burden increases.

The district court held a Saturday session on October 23, and some of the witnesses who had previously testified were recalled. The defense scored some points when it established that there were times during the preparation of the jury list when only Alston and Linton were present.[11]

On Monday morning there was only a brief evidentiary presentation. Percy Metz made his first active appearance, conducting a very brief examination of C. C. Ellis.[12] Then the real fireworks began as each side presented its closing arguments.

The defense showed that it would not hesitate to drive home its view that the actions of the grand jury were illegitimate. J. L. Stotts of Sheridan, known as "Judge" Stotts, opened for the defense and declared that the jury commission had "absolutely ignored" the law. He spoke of the "tampering" that had occurred, resulting in the preparation of an "illegal" jury list.[13]

E. E. Enterline responded first for the prosecution. Enterline's presentation was much more scholarly, much less emotional than the argument of Judge Stotts; he forwarded the state's case so effectively it even impressed

the *Republican*. Enterline suggested that the court could rectify any problem with the selection of the jury by simply replacing the names removed.
He asserted that the defense contention that Felix Alston had altered the
jury list was to "attribute clairvoyant powers to the Sheriff," because any
such action would have far preceded the raid.[14]

Will Metz followed Enterline and also made an unemotional, closely
reasoned argument. He carefully reviewed the evidence, pointing out that
every member of the board believed he had properly discharged his duties,
and concluded that although someone may have removed some names
(Metz all but admitted that something akin to tampering occurred), the
defense had not shown that this was in any way aimed at Saban or that it
negatively affected him.[15]

H. S. Ridgley closed for the defense, and he resumed the harsh tone
taken by Stotts. "The polluted jury box," he declared, "cannot be purified
by the court returning the abstracted names." He "excoriated" Felix
Alston, pointing out that Alston was present at each session at which the
jury list was being compiled and saying that the law was designed specifically to prevent sheriffs from doing so. Ridgeley concluded his argument
with a dramatic appeal:

> I have called the attention of this honorable court to this not because
> we are not ready for trial, for we are. We could go to trial and the supreme
> court would reverse this court. I do it because a great wrong had been
> done this county, and all who would have to plead in this court, and,
> before juries drawn from that dirty box.
>
> I do it because it will save this already heavily in debt county
> thousands of dollars. I do it because the lives and liberty of my clients
> are involved. May it please your honor, then, in view of the testimony
> and the law to grant this motion as asked for by the defendant, Saban.[16]

When Ridgeley completed his argument, Judge Parmelee asked him
for the legal authority he had quoted. The attorney handed it to the judge,
and Parmelee started reading it as the attorneys and spectators quietly
watched.[17] Such moments of oppressive silence mask almost unbearable
tension, stirring and surging behind impassive faces.

Finally, Judge Parmelee looked up and began to announce his decision.
He said that the only serious question before the court was the exclusion
of a large number of names from the jury list; the other questions merited
little attention. He discarded the charge that there were no cattlemen and
no residents from the east side of the river on the jury. There was no proof,
the judge said, of any participation of the sheriff in selecting jurors; he

simply wrote off the names. The offense at Spring Creek had not been committed at the time the list was prepared, so there could have been no effort to discriminate against the defendants. It did appear there had been carelessness by officials, and it was clear that the jury list had been tampered with. No proof was introduced to prove who was responsible, however, and neither side could charge the other with the crime.[18]

But all of this still left the serious question of the existence of a jury list containing only half of the qualified jurors. Judge Parmelee pronounced the key finding:

> A list must be obtained which is above suspicion.
>
> The prosecution must proceed without the suspicion of unfairness; it is better, therefore, that the prosecution go forward by information than under these indictments returned under circumstances where suspicion rests, and that they should charge that they have been improperly drawn.
>
> I therefore sustain the plea of abatement of the defendant Saban and direct the county attorney to file the information necessary.[19]

The defense was jubilant and the prosecution crestfallen. The prosecuting attorneys had been badly embarrassed, even with the court's discarding all but one of the claims in the plea of abatement. Of course, informations were immediately filed against all five defendants. They never left jail, and the prosecution immediately set to compiling a complete jury list. But when court was convened again on Wednesday, October 27, the prosecution felt it had to ask the court to specifically list Felix Alston as having been exonerated. Apparently the judge's order, which stated, "there was no fraud, discrimination or intentional wrongdoing by the jury commissioners, or by any one assisting them." was not sufficient to avoid the blight of the overall ruling. Judge Parmelee did not change his order.[20]

On that Wednesday, all of the defendants were arraigned, and they all pled not guilty. It was made known that Herbert Brink would be the first defendant tried and that the trial would begin on November 4.[21] So after Judge Parmelee's ruling, the trials would still go on, albeit a week later than expected. But this did not dim the defense's euphoria over its victory. The defendants had felt all along that the indictments were a put-up job by sheepmen on a grand jury from which cattlemen were deliberately excluded. Judge Parmelee had revealed to the whole world that these indictments were bogus.

Again the Basin newspapers reflected the contrasting attitudes of sheepmen and cattlemen. The *Rustler* article about Judge Parmalee's ruling was succinct, factual, and subdued. But the story exploded on the *Republican's* pages. There were two sets of headlines. One read: "JUDGE DECIDES PLEA — And He Sets Aside the Indictments. Judge Parmalee Approved by People Everywhere — RIDGELEY MAKES A BRILLIANT ARGUMENT." The second: "SABAN CHARGES WIN — Testimony and Opening Jury Boxes Shows It. Crime Committed by Someone — PROSECUTION FALLS DOWN ON PROOF."22 In both stories the *Republican* abandoned any pretense of objectivity.

The articles were very long; the one headed "Judge Decides Plea" covered two complete columns on the first page and about a column and a half on the second. It described in lavish detail the drama of the ruling by Judge Parmelee and was unstinting in its praise of the judge ("Here was the personification of judicial impartiality. . . . It [the decision] met the requirements of the hour, and its spirit of fairness, exact impartial justice came like a zephyr of cooling and refreshing ozone."). The second story also offered great detail, but it concentrated on the presentations of evidence and argument. The writer certainly did not refrain from making editorial comments, however:

> That a fearful crime was committed in the murder of the three sheep men is a fact. That men could do such things to their fellow men is deplorable and is profoundly regretted by every law abiding citizen of every commonwealth or community.
>
> But as fundamental as this sentiment, equally as strong, equally as important, if justice is to dwell in the land, if organized government is to stand or to endure, and the proper administration of law is to follow, such deadly assaults upon the machinery of justice should be halted and not pass unnoticed.23

One would think that the two front-page stories sufficiently expressed the *Republican's* editorial posture, but a third article, more clearly submitted as editorial, was also run:

> The thought may have occurred to some persons that the plea in abatement made by counsel for the defense in the Tensleep murder cases was the usual, perfunctory and technical one. As the witnesses testified, and their evidence fragmentary though it was, filtered from the court room, it was a dull or deeply prejudicial mind that did not see that a crime had been committed. The prosecution admitted it before the end of the week. Judge Parmalee, deeply entrenched in the good will, the love, the respect and the confidence of the people of this part of the state of Wyoming has added to all three if that be possible by his most

righteous decision in granting the motion prayed for by the defense. Not because some individual or individuals might be hurt thereby, but because the people of this county must not suffer a great wrong to their property rights or to their liberty and perchance their lives, by the pollution of the jury box. Some one has perpetrated a crime most heinous in the eyes of the American people. None is so despicable in their estimation. None strikes so deadly a blow to a most vital part of our machinery of our government. None deserves the severest condemnation of all more and none there is that merits the heavy hand of the law more than pollution of the jury box.[24]

All in all, it was a remarkable display by the *Republican*. But it wasn't just the *Republican* that reacted this way to Judge Parmelee's decision. The *Worland Grit* carried several front page articles that, if anything, were more strongly pro-cattlemen than those in the *Republican*. Indeed, the same person who wrote the *Republican's* articles probably wrote two long stories for the *Grit*. They were noted as "Special to the *Grit* from Basin," and certain phrases, such as "most righteous decision" and "a zephyr of refreshing and cooling ozone," made a reappearance. The *Grit* articles all but charged Felix Alston and the prosecution of fostering a scheme to control all juries in the county. But fortunately, the *Grit* said, "Judge Parmalee's decision destroyed the cunningly devised scheme."[25]

County officials prepared a new jury list, which contained more than 2,600 names, over three times the earlier number of only 755. In its headlines, one of the *Grit* articles made sarcastic reference to this great increase: "THE RAPID GROWTH OF BIG HORN COUNTY. — THE JURY LIST HAS INCREASED THE PAST TEN DAYS FROM 755 TO 2600." The article following these headlines had an especially harsh tone:

> Some one has committed a gross violation of the statutes of Wyoming.
> A crime has been done. It is not enough to say, that because the Tensleep murders were not committed until April, and, that these lists were made long before that, no wrong was intended them ` — the defendants.
> For whom was the wrong intended? . . .
> The grand jury was called in April, eighty-one names taken off.
> When?
> By Whom?
> By what authority?
> For what purpose?

For whom was the wrong intended? The more the man and his clique tries to explain this dastardly work, the deeper he puts himself and his clique.[26]

It is not clear whether the article was referring to Felix Alston or Percy Metz as the "man and his clique," but either would have sufficed for the *Grit*'s purposes.

The strange thing about the whole reaction to Judge Parmelee's decision is that it seems so disproportionate to the event. Looking back eighty years, the event appears to be a garden variety example of county officials being careless about keeping their jury lists current. But these officials did not intend to jeopardize anyone's rights, and the defense victory did not represent a moral triumph over forces of evil.

The defense did win an apparent advantage when the judge ruled for them, but it didn't mean that the trials would not proceed (that was never more than wishful thinking). All the witnesses and all the evidence of the prosecution were still intact and would be presented to a jury. Perhaps the key to understanding the reaction is that the people involved were not viewing the event from a lofty objectivity of eighty years. They were living it; they were the ones fighting with their neighbors and feeling that their lives and property and reputations were at stake.

Before these feelings began to fade, another emotional issue arose. As early as October 16, the question of adding more militiamen was being addressed. On that date, William Simpson wrote a letter to the governor. He indicated that he was writing after discussing the case with the other prosecuting attorneys, and he stated his belief that more troops should be brought in. He explained that

> the defense intends, with out question to place at Basin, a great many sympathisers, for the purpose of intimidating witnesses and influencing jurors. . . . It is expected to duplicate the conditions, that existed in Weston County or Crook County cases. Already this method is being urged and last night, two sheep men from the Grey Bull Country, were assaulted here in Town, to the extent of being advised that they had better get out of Town, and at once. and were abused shamefully by a couple of cattle men sympathisers. . . .
>
> I am looking for trouble in this County during the trial of these cases and I don't believe I guage conditions from alarm for my own personal safety, but it is in the air, and being forced along and sooner or latter will brak [sic] out.[27]

Governor Brooks responded immediately, sending the adjutant general of Wyoming, P. A. Gatchell, to Basin with "full authority to take whatever steps are necessary to see that the laws are impartially enforced."[28] Will Metz, writing his wife on October 21, remarked that "we expect about 50 soldiers and about 15 deputy sheriffs here next week," but it is not clear whether that information came from a conversation with Gatchell.[29] Metz did confer with Gatchell on October 23 and learned that the adjutant general was planning to be in Basin during the trial and "take active command if necessary." He dutifully reported this information to his wife. Metz also commented upon something that other observers noted: It had been an unusually fine autumn, one beautiful, warm day stretching after another. Metz said it was the finest fall he'd ever seen in Wyoming, and he was sorry he could not have tried the cases during such fine weather.[30]

Gatchell stayed for a few days and then left Basin. The prosecution understood that troops would be added, bringing the total to about thirty men. But on October 28, Alston received a telegram from the adjutant general, and it seemed to indicate that more troops might not be forthcoming. E. E. Enterline then wrote a long letter to W. E. Mullen, the Wyoming attorney general. The letter is well written and shows the qualities of mind that made Enterline an impressive attorney; it is an explanation and a plea for more troops.

> Now the situation is simply this: The cattlemen and cow-boys from the east side of the river intend to swarm in here during the trial and no doubt in every manner, seek to impede the administration of justice. They intend to move their round-up wagons into the town, or in a park adjacent to the town and camp there. There is already one outfit here having some thirty camp beds, and we are reliably informed that there are seven more to come just as soon as the trial commences. You will observe therefore, that there will be several hundred men here whose interests and feelings will be hostile to the State. The two men who participated in a measure in the raid, and whom we expect to use as witnesses here, are now confined in the Sheridan County jail. They will have to be brought here to attend the trial, and will have to be guarded while here. It will never do to put them into the county jail where the other prisoners are kept. If we did, influence would be brought upon them to go back upon the prosecution. We cannot use the city jail because the mayor and the officers under him are in sympathy with the defense.[31]

Enterline went on to say that if the sheriff could not muster sufficient force, sheepmen would begin to come in "for the purpose of seeing fair play," thus creating two contending factions.[32] The prosecution was afraid that the main street would become a battlefield, with a lot of people being killed.[33] A decision was finally made, and on Saturday, October 30, a train arrived from Sheridan, bringing ten privates, Capt. Arthur Parker, and Col. C.Z.A. Zander.[34]

Will Metz was not dissatisfied with the extra men sent. On October 31, he wrote his wife: "The soldiers under 'Col Zanders' came in yesterday and are 'tenting on the old camp ground' and the cattlemen are hot. I do not look for any trouble now."[35]

The cattlemen were indeed hot, and as the trial came closer and closer, they seemed to grow increasingly rigid. On October 31, the same day Metz wrote his wife Jennie, a Basin citizen also wrote a letter. It was to Governor Brooks, and it provides insight into the cattlemen's collective state of mind on the eve of trial. Mr. C. M. Jones told Governor Brooks that he had lived for twenty-four years near Ten Sleep and "know whereof I speak." He said that the country between Shell Creek to within ten miles of the head of Nowood was well organized against sheep and sheepmen, and whenever these subjects were brought up the reaction could only be explained by saying these people were "insane." Jones stated that men he considered his neighbors and friends would "look me square in the eye and say that no crime was committed at Spring Creek, that what was done there was justifiable and right."[36]

Jones mentioned the round-up wagons that had been gathering in large numbers since Mr. Whaley (George Saban's father-in-law) got a permit from Mayor Collins to camp on the edge of town. He thought that too much political influence was involved and told Governor Brooks (who was a Republican) that he was a lifelong Republican but wasn't going to take sides on the case "measured by the political complexion of some of our county officers whom I did not vote for."[37]

Jones was certainly correct that the trials had become political, with the cattlemen feeling that Democrats were persecuting them and that Republicans should be helping them. (The Johnson County War also had political overtones; there was a strong Republican association with the big cattlemen who were responsible for that raid. The voters punished the Republicans severely in the next election, in 1892.) The people making these appeals to Governor Brooks assumed that he would have more sympathy for their positions because of this Democratic harassment. They also assumed that somehow these Democrats, the sheriff and the county attorney and all their "clique," had misled the governor.[38] That is exactly what was asserted by the *Republican* after the first contingent of troops arrived in June.[39]

Even this late, the cattlemen and their allies still believed there was a chance Governor Brooks would pull the militia out if he just understood the true state of affairs. On November 2, Mayor Collins sent the governor a telegram, which read as follows:

> As Mayor of town of Basin and in name of great majority good citizens I respectfully request you to remove the detachment of state militia. Posted here situation does not warrant their presence never had militia here is menace to the peace and quiet of the town if sheriff will not do his duty I as Mayor will guarantee to see that peace and good order shall be maintained,
>
> W S Collins Mayor[40]

The *Republican* came out on November 4, and its article about the militia was not presented as news but as a declaration of position. The headlines read: "RECALL THE MILITIA — Mayor Collins Telegraphs Brooks. The Citizens Remonstrate Presence of Troops — WHY DID THE GOVERNOR SEND THEM IN?" The article was unequivocal in its condemnation:

> Who has asked for these troops to be quartered here during a time of profound peace? What has occurred at any time in the past year to warrant or to justify in this fair city and peaceful valley armed militia?
>
> Who made such statements that Governor Brooks felt justified in his issuing an order directing troops to be quartered here? Will Governor Brooks inform the citizens of Basin who made such statements to him that resulted in the national guard being quartered here?"[41]

As this article implies, the cattlemen had become very dubious about Governor Brooks' allegiance, despite his Republican credentials. They intended by their actions to challenge him to either declare martial law or remove the troops.[42] The governor would do neither. He did not even reply to Mayor Collins' telegram until November 8, when the trial of Herbert Brink was well underway, and his reply was terse and direct: "Troops there at request of sheriff and Prosecuting Attorney and will remain as long as they seem necessary to preserve order."[43]

So the militiamen in Basin would remain in Basin, and one more threat to the fair trial of the raiders was removed. There was still another threat, though, and it was the most serious of all. The cattlemen had been alluding to it frequently, and the last paragraph of the Republican's "RECALL THE MILITIA" story again raised it: "And, finally, the taxpayers want to know who is to foot the enormous bills to pay for these troops that they say are not now, nor ever were needed. Is the county not heavily enough in debt now?"[44]

It was true the county was heavily in debt, and for over two weeks that had been a matter of the deepest concern to the prosecution. When William Simpson wrote the governor on October 16, he spoke of this "serious matter." The county had already exceeded its limit of indebtedness for 1909, and the local banks announced they would not honor the county's scrip (a promise to pay from the next year's revenues) in payment of juror and witness fees.[45]

This problem could have prevented the trial altogether; if the state had no money to subpoena jurors and witnesses, it would be impossible to have a trial. The two Basin banks were pro-cattlemen, and their refusal to honor the county's scrip had more to do with their disapproval of monies spent on these trials than with prudent banking practices.[46]

But the sheepmen of Wyoming were not going to let the case die this near to trial. A number of them came forward and took much of the scrip, and at least some of the wages and expenses of the troops were paid by sheepmen. On November 3, the day before the trial was to begin, the First National Bank of Meeteetse, probably acting with the support of sheepmen, wired Simpson that it would buy all of the scrip issued by the Big Horn County Commission, albeit for an 18 percent discount. Simpson announced: "There has never been any doubt about the prosecution of the cases." This was a braver tune than he sang on October 16, and he was no doubt relieved that the problem was put to rest.[47]

With this final resolution there was, at last, nothing to impede the trial from beginning on November 4.

Strangely, the eve of a trial, even a very big trial, is not usually a time of great anxiety for lawyers. No doubt every one of those small-town attorneys who were to rise when Judge Parmelee first entered the courtroom on November 4 was acutely aware that he would never again be part of a bigger case. But most of the anxiety had already been worked out in the tedious hours, weeks, and months of preparing witnesses, gathering evidence, planning strategy, and researching the law. By the time the case was to begin, Metz and Enterline and Ridgeley, the primary trial counsel, had surely assumed that "war horse" mentality that every good attorney embraces just before trial. Indeed, these lawyers were probably eager to begin, each convinced that his side would prevail brilliantly.

There were aspects, of course, to *State v. Brink* that were very different from other cases. One of them was that the lead attorneys carried the banner for a large group of people, almost as if heading a crusade. Ordinarily, an attorney fiercely focuses on one client and the protection of that client's rights. But when a case becomes a cause and that cause becomes symbolic, it is impossible to so concentrate on the client, and many things must be done to accommodate a constituency while still protecting the client's rights.

Another unusual aspect of *State v. Brink,* was fear for the prosecuting attorneys' personal safety. Percy Metz spoke of attorneys who carried guns, but the prosecuting attorneys also made it a practice to walk in the middle of the street at night to avoid ambush, and Joe LeFors frequently acted as their bodyguard. In one of his talks, Metz told of something he had never mentioned before: During much of the time before the trial LeFors stationed himself in a second-floor room of the Mountain View Hotel, an establishment directly across the street from the Big Horn County Courthouse. He sat in a chair next to a window, scanning the courthouse square, with a Winchester across his knees.[48]

Throughout this time, Will Metz and his wife Jennie maintained a steady stream of correspondence. Ironically, Metz wrote his wife just before the trial and gently scolded her for her fears for the safety of her husband and son. On November 3, he wrote:

> My dear Scared Girl,
> Your scary letter just at hand — you certainly must know that the newspaper correspondents in their grafic reports are trying to earn their salary — and the one who can make the greatest sensation out of the reports of this trial & the surroundings gets the highest salary.
> There is absolutely no danger to counsel. The only possible reason for troops & for the reports — is to prevent the cattlemen from intimidating the witnesses & getting them to go back on their statements & to keep the men safely in jail.[49]

Will Metz was suppressing facts, being protective of his wife to keep her from worrying. But she must have worried anyway, especially after learning that on October 30, and for the next three days, Percy had joined a posse chasing down three men implicated in the murder of a man in Lovell.[50]

The beautiful fall of 1909 had continued into November. Dry, windless autumn days in the Big Horn Basin are exquisite in any year; if one could bottle a single day and keep it through the whole year, it would be a day in October or November. But such days have a touch of sadness, with their long, haunting sounds and foreboding sense of calm before the winter. Perhaps, on November 3, 1909, there was an extra touch of melancholy, because November 3 was surely the last lovely day of the frontier in Wyoming.

## NOTES

1.  A term of court is simply the interval of time during which the court holds a session.
2.  Plea in Abatement, *State v. Saban*, Case No. 401, Records of the Big Horn County Clerk of the District Court.
3.  *Basin Republican*, 10/22/09.
4.  Ibid, 10/29/09.
5.  *Big Horn County Rustler*, 10/22/09.
6.  *Basin Republican*, 10/29/09, from the remarks made by Judge Parmelee upon announcing his decision. See also speeches of Percy Metz before the Park County Historical Society, 6/9/61, and the Big Horn County Historical Society in Lovell, 3/2/62.
7.  *Big Horn County Rustler*, 10/22/09.
8.  *Basin Republican*, 10/22/09.
9.  Letters of 10/21/09 and 10/24/09 from Will Metz to his wife, Jennie, Metz Collection.
10. *Thermopolis Record*, 10/23/09.
11. "Saban Charges Win," *Basin Republican*, 10/29/09.
12. Ibid.
13. *Big Horn County Rustler*, 10/29/09.
14. *Basin Republican*, 10/29/09. Percy Metz, in his 1961 and 1962 speeches, indicated that he was the one who made the primary arguments to the court, because the prosecution really wanted to lose this motion. The *Republican* (and other newspapers) directly contradict this. It was the "big guns" who argued the motion, not Percy Metz, and there is every indication that, at least at that time, they wanted to win the motion.
15. *Basin Republican*, 10/29/09; *Big Horn County Rustler*, 10/29/09.
16. *Basin Republican*, 10/29/09.
17. Ibid.
18. Ibid; *Big Horn County Rustler*, 10/29/09.
19. Ibid.

20. *Denver Post*, 10/26/09, p. 4, col. l; "Judge Decides Plea," *Basin Republican*, 10/29/09; October 25, 1909 order by Judge Parmelee, *State v. Saban*, Big Horn County Case No. 399.

21. *Basin Republican*, 10/29/09.

22. An item of note is the spelling of Judge Parmelee's name. The *Republican* spelled it with an "a," as in "Parmalee," but the judge himself spelled his name with an "e," i.e., "Parmelee." Folks in 1909 were apparently not as concerned about the correct spelling of a name as they are today.

23. Ibid.

24. Ibid.

25. *Worland Grit*, 10/28/09 and 11/4/09.

26. Ibid, 11/4/09. The *Grit* said there were 755 names on the original jury list, the plea 731. The numbers flopped around as the list was scrutinized and tinkered with.

27. Letter of 10/16/09 from W. L. Simpson to Hon. B. B. Brooks, Sheep Raid File

28. Letter of 10/18/09 from Gov. B. B. Brooks to W. L. Simpson, Sheep Raid File.

29. Letter of 10/21/09 from William Metz to Jennie Metz, Metz Collection.

30. Letter of 10/24/09 letter from William Metz to his wife, Jennie, Metz Collection.

31. Letter of 10/29/09 from E. E. Enterline to Honorable W. E. Mullen, Attorney General, Metz Collection.

32. Ibid.

33. Speech of Percy Metz before the Park County Historical Society, 6/9/61.

34. *Denver Post*, 10/30/09, p. 3, cols. 3–4; 10/31/09, p. 7, sec. 1, col. 1–3.

35. Letter of 10/31/09 from William Metz to Jennie Metz, Metz Collection.

36. Letter of 10/31/09 from C. M. Jones to t he Hon. B.B. Brooks, Sheep Raid File.

37. Ibid.

38. *Denver Post*, 11/3/09.

39. *Basin Republican*, 6/11/09.

40. Telegram of 11/2/09 from W. S. Collins, Mayor, to B. B. Brooks, Governor, Sheep Raid File.

41. *Basin Republican*, 11/4/09.

42. *Denver Post*, 11/3/09.

43. Telegram dated 11/8/09 from B. B. Brooks to W. S. Collins, Mayor, Sheep Raid File. Adjutant General Gatchell was in Basin and gave his very strong opinion to the governor that the troops were necessary and Mayor Collins was misusing his position. Undated Gatchell letter to B. B. Brooks, id.

44. *Basin Republican*, 11/4/09.

45. See Note 29, this chapter.

46. See the *Denver Post* article, 11/3/09.

47. *Denver Post*, 10/31/09 and 11/3/09.

48. Speech of Percy Metz before the Natrona County Historical Society, 11/2/61.

49. Letter of 11/3/09 from Will Metz to Jennie Metz, Metz Collection.

50. Letter of 11/1/09 letter from Will Metz to Jennie Metz. Entries from the 1909 diary of Percy Metz, Metz Collection. Percy was chasing three Mexicans, including the murderer, Paseo. In his letter, Metz also spoke of the reporters from all the newspapers and how insistent they were about pictures and information; he said he put them all off except for the *Denver Post*.

# The Trial Starts CHAPTER 12

The trial was convened Thursday morning, November 4, but not at the site of the regular courthouse. That building had been condemned by the grand jury after it noted such things as "large fissures appearing in every room occupied by the county officers."[1] Besides, the small courtroom would not begin to accommodate the large crowds of people expected at the trial. Therefore, *State v. Brink* was heard at Fraternal Hall, a public auditorium that, the *Cheyenne State Leader* observed, "some people with riotous imaginations, dignify by the name of opera house." The *Leader* also noted that the building was "not too palatial," apparently meaning that the facilities were rather dingy.[2] Percy Metz referred to Fraternal Hall as "a big dance hall."[3] Nevertheless, it was the best Basin had.

In 1909, Basin, Wyoming was a neat, quiet little town of about 1,000 people. In many ways it was remarkably progressive, with "splendid" water and sewerage systems, a nascent electric light system, and a natural gas plant.[4] The town's systems were going to be severely tested, however, because as the first of the Spring Creek raid trials began, Basin had exploded to twice its normal population.

During any term of court the number of people in Basin would increase, what with jurors, judges, litigants, lawyers, and witnesses coming in. The term of court was treated as a major social occasion. Percy Metz spoke of how a big platform had been constructed down by the river and how everybody — opposing attorneys, opposing parties, even the judge — would set aside their differences and come down and dance and have a good time.[5]

In addition to large numbers of cattlemen, large numbers of sheepmen had arrived in Basin, as well as newsmen and, probably the largest group, people who were just plain curious about the trial. It had been very well publicized, of course, and besides offering coverage directly about the case, at least two of the area newspapers had run long articles with biographical information about all the lawyers who were involved.[6]

None of the many people reporting about the trial indicated that the mood was ugly. At the outset, anyway, the normal festive atmosphere probably prevailed. Any zeal for a dispute was no doubt dampened by the presence of so many soldiers and lawmen. Moreover, as noted by Dick J. Nelson, guns were collected. Nelson wrote that the center for this collection was Allen's Livery Barn and that "six-shooters by the bushel, were held in the Allen Barn Office."[7] The regular citizens of Basin didn't feel festive, though; they were a little cowed by all these strangers descending on their town. Dr. Carter spoke of this period and said: "Folks talked in whispers, afraid if they spoke aloud, they would either be called on the witness stand or be shot in the back."[8]

The city fathers were concerned about the image Basin was getting from all this notoriety. The editor of the *Rustler,* in a guest editorial published in Denver's *Rocky Mountain News,* insisted that despite the Spring Creek murders, Basin was not "an outlaw town in an outlaw country" and that its streets were as peaceful as "any village of Puritanical New England." He assured the readers of the *News* that "those who have friends in the Basin country need have no fear as to their safety."[9] There were, however, aspects of Basin to make a thoughtful person worry about the peacefulness of the town's streets. About twenty soldiers, camped in tents about the courthouse, had their weapons at the ready and would challenge anybody who came too close.[10] They were guarding the jail so that deputies could attend to the witnesses and attorneys at the trial.

The attorneys alone presented a crowd as they arrived at Fraternal Hall: for the prosecution, Enterline, Simpson, and Will and Percy Metz; for the defense, nine attorneys appeared — Ridgeley, R. B. West, W. S. Collins, Thomas M. Hyde, and C. A. Zaring of Basin; C. F. Robertson and J. T. Jones of Worland; W. L. Walls of Cody; and J. L. Stotts of Sheridan.[11] Of course, not all these attorneys represented Brink, but the attendance of the attorneys representing the other defendants was essential. They knew the prosecution was leading off with its strongest case; in a sense, then, the fate of their clients hung on the fate of Brink. If Brink was acquitted, even if there was a hung jury, their clients would probably go free. But if Brink was convicted and the evidence was strong, their clients were in deep peril.

The first job was the selection of a jury. Many attorneys, especially the great ones, believe that selection of the jury is the single most significant stage of a trial.[12] It undoubtedly was in *State v. Brink.* With the passionate divisions existing in Big Horn County, the biggest challenge the prosecution faced was finding an unbiased jury. Only one or two cattlemen could hang a jury, and a hung jury was as good as a loss. Big Horn County had neither the money nor the stamina to begin the process again and possibly face another hung jury. It was the prosecution's nightmare. They could present a perfect case, could bring to fruition seven months of anguish and hard work in a brilliant presentation, and still have one or two jurors refuse to convict. It was also a very realistic fear; even the *Big Horn County Rustler* observed that "disinterested persons predict that the outcome will be a mistrial, resulting from a hung jury."[13]

From the new, much larger jury list, about a hundred names were drawn and subpoenas were issued.[14] Thursday morning, about ninety men appeared.[15]

They were chosen at random from places throughout Big Horn County, but only about twelve were from that area of the eastern Big Horn Basin described by C. M. Jones in his letter to the governor.[16] One of these men, Jacob Becker from Nowood, was a sheepman, while another, F. M. Sheldon of Big Trails, was Joe Allemand's brother-in-law.[17]

This panel must have been a profound shock to the defense. There were so few of their devoted friends among the veniremen that the prospect of getting many cattlemen on the jury was remote. Instead of cattlemen — or sheepmen, for that matter — most of those on the jury panel were farmers. An awful reality began to dawn on the defense: By having all those names added to the jury list, they had diluted the pool of cattlemen. Perhaps that glorious victory, Judge Parmelee's granting of the plea in abatement, was not so glorious after all.

When the clerk of court started drawing names, however, the very first man selected probably made the defendants more optimistic. He was Mark Warner, a staunch cattleman who had testified before the grand jury.[18] This was like the first batter in the World Series getting a triple — perhaps it was a portent of a lucky draw of cattlemen. But it was not to be.

From that ninety-man pool, eleven more names were drawn. Warner was followed by C. C. Shaw, a carpenter from Worland; Robert Carroll, a farmer from Penrose; Leo H. Pfaff, an undertaker from Cody; J. J. Davis; C. R. Jones of Basin; William Lewis, a farmer from Greybull; Elmer Yarnell from Burlington (probably a farmer); Clause Andrieu, a sheepman from Marquette (west of Cody); J.H. Smith from Ionia (east of Lovell; he also was probably a farmer), J. T. Hurst of Basin (soon to be a very wealthy oilman, although that knowledge was hidden from him in 1909); and W. H. Packard, a beekeeper and farmer from Burlington.[19]

These twelve men were probably called to the jury box, and all would have come forward and sat in chairs reserved for the jurors. Then, voir dire was conducted. "Voir dire" refers to the questioning of prospective jurors for the purpose of determining their impartiality. An individual may be accepted as a juror, challenged for cause, or challenged peremptorily.

In *State v. Brink* the twelve prospective jurors were questioned and first challenged for cause. If facts were drawn out during questioning to show that the juror had a bias that would keep him from rendering a fair decision, the judge sustained a challenge for cause. The juror left the jury box, and a new one was selected to assume the old juror's place. Only when all jurors were passed for cause (and there are no limitations on the number of challenges for cause) were peremptory challenges made.

A peremptory challenge is one in which no reason for the challenge is given. On its face, this process seems to be based on pure whim, and at times it is. But most peremptory challenges are made from the deepest and most telling instincts of the trial lawyer; a good trial lawyer will sense, from any of a hundred sources, that a juror may not be, cannot be, impartial.

It appears that in the *Brink* case, there were successive rounds of peremptory challenges. The prosecution would exercise its peremptory challenge (it only had a total of six) and then the defense would exercise two (Brink had twelve). Then the new jurors would be questioned and challenged or passed for cause. Once all were passed for cause, another round of peremptories would take place. This whole process can drag on interminably; it was widely predicted it would take many days to secure a jury to hear the case against Herbert Brink, even that, perhaps, it couldn't be done.[20]

Will Metz handled the questioning for the prosecution, H. S. Ridgeley for the defense. These old pros were smooth, and the newspapers favorably noted their techniques. The *Republican* was especially impressed by Ridgely: "The latter [Ridgely], bending forward in his seat would take a juror and in soft, mellow tones, soothing and winning, would quickly and deftly draw from the man innermost thoughts, the thing concealed, and then quickly came the challenge and rejection."[21]

Surprisingly, the questioning was not extensive; the veniremen were only asked general questions about their acquaintance with the raiders and their opinions reflecting bias or prejudice.[22] It may have been that both the prosecution and defense teams felt they already knew every juror's position about the raid — a great deal of information could be quickly gathered on every member of the panel because of the many people associated with each side. By and large, there were not many challenges for cause, and that was also not expected. Neither the prosecution nor the defense had foreseen the large number of neutrals, people who were neither cattlemen nor sheepmen and who did not have passionate feelings about the raid.

Of the twelve original jurors, only two were excused for cause. One was C. A. James. The exact basis for the challenge is unknown, but three of the eight veniremen (including replacements) excused for cause had scruples against the death penalty.[23] The other original juror challenged for cause was very significant: Mark Warner. Before the grand jury, Warner had stated that he "was opposed to seeing sheep come in there," meaning the Upper Nowood.[24] This statement was probably enough for Will Metz to establish that Warner had views that would make it hard for him to fairly judge Herb Brink's case, and so Warner was excused for cause. The prosecution didn't even have to use one of its six peremptory challenges. This development must have discouraged the defense; it was as if that promising leadoff batter had been picked off third by the pitcher.

Warner was replaced by Frank Young, a barber from Meeteetse, and James by L. E. Brown, a farmer from Clark.[25] They were passed for cause, and the peremptory challenges began.

The prosecution's first peremptory challenge was J. T. Hurst.[26] Hurst wasn't a cattleman, but judging by his later successes he was an energetic and forceful man, and perhaps he'd strongly expressed sympathy for cattlemen. (He and his wife were original locators in Elk Basin in 1916, and he took the fortune thereby earned to Denver, where he formed a large oil company.[27])

The defense challenged C. C. Shaw and Elmer Yarnell. Again, the reasoning behind these challenges is not known; the defense simply had to make challenges. They had to do everything they could to get cattlemen on that jury. It is surprising, though, that one of the first challenges was not W. H. Packard. Perhaps the defense simply viewed him as an innocuous beekeeper. But Packard was a man who had displayed strong leadership qualities in Burlington. The Mormons who colonized Burlington had elected him as their first bishop. A few years later, this election was ratified when church authorities from Salt Lake City appointed Packard to that position.[28] As a bishop of the Mormon church, Packard would not be expected to have much tolerance for the exuberance of sheep raiders. The cattlemen supporting Brink probably knew that Packard was "one of those Burlington Mormons," but they did not have much association with the farmers in the center of the Basin and obviously did not realize what a potent personality Packard was.

The three men challenged were replaced by Charles Duncan, Lee Walters, and W. J. Morris. It is not clear how it came about, but another juror was then drawn: C. H. Gardner. All these men were passed for cause, although the prosecution must have tried hard to show the prejudice of Gardner. Clarence Gardner was a cattleman, ranching on Paintrock Creek near Hyattville. He had been outspoken against sheepmen, and one witness even told the grand jury he thought Gardner might have been involved in the raid.[29] Gardner testified before the grand jury, but the prosecution was not able to pull any information out of him regarding the raid.[30]

Men such as Clarence Gardner are the reason peremptory challenges are so important to assure fairness in a jury trial. The prosecution quickly had him removed from the jury. The defense then challenged Morris and J. H. Smith.

Remarkably, the selection of the jury moved very rapidly. At noon on Thursday, Will Metz said: "If the work goes as smoothly in the afternoon as it did in the forenoon, the jury will be completed before adjournment."[31]

In the third round of peremptory challenges, the prosecution challenged J. J. Davis, the defense M. H. LaFollet and A. A. Pulley. After these men were replaced, the jury selection had evolved so favorably for the prosecution that it waived its fourth challenge. The prosecution was quite happy with the jury as it stood. The defense was certainly not: It still had no cattlemen. Therefore, two more peremptory challenges were made, to men named Shoumaker and Johnson.

On the fifth round of peremptories, the prosecution again waived its challenge! The defense must have been getting desperate, even fighting panic. It once again challenged two men, Ackerman and Andrieu. New names were drawn for these two, and this time, at least, the defense got someone on the jury the prosecution felt it had to challenge: Dan Winslow. Known as "Denver Jake," he was a man with a seamy reputation. Winslow ran a livery stable in Worland, but for years before that he had been a working cowboy.[32] The prosecution must have felt he was prejudiced in favor of the raiders and used its last peremptory challenge to remove him. The defense used its last two challenges upon Angus Beaton and P. C. Everett.

The time after all peremptories are exhausted is a time of insecurity for the trial lawyer. Indeed, a lawyer tries to avoid ever being in this situation, although it apparently was not possible in *State v. Brink*. Without peremptory challenges, a juror can only be removed for cause; that is, if the lawyer can affirmatively demonstrate prejudice. This is difficult in the best of circumstances, because most prospective jurors are very reluctant to admit that they cannot be fair. And the worst calamity, the one that jerks the trial lawyer awake at 3 a.m. in a cold sweat, can arise after all peremptory challenges are exhausted.

Some jurors are deeply committed to one side in a case and are determined to conceal their predisposition, wanting very badly to get on the jury and enforce their views. C. H. Gardner is a good example; if he had been selected after all peremptory challenges were used, it would have meant complete disaster for the prosecution. As it was, two names were drawn that the prosecution feared might be just as bad: John S. Rutrough and John Donahue.

John Rutrough was a sheepman from Cody. That would seem to be very good for the state, but the prosecuting attorneys knew that after he had been served with a summons for jury duty, Rutrough had visited the office of W. L. Walls, one of the defense attorneys and Percy Metz's opponent in the 1908 election. Just before the trial charges circulated that the defense had tried to tamper with more than one juror, and the prosecution suspected that here was an example.[33] Rutrough said, however, that when he visited Walls' office the murder trial wasn't discussed, and after some sharp questioning, he was passed.

It was the second man who really frightened the prosecution. John Donahue was a rancher and farmer from Hyattville who knew all of the defendants; George Saban and Milton Alexander had frequently stopped at his house overnight.[34] This by itself was not significant — in those days when men traveled they stopped at the nearest ranch when night fell — but it did heighten fears that Donahue shared the seemingly pervasive insanity against sheep that prevailed in his part of the county.

The prosecution went into a huddle. Some of the attorneys knew Donahue and felt he was honest and independent, that if he heard the evidence he would bring in a verdict of guilty. They therefore decided not to try to disqualify him. They felt they probably could not get the job done and would just irritate Donahue. The defense was extremely pleased. As Percy Metz later told it: "Ridgely was thrilled beyond words. He figured, 'Well, here's a fellow to hang the jury.' There was no question in his mind that the jury would be hung."[35]

Still, when the jury was finally selected, Donahue was the only juror who might hang the jury, and he had never been identified as one of the diehard cattlemen. If the defense had three or four cattlemen on the jury, it would have had considerably more cause for optimism.

The unavoidable conclusion is that there probably would have been three or four cattlemen on the jury had the plea in abatement not been made. In light of this probability, the plea has to be viewed as a major tactical blunder by the defense. Percy Metz later said the prosecution recognized as much. Metz even asserted that they *tried* to lose the plea in abatement, but this seems a revisionist perspective, made considerably after Judge Parmelee's ruling.[36]

The jurors finally selected were:

Robert Carroll, a farmer from Penrose
Leo H. Pfaff, an undertaker from Cody
Wm. Lewis, a farmer from Greybull
W. H. Packard, a beekeeper and farmer from Burlington
Frank Young, a barber from Meeteetse
L. E. Brown, a farmer from Clark
Charles Duncan, a farmer from Lovell
Joseph Vogel, a farmer from Cody
C. E. Nielsen, a farm laborer from Cody
Charles Walter, a farmer from Cowley
John S. Rutrough, a sheep raiser from Cody
John Donahue, a farmer and rancher from Hyattville[37]

What was astounding was that these jurors were selected in only six hours, jury selection being completed about 3:30 p.m. When Will Metz made his remark about getting a jury before adjournment, many people thought he was "entirely wrong," and when he turned out to be right, "there was genuine surprise on all sides," as the *Cheyenne Leader* noted.[38] Indeed, there would have been time to begin the main body of the trial, but the lawyers asked that it not begin until the next morning (Friday), and Judge Parmelee grudgingly agreed.[39]

On that Friday morning, Fraternal Hall was packed with people. Standing room was not available, as the crowd pushed back into the front doors; if anyone left his or her seat, it was immediately lost.[40]

There is an old saw that declares that a trial lawyer need only do three things: 1) Tell 'em what you're going to tell 'em. 2) tell 'em; 3) tell 'em what you told 'em. The opening statement is when the trial lawyer meets the first requirement, and E. E. Enterline certainly did tell 'em what he was going to tell 'em. His statement was an hour and a half long, and he laid the whole case out, all those things people had been guessing and gossiping about the past several months.[41]

Enterline began his presentation by making the bold assertion that the plans and operations of the murderers were known to the state down to the smallest detail and that the evidence, when unfolded, would leave no room for doubt as to the guilt of the accused, Brink. The prosecutor traced the whereabouts of Brink throughout April 2, finally leading to Keyes' ranch. He said the raid was planned there by Saban and Alexander, and seven men left the ranch on a mission that was originally intended only to "ditch the sheep" and burn the wagons. Enterline told the jury that the state had prevailed upon Faris and Keyes to turn state's evidence in light of the part they had taken and had granted immunity to them (thereby confirming the accuracy of those April news stories).[42]

The attorney painstakingly described details such as the calibers of the weapons each raider carried, the exact route followed to Spring Creek, and the exact plan of attack. He told how the plot was carried out at the scene and quoted Faris' question — "Where are your men?" — and Saban's reply: "I guess they're dead." Enterline also repeated Brink's statement after he gunned down Allemand: "This is a hell of a time of night to come out with your hands up."[43] The surveyor's map first employed before the grand jury was used by Enterline, and he showed photographs of the burned bodies and camp wagons.[44]

It is not clear whether Enterline included it in his opening statement, but that morning the state also announced that Billy Goodrich and his wife and Charles Helmer would be there to testify against Brink.[45] (It was believed by many people that the Goodriches and Bounce had left the state to avoid testifying; some sheepmen even accused cattlemen of tampering with witnesses by frightening Billy Goodrich away.[46])

All of this must have made a powerful impression upon the jury. It certainly made an impression on Herbert Brink. The *Cheyenne State Leader* described the defendant during Enterline's address:

> Brink, who sat behind his lawyers, listened with rapt attention to the argument of Judge Enterline. Brink is rather a good looking young fellow and a Lombrosa or a Sherlock Holmes would be at a loss to find on his open, ruddy countenance any lines denoting murderous propensities. That he takes an intelligent and vital interest in the proceedings was evidenced by numerous whispered suggestions to Mr. Collins and Judge Stotts of the defense.[47]

After Enterline completed the opening statement, it was time to "tell 'em," to call witnesses to the stand and prove the state's case against Herb Brink.

## NOTES

1. *Worland Grit*, 5/13/09.

2. *Cheyenne State Leader*, 11/6/09.

3. Speech of Percy Metz before the Natrona County Historical Society, 11/2/61.

4. *Denver Post*, 11/6/09, p. 3, cols 4–6.

5. Speech of Percy Metz before the Natrona County Historical Society, 11/2/61.

6. See the *Basin Republican*, 10/29/09, and the *Worland Grit*, 11/2/61.

7. Nelson, *The Big Horn Basin*, 43.

8. "C. Dana Carter, Pioneer Doctor," Wyoming Division of Parks and Cultural Resources, Historical Research and Publications Division, Cheyenne, WPA File #619, 13.

9. *Rocky Mountain News*, 11/5/09, editorial page.

10. *Basin Republican*, 11/5/09.

11. Appearance page, trial transcript, *State v. Brink*.

12. For instance, G. L. "Gerry" Spence of Jackson, Wyoming, one of the great trial attorneys in the United States, owes much of his success to his mastery of this process.

13. *Big Horn County Rustler*, 11/5/09.

14. *Basin Republican*, 11/5/09.

15. See the Appendix herein. Surprisingly, only men served on juries in Wyoming in 1909. Although Wyoming established woman suffrage when the territory was first established in 1869 and several women served on petit and grand juries in 1870 and 1871, the practice had been discontinued. T. A. Larson, *History of Wyoming*, (Lincoln: The University of Nebraska Press, 1965), 84, 85.

16. These included Jacob Becker, R. W. Burington and W. J. Hartman of Nowood; H. H. Carstensen, J. L. Van Buskirk and M. H. Warner of Ten Sleep; C. H. Gardner, W. E. Morris and John Donahue of Hyattville; W. W. Rhea of Shell; and Joseph Leishman and F. M. Sheldon of Big Trails. There may have been other cattlemen from the eastern part of the Basin, but those missing from the Metz lists (see Appendix) were apparently almost all from other parts of the Big Horn Basin.

17. *Denver Post*, 11/5/09, p. 9, col. 1; Sheep Owners of Wyoming, 1910 Directory.

18. Record of Challenges, *State v. Brink*, Case No. 443, Records of the Big Horn County Clerk of the District Court.

19. Homsher Collection; Record of Challenges, *State v. Brink*; Sheep Owners of Wyoming. See Notes 16 and 17, this chapter.

20. *Cheyenne State Leader*, 11/5/09.

21. *Basin Republican*, 11/5/09.

22. *Big Horn County Rustler*, 11/5/09.

23. Ibid, 11/5/09.

24. Grand jury testimony of Mark Warner, 1.

25. For all jury selection maneuvers, see Record of Challenges, *State v. Brink*.

26. Ibid.

27. For the story of Elk Basin and some of J. T. Hurst's later activities, see Davis, *Sadie and Charlie*, Chapter 4.

28. Andrew Jensen's field notes, Church Historical Department, Church of Jesus Christ of Latter Day Saints, Salt Lake City, Utah. A letter from James R. McNiven in the *Deseret News Weekly* of 3/21/96, refers to Packard as Bishop or presiding elder; a letter from Ambrose Hibbert, published in the *Deseret News Weekly* of 3/26/97 refers to organized worship since 1894. The Burlington Ward was formally organized on July 30, 1899, with William H. Packard as Bishop and David P. Woodruff as first counselor.

29. Grand jury testimony of C. C. Shaw, 3.

30. See grand jury testimony of Clarence Gardner, and recall.

31. *Cheyenne State Leader*, 11/5/09.

32. See John W. Davis, *Worland Before Worland* (Worland: Northern Wyoming Daily News, 1987), 2.

33. *Denver Post,* 11/5/09, p. 9, col. 1; 11/4/09, p. 3, col. 1.

34. *Big Horn County Rustler,* 11/5/09.

35. Speeches of Percy Metz before the Natrona County Historical Society, 11/2/61, and Big Horn County Historical Society in Lovell, 3/1/62.

36. Speeches of Percy Metz before the Natrona County Historical Society, 11/2/61, and the Big Horn County Historical Society, 3/1/62.

37. Big Horn County Rustler, 11/5/09; *Thermopolis Record,* 11/6/09; *Denver Post,* 11/5/09.

38. *Cheyenne State Leader,* 11/5/09.

39. *Big Horn County Rustler,* 11/5/09.

40. *Basin Republican,* 5/11/09; *Denver Post,* 11/6/09, p. 7, cols 4–6.

41. *Big Horn County Rustler,* 11/5/09.

42. Ibid.

43. Ibid.

44. Denver Post, 11/5/09, p. 9, col. 1.

45. Ibid.

46. *Big Horn County Rustler,* 11/5/09; *Denver Post,* 11/30/09, p. 3, cols. 3–4; *Thermopolis Record,* 11/6/09; see statements of Percy Metz re Bounce Helmer in Chapter 11.

47. *Cheyenne State Leader,* 11/6/09.

The Sheep Herd. Before the Allemand-Emge sheep herd was driven east from Worland to Ten Sleep and Spring Creek, several photographs were taken, including these two. A puppy is held in the top picture, and it is probably one of those later found on Joe Allemand's body. The man standing in the buggy in the picture below is Joe Emge. Courtesy Washakie County Museum and Cultural Center.

The North Wagon. On April 2, 1989, a sheepwagon was wheeled onto the place where another sheepwagon stood on April 2, 1909. Jack Seaman took this eastward-looking photograph about 9 o'clock that evening. There was a full moon and Mr. Seaman used full exposure. Courtesy Jack Seaman.

The Gully. The small gully east of where the north wagon stood. The photograph looks south to the area where the south wagons stood, about one-quarter mile away. Photograph by the author.

Looking North. Photograph taken from the site of the south wagon, looking north. Photograph by the author.

Fred Greet. Mr. Greet is standing next to the ranch house he was vacating on April 2, 1909. The raid occurred to the east (Mr. Greet's left) and it was at the east end of the house, where Greet and three other men stood watching the evening of April 2. This photograph was printed originally in Ten Sleep and No Rest, by Jack Gage. Courtesy Jack Gage, Jr.

The Graves. These three crosses stood over the graves of Allemand, Emge, and Lazier on Spring Creek. This photograph was also printed originally in *Ten Sleep and No Rest*. Courtesy Jack Gage, Jr.

Joe Lefors: The infamous lawman, Joe Lefors. Another of the pictures taken at the time of the trial. Courtesy Washakie County Museum and Cultural Center.

Fraternal Hall. This photograph shows the hall many years after the trial, when it had been moved. Courtesy Jack Gage, Jr.

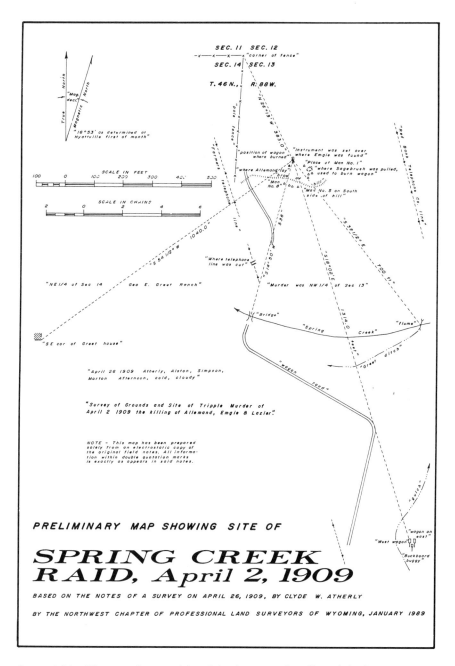

Surveyor's Map. This is a replication of the exhibit that was used so effectively by the prosecution at the trial; it was drawn from the original survey notes of Clyde Atherly, the Big Horn County surveyor in 1909. Courtesy Northwest (Wyoming) Chapter of Professional Land Surveyors.

The *Denver Post*, November 4, 1909. The *Post* printed photographs on November 4, 1909, showing Basin Mayor W. S. Collins, militia about the Big Horn County Courthouse, W. S. Metz and H. S. Ridgeley. Courtesy Colorado Historical Society.

The Militia. Another November 1909 photograph of the militia camped about the Big Horn County Courthouse. Courtesy Washakie County Museum and Cultural Center.

E. E. Enterline. From the November 13, 1909, edition of the Denver Post. Courtesy Colorado Historical Society.

W. L. Simpson. This photograph of Billy Simpson was printed in the November 5, 1909, issue of the *Denver Post*. Courtesy Colorado Historical Society.

The Spring Creek Five. The five defendants at the time of trial. Proceeding clockwise from top left: Herb Brink, Ed Eaton, George Saban, Tom Dixon, and Milton Alexander. Courtesy Washakie County Museum and Cultural Center.

# The Parade Begins

## CHAPTER 13

The state of Wyoming first called Felix Alston.

The prosecution had a plan of action and the first part was to establish the corpus delicti. "Corpus delicti" is Latin, and it refers to proof of the essential fact that a crime has been committed.[1] There would be five corpus delicti witnesses, including Alston.

The sheriff laid a grim groundwork of facts, describing what he found on April 3. He also told of the rifle and pistol shells picked up the next day and of the various tracks at the scene.[2] Will Metz handled the direct examination of Sheriff Alston. (The day was significant to Metz for another reason; it was his fiftieth birthday.)[3] It only took about an hour; then came the cross-examination.

The real test of a witness is not during direct examination but under cross-examination. It is the difference between shooting practice and combat. And H. S. Ridgely was a lawyer who could provide a real test under fire. Ridgely first asked about the shells, whether there was anything unusual about them or if Alston had marked them. Alston said that they were the "regular standard .25-35, .35 automatic and .30-30 shells" and that there were no marks to show these were the shells picked up at Spring Creek.[4] Then Ridgely started emphasizing the .30-30 shells, asking how many Alston had found and where. Were any loaded cartridges found, and had he given any of them away (as Alston had some loaded .25-35 shells)? Alston knew he'd only found .30-30 shells to the south of the north wagon, but most of his other answers were vague. The sheriff must have wondered why Ridgely was concentrating so much on .30-30 shells.

Ridgely picked at little points to raise doubts. Did any one else pick up any shells there? (Real point: Who knows how the scene was picked over?) How large an entrance hole did the wound in Allemand's side make? (Perhaps this wound didn't match Brink's rifle.) Didn't you run into other horse tracks? (Those range horses probably completely threw your tracking off.) Weren't there fairly heavy snows on April 3 and 4? (How could you possibly follow tracks after that snow?) In each case, Alston provided a more or less satisfactory answer, but all of it could have raised questions in a juror's mind if he were so inclined.

Interestingly, it was Ridgely who raised the matter of a boot with a "turned-over" track; nothing had been said about distinctive boot tracks during the direct examination. It seemed that Ridgely wanted to draw the prosecution into making claims based upon the boot tracks and that Alston wanted to avoid doing so.[5] Perhaps the defense had heard something about a possible identification based upon boot tracks and was prepared to rebut it.

Ridgely was skilled at making witnesses appear fumbling and ignorant of essential facts. He would ask a series of questions about details that were not particularly significant but that Ridgely wanted the jury to believe were important. The prosecution was aware of Ridgely's propensities and no doubt worked hard with Alston and other witnesses to prepare them for that. Something that greatly aided Alston and blunted Ridgely's attempt to show him an ignorant witness not worthy of credence was the survey map. In most cases, a jury has a lot of basic questions about the facts of the case. Attorneys who have lived a case for months forget that jurors have not, and they sometimes debate esoteric points while the jury is back at the beginning, wondering where the crime occurred and who and what was where. In this situation tactics such as Ridgely's are especially effective. The prosecution must present facts distinctly showing a clear violation of law; if it fails to do so and the jury is confused, an acquittal follows. The map, however, cleared away most of the fundamental questions. It undeniably established where the wagons and the bodies and the shells and the creek and the road and the Greets' ranch house and the telephone lines all sat. Given a lawyer with Ridgely's obfuscating tactics, such a map was a godsend.

It seems, however, that Felix Alston was susceptible to such tactics, and Ridgely still attempted them. For instance:

Q: Did you measure the distance from the wagon to the round dot here that is furtherest [sic] to the north beyond the brow of the hill along this gully? (indicating).
A: I did not.
Q: Did you measure the distance from the wagon to the second black dot?
A: I did not.
Q: Did you measure the distance from the wagon to the third black dot?
A: I did not.

Q: Did you measure the distance from the wagon to the black dot
    furtherest south?
A: I did not.
Q: Did you measure the distance from the wagon to either of the dots
    on the south side?
A: No sir.
Q: Did you measure the distance from the place where the double circle
    is located on the map representing the place where Allemand's body
    lay to any of the black dots to the east or to the south?
A: I did not.
Q: You don't know the exact distance?
A: I do not.[6]

Ridgely was not all smoke and mirrors, though, and when it was his
intent to clarify rather than confuse an issue, his questioning could do that
very well. Ridgely closed his cross-examination with very pointed questions, the significance of which was quite clear:

Q: Now you don't know when Allemand was killed do you?
A: Oh no.
Q: And you don't know who killed him?
A: No sir.
Q: And you don't know who pulled up the sage brush here from your
    own knowledge?
A: No sir.
Q: Nor you don't know who fired the shells that you found there on the
    ground from your own personal knowledge?
A: No sir.
Q: Now there had been quite a number of people before you arrived?
A: Yes sir, there were some six or eight when I got there, and I don't
    know how many more had been there.
Q: And you don't know whether there had been a number of shells
    picked up before you arrived or not?
A: I do not.[7]

When it was Will Metz's turn again on re-direct examination, he did
what a lawyer is supposed to do after cross-examination — clean up the
messes left by the cross-examiner. Metz had Alston explain that he had
contacted Al Morton the morning of April 3 and had him go immediately
to the scene to keep people on the west side of the north wagon. Metz also
had Alston explain that although snow had fallen, it had all melted off by
noon on Sunday and that the snow had only had "some" effect on tracks.[8]

Metz also raised some matters overlooked during the direct testimony. He had Alston testify about sheep and dogs that had been shot (two at the north wagon) and about those little woolly puppies found on Alle-mand's body. Alston told of seeing Brink at the scene Sunday night. Brink had arrived with Billy Goodrich, and it seemed to the sheriff that Brink was "a little more serious when he first came than he did when he went away." The sheriff made it clear that sagebrush that had been pulled up on the east side of the north wagon "looked as though it had right recently been pulled."[9]

Ridgely had one last shot at Alston. He made some points similar to those raised during the initial cross-examination, but his primary focus was on the empty shells in the burned wagons. Alston's answers showed there had been a lot of cartridges in the wagons; many had been exploded from the heat of the fire, but eight or ten were exploded from a gun.[10]

The press only mentioned Alston's testimony in a perfunctory man-ner, apparently viewing it as mundane. But what the press did not realize was that through Alston, both the prosecution and the defense were sounding themes that would be echoed throughout the trial.

The county surveyor, Clyde Atherly, was the second witness called, and he explained how he had constructed the map. He told the jury that he had made a survey of the crime scene accompanied by Sheriff Alston, Al Morton, and William Simpson and that the plat had been drawn from that survey. Ridgely did not challenge Atherly's plat, but after the sur-veyor's testimony, he did challenge another part of the state's case: "Defendant moves to strike out of the evidence the shells received in evidence for the reason that on cross-examination of the witness it was discovered there was no proper identification of the shells."[11]

Judge Parmelee sustained the motion. All of those shells picked up at the scene on April 4 were thrown out of evidence: the jury could not consider them. This was a blow to the prosecution, but the case had to go on, and the prosecuting attorneys made no immediate response.

The next witness was Al Morton. Morton's testimony was very similar to Alston's; he confirmed what the sheriff had testified to but added many details. Morton told of his instructions to go to the scene and said that after he arrived no one was allowed around the wagons. He told of finding the gold teeth and of seeing three dead dogs, two of which had been shot and the third of which had apparently died of some cause other than a gunshot wound. He testified that he had been with Alston when the shells were picked up and that the sheriff had taken all of them. He also said he had tracked horses without the sheriff and that this trail, the one taken from the big sagebrush along Spring Creek after the raid, went back to the southwest.[12]

Ridgely's cross-examination of Morton, as with Alston, was comprehensive, but some of the answers were probably not to his liking. He tried to push Morton to say that he had not been able to prevent people from tracking up the area around the north wagon. But as Ridgely asked questions, Morton became stronger in his responses, finally declaring that no one was at that wagon ahead of him (except the Greets and Lamb) and that no one was allowed there until the sheriff went over the ground. With respect to the shells, Morton would not agree that someone had coached him in his testimony, specifically not Joe LeFors. (Ridgely gratuitously threw in a question about LeFors, invoking the name of a man viewed by the defendants as a hireling beast of the sheepmen.) Nor would Morton agree with Ridgely that there had been a thousand shells in the north wagon. Morton further testified there were exactly seven raiders headed southwest, back toward Keyes' ranch, and that he was not misled by tracks of the range horses — it was a very clear trail.[13]

Perhaps in frustration, Ridgely accosted Morton over alleged improprieties in the coroner's report prepared by Morton, but Judge Parmelee refused to allow Ridgely's questions.[14]

The defense attorney asked a series of questions about Allemand's wound. Morton testified that the bullet had struck Allemand in the left side just above the waist, exiting on the right two to four inches higher, and had slightly mushroomed becoming about twice as large. Surprisingly, Ridgely again raised the matter of the "turned-over" or "run over" heel; Morton, like Alston, made no conclusions from these tracks.[15]

Deputy Morton was a good witness for the state, significantly strengthening the corpus delicti showing. There was still the matter of the shells, though, but the prosecution was soon to fix that problem. The next witness called was Percy Metz, Big Horn county attorney.

Young Percy was examined not by his father, as had been all of the previous witnesses, but by Enterline. The transcript shows a confident, even brash young man. The direct examination was very brief, simply establishing that he was at Spring Creek at the time Sheriff Alston collected the shells and culminating in two decisive questions:

Q: You may state Mr. Metz whether the cartridges and cartridge shells I exhibited to you are the shells that were delivered to you by the sheriff, the same shells?
A: They are.

Q: You may state to the jury whether or not they are the same shells you
   delivered to the sheriff to be used as testimony this morning.
A: They are.[16]

Mr. Enterline then reoffered the shells in evidence. But Ridgely wasn't
going to let the prosecution off so easily, and before responding to the offer
he cross-examined the young county attorney. The questioning, however,
merely strengthened the previous testimony. Percy testified that the shells
had been in his possession since Alston had given them to him, that he
had marked "one or two at that time and I marked some since," and that
the shells had never been out of his possession (except when delivered to
Alston for his testimony). He carefully pointed out the lead pencil marks
he had made at the time. Ridgely did score a point when he brought out
that Metz had only marked four shells, and he used that as a basis to object
to the shells being admitted into evidence "except the four that bear
identification marks for the reason they are not properly identified." Judge
Parmelee, however, apparently felt that Percy's other testimony was sufficient to establish proper identification, and he received all the shells in
evidence.[17]

Dr. George Walker was the next witness called and the last corpus
delicti witness. Dr. Walker, a well-qualified physician, had practiced in
Hyattville for several years, and he provided a dispassionate, detailed
description of the condition of the bodies found. Among other matters,
Dr. Walker testified that the entrance wound was about three-tenths of
an inch in diameter. He also concluded that the wound to Allemand's
collarbone was from a bullet that had mushroomed after striking some
other object.[18] This conclusion should have laid to rest the supposition
that one of the raiders had hacked at Joe Allemand's neck with a shovel,
but this tale was still being circulated years later.

The cross-examination was contentious, a battle of wills between
Ridgely and the doctor. Ridgely held up a blue pencil and asked Dr. Walker
whether the wound was the size of the pencil. When Walker said he
couldn't say, Ridgely confronted him with a conversation held only the
night before in which he had supposedly agreed to the comparison. Dr.
Walker said he didn't recall that, and attorney and physician bickered
about the doctor's memory.[19]

Doctor Walker testified that the bullet had exited Allemand's body
about one inch higher than the point of entrance and, after much jousting
with Ridgely, agreed that it would not have exceeded one inch. The two
men struggled back and forth over the question of where Joe Allemand's

arm had to be in order for the bullet that passed through the body to hit the forearm as well. Ridgely seemed to score a point with the following exchange:

> Q: Then doctor it would have been impossible for that bullet that passed through the body of Allemand to have made the wound in the arm if he had his hands up in that manner would it (indicating)?
> A: Yes sir.[20]

Will Metz obviously felt Ridgely had done some damage, and his first inquiry on re-direct examination related to the position of Allemand's shoulder and arms necessary to create the described wounds. He was only partially successful; after Dr. Walker's answers, it was still not completely clear how all the wounds had come about.[21]

Dr. Walker's testimony was completed late in the afternoon of Friday, November 5. From the prosecutor's standpoint, it would have been a good time to recess. But the prosecution's categories (such as "corpus delicti") did not dictate the progress of the trial, and so another witness had to be called. The prosecution was prepared next to call several eyewitnesses to the raid, and the first one from that category was Fred Greet.

Fred Greet was in a terrible position. He was a rancher at the vortex of this emotional controversy, and he no doubt felt a great deal of pressure from the cattle ranching community. At the same time, he also got along well with the murdered sheepmen and surely felt deep regret over their deaths. So Greet did what many people do in this situation: He told the truth and discharged his duty, but he did so only in response to direct questions, not elaborating at all. Greet's testimony was direct and terse.

As he had before the grand jury, Fred Greet told what he knew of the terrible night of April 2 and of the anguishing discoveries the next morning. E. E. Enterline sought to have Greet make the conclusion that the rapid firing he had heard was from an automatic. The defense made several objections, which were overruled but which might have been intended to induce Greet to avoid making this conclusion. If the thought occurred to Greet, he declined it and readily, but succinctly, gave his opinion that the rapid shots were from an automatic.[22]

Greet's testimony showed what an unusual amount of light there had been at the crime scene. In addition to there being a clear moon, the fire from the north wagon was very bright, as was that from the south wagon. Greet could not see the south wagon fire from the ranch house, but he could still see the reflection of that fire, which was a quarter-mile away.

As Greet testified, Enterline made good use of the surveyor's map, having the witness demonstrate where he had seen two men near the north wagon, where the four men in the Greet ranch house had walked the morning of April 3, and where he found the telephone wire cut.[23]

Greet also provided general corroboration to Alston and Morton's testimony. He told about the shells he had seen and said he had noticed where there had been men south and east of the wagon, and pointed out where some person had pulled sagebrush. Greet also made the important point that he had *not* gone on the east side of the wagon the morning of April 3. In one minor way, Greet's testimony was inconsistent with Alston and Morton's: He said there were *four* dead dogs around the north wagon.[24] It was also notable that Greet was never asked about the warning shot that had been fired toward the ranch house by the raiders.

In addition to recalling the events of the evening of April 2, Greet told the jury that at about 3 o'clock that afternoon he had seen Herbert Brink riding a sorrel horse south toward Joe Henry's.

After Fred Greet completed his direct examination, the case was finally recessed for the day, giving poor Fred a night to think about the cross-examination he would have to endure in the morning. The trial was to continue the next day, Saturday.[25] It was a day in which the key witnesses for the prosecution were scheduled to testify: Bounce Helmer, Bill Keyes, and Charlie Faris.

## NOTES

1. Trial notes from the Homsher Collection.
2. Trial testimony of Felix Alston, 2–17.
3. Letter of 11/1/09 from Will Metz to his wife Jennie, Metz Collection; Lawrence M. Woods, *Wyoming Biographies* (Worland: High Plains Publishing Company, 1991), 133.
4. See Notes 1 and 13, this chapter. The subsequent discussion is taken from pp. 17–34 of the trial transcript, which is the cross-examination of Felix Alston by Ridgely.
5. See the testimony at 32, 33, and 40 of the trial transcript.
6. Trial testimony of Felix Alston, 22, 23.
7. Ibid, 33, 34.
8. Ibid, 34–37.
9. This discussion is taken from 34–39 of the trial transcript.
10. Ibid, 44, 45. Alston testified that two or three of these were .41 pistol shells. Apparently, though, the remainder were .35 automatic shells.

11. Trial testimony of Clyde W. Atherly, 47–50 of the trial transcript; Atherly survey map.

12. From the direct testimony of Al Morton, 51–61 of the trial transcript.

13. Trial transcript, 63, 66, 78–82.

14. Morton had called a coroner's jury consisting of George Pickett, Perry Miller, and Fred Winsor. The witnesses included the Greet brothers, F. S. Howard, and Pete Cafferal. Ridgely was critical of Morton for not writing down the evidence presented as part of this report, but Judge Parmelee ruled this was irrelevant. Trial transcript, 70–71.

15. Trial transcript, 67–68, 72–74.

16. Ibid, 86.

17. Ibid, 86, 87, 88.

18. From the direct examination of Dr. Walker, 88–96, trial transcript.

19. Ibid, 97–98.

20. Ibid, 98, 100, 101.

21. Ibid, 101–103. Dr. Walker did not testify to conversations with Alexander, but they no doubt would have been presented at a trial of Alexander.

22. Ibid, 111.

23. Ibid, 114, 115, 118, and 120; Atherly survey map.

24. Ibid, 118, 119, 121.

25. This was apparently a common practice in 1909.

# The Heavyweights Testify CHAPTER 14

On Saturday, the biggest crowds yet congregated at Fraternal Hall. The *Rocky Mountain News* claimed that 700 people were crowded into the courtroom, which seems an exaggeration.[1] There were a lot of people, though, if not 700; the crush was so bad that many people stood on chairs, and the crowd had to be slowly pushed aside so deputies could bring witnesses to the stand. Saturday, November 6, was a day in which Basin was consumed by the trial. The *Republican* wrote: "Practically all business in stores was suspended, and those who could not gain admittance gathered on the streets and discussed the case in all its phases." The crowd was there for the testimony of the prosecution's most important witnesses, anticipating that this would be the most dramatic day of the trial. They would not be disappointed.[2]

The first matter was Ridgely's cross-examination of Fred Greet. Initially, the inquiry was desultory, a general discussion of odds and ends details. But then, suddenly, there was an eruption, perhaps the most emotional point in the trial, when Ridgely's seemingly bland questions were interrupted by forceful objections from the prosecution. Quoting from the transcript:

Q: What were they doing in that country there?
A: Trailing sheep.
Q: How many bands of sheep?
A: Two bands.
Q: Was that range a sheep range in there?
   Plaintiff objects as wholly immaterial, incompetent, and irrelevant.
Objection sustained. Defendant excepts.
Q: Did the sheep men run their sheep in on that range and feed their
   sheep?
   Plaintiff objects as wholly incompetent, irrelevant, and immaterial.
Not proper cross examination. Objection sustained. Defendant excepts.
   Defendant offers to prove —

Plaintiff objects to the offer being made in the presence of the jury. Objection sustained. Defendant excepts.

Q: What character of animals was it they had brought in there, that they
    had with them?

A: Sheep.

Q: And you say there were two bands of sheep?

A: Yes sir.

Q: What character of sheep usually ranged in that vicinity?

    Plaintiff objects as wholly immaterial. Objection sustained. Defendant excepts.

    Defendant offers to prove by the witness on the stand on cross-examination that that was a cattle range country, that no sheep ranged in there and that —

    Plaintiff objects as wholly immaterial, irrelevant and incompetent, and not proper cross-examination. Objection sustained. Defendant excepts.

Q: You say you have lived in that country eighteen years?

A: Somewheres near there.

Q: I will ask you if it is not true that there was a line drawn and agreed
    upon between the sheepmen and the cattlemen in that country
    which excluded the sheep from coming into the country where the
    sheep were that night?

    Plaintiff objects as not proper cross-examination, irrelevant and incompetent, and in no sense a justification for murder. Objection sustained. Defendant excepts.

    Defendant offers to prove by the witness on the stand that prior to the time of this killing and of the time that Allemand and Emge had their sheep at the place where the killing occurred that there was an agreement between the sheep and the cattle interests as to the range that each should occupy, and by the agreement it was agreed that this range was a cattle range and not a sheep range, and that no sheep under the agreement had a right to range or feed in that vicinity or travel through that country.

    Plaintiff objects to the offer as not proper cross-examination, incompetent, irrelevant, and immaterial, and for the further reason it would in no sense be a justification for the crime of murder. Objection sustained. Defendant excepts.[3]

Ridgely was forwarding the core defense — that the sheepmen were aggressive invaders violating the cattlemen's rights and were justly expelled. The *Denver Post* said: "The defense will attempt to show that Emge, one of the slain sheepmen, had given word that he had armed himself for any cattlemen who might cross his path."[4]

Ridgely probably felt that Fred Greet, as a cattleman, was a good witness before whom to raise all this, someone likely to know of and perhaps even accept the deadline. But the defense attorney did not really expect Judge Parmelee to allow his questions, and he was well prepared to get his message before the jury anyway. Parmelee's rulings were correct from a legal standpoint (cattlemen were not entitled to use deadly force to repel the sheepmen, even if the sheepmen had been trespassing), and it was manifestly improper to fling out all those offers of proof. Ridgely knew all this but didn't care a whit. He was determined to get his message before John Donahue and other jurors he hoped would be sympathetic, and in the end he did. Whether Ridgely would get the response he wanted remained to be seen.

The exchange between Ridgely and Enterline was undoubtedly very heated, but it subsided as quickly as it had arisen — a violent but brief squall — and Ridgely resumed an understated and competent cross-examination. He kept nicking away at the many guns and shells found at the north wagon (including a Remington automatic) and established that Greet did not know what kind of automatic he had heard or who had done the shooting, thereby leaving open the possibility that the gunshots had come from the *sheepmen,* not the cattlemen. Then Ridgely again raised the matter of the "run over" boot track. His persistence on this point indicated that the defense had some evidence they wanted to use.[5]

. The most effective part of Ridgely's cross-examination came when he skillfully demonstrated what Greet did not know: He did not know just where the shooting occurred, who had done it, who killed Allemand or the others who killed the sheep or the dogs, nor who burned the wagon.[6]

Porter Lamb was the next witness, and that was logical, but the prosecution must have called him with some trepidation. The defense had issued subpoenas to summon those witnesses who would probably be called to testify on behalf of Herbert Brink. The state had done likewise for its witnesses.[7] Both Brink's and the state's list, however, included Porter Lamb and Lizzie Lamb. This had ominous implications. Throughout the case, the prosecution had been deeply worried that cattlemen would "get to" its witnesses; Porter and Lizzie Lamb's appearance on a list of defense witnesses raised that distinct possibility. The prosecuting attorneys probably handled this problem by simply asking Lamb why he was listed as a witness for the defense. However they proceeded, the state obviously decided that calling Lamb was worth the risk.

However, it was not very far into the questioning before Lamb began to stray from his grand jury testimony. Enterline asked him what time on

April 2 he had been awakened by shooting. Before the grand jury, Lamb
had said "about half past ten" without hesitation. Now it was: "I can't say
of my own knowledge more than what Frank Greet told me."[8] It was not
a big point, but to the trial lawyer such a change heralds serious problems
on points that do count. Still, Lamb generally followed his prior testimony,
concluding that he had heard an automatic and describing the fires at the
wagons. He also repeated that he had seen two men go up toward the south
wagon and back and that he saw two shots. But when Lamb was asked
from what direction those two shots had come, he said: "I would not say
just from what point they did come."[9] Before the grand jury he had
answered the same question quite differently: "I should say towards where
Allemand was found."[10]

Enterline made another try, asking the question another way. Lamb
responded: "It would be hard to say from the distance we were from the
wagon."[11] Enterline moved on to other questions, but he was undoubtedly
a very irritated lawyer. The grand jury testimony of Lamb had been good
corroboration that the killing shots had come from east of the wagon, but
that testimony was of no help when Lamb refused to repeat it to the trial
jury.

On cross-examination, the rancher told of an explosion at the south
wagon, which the *Denver Post* thought significant because it was "evidently from ammunition stored within." Lamb also made another statement that hurt the prosecution's case: He said he walked completely
around the wagon on Saturday, April 3. This gave some support to the
defense contention that the area was too tracked up for Alston to have
made the conclusions he did. The statement was mitigated, however,
when Lamb testified that he didn't think anyone else went around the
north wagon.[12]

One interesting observation Lamb made was that he had heard "heavy
shooting," presumably from the discharge of a large rifle.[13]

Overall, the testimony of Porter Lamb was generally consistent with
Fred Greet's testimony, and it could not fairly be said to have been harmful.
It was not what it should have been, however, and this kind of experience
will shake a prosecuting attorney.

Pete Cafferal, a more important witness, was next, and perhaps the
prosecution could regain momentum from the Frenchman's testimony.
The attorney asking Cafferal questions was William L. Simpson, or, as he
was widely known, "Billy" Simpson.[14] Simpson was only forty-one in
1909, but he had already been in Wyoming twenty-six years; the *Denver
Post* referred to him as an "old range rider." The *Post* carried an article

featuring Simpson, and the theme of the piece was that it was time for the kind of violence perpetrated at Spring Creek to stop, that "Wyoming has passed the border stage of her history." The *Post* article asserted: "The progress of Northern Wyoming from the days of Indian warfare to the present has been marked with blood" and quoted Simpson:

> There are graves of my relatives and friends up here in Northern Wyoming, made as the result of Indian bullets. After the Indians came the big cattle barons with their hired killers. I remember a dozen years ago when two small cattlemen were bound over by a justice of the peace in this town on a trumped up charge and shot in cold blood while they were being taken across the range to Buffalo. They had been tied to their horses and were helpless. One of the cattle company killers waited in ambush for them at the canon down below here and murdered both of them.[15]

It was not easy for Simpson to present Cafferal's testimony, because the witness did not have a strong command of the language. Several times Cafferal misunderstood a question; Simpson would then ask another question suggesting the answer, and the defense would object that Simpson's new question was "leading." But Simpson gradually pulled all the basic information from Cafferal — the setting of the sheep camp at Spring Creek, the men who were present, and what happened that fateful night.[16]

Pete had trouble with more than the language. The *Post* commented: "As he progressed with his story he was affected with violent emotion. He seemed to be living over again the hours last April, any second of which he felt might be his last."[17] In truth, Cafferal *was* recounting terrible memories, how he had "heard shots all of the time," how a cowboy had "push me twice in the ribs with a gun," and another had said: "Turn your face to the other side you son of a bitch. Keep your face straight." When he was lying on the ground in the road, Cafferal had heard sounds coming from around the north wagon: "I heard a groan, somebody do that way, 'Oh, Oh,' and I don't know how many times, I no counted them."[18]

Cafferal also recalled some less frightening but very significant details. He testified that he saw one man near the south wagon throwing harnesses and saddles in a pile; the man was wearing gray pants that looked like corduroy. Cafferal also remembered that one of the raiders had asked Bounce about coal oil and that Bounce had said there was a little bit back at the south wagon. More important, Cafferal testified that at one point during the night, he saw seven men.[19]

Ridgely's cross-examination of Pete Cafferal was not particularly effective, perhaps because Cafferal's statements and descriptions were limited to things he was quite sure of. Ridgely did underline that Cafferal had not recognized any of the men, didn't know who they were.[20]

Cafferal was an important witness, providing direct information as to what took place at the wagons during the raid. But his most important function was to prepare the way for Bounce Helmer's testimony, and from that standpoint, Cafferal's appearance was successful.

Bounce was a crucial witness because of his identification of Ed Eaton; the prosecuting attorneys had a mountain of evidence linking Brink and Eaton the day of the raid. The prosecution and defense knew — or the defense at least assumed — that Bounce could identify Ed Eaton, and they had both known it for months. The prosecuting attorneys surely spent hours and hours preparing Bounce. Still, having so much of a case depend on a very young man who was unpredictable, scared, and no mental giant had to be an unnerving prospect. What would Bounce say under pressure? Would he claim that Jake Frison was on the scene? Or that George McClellan's lumber wagon was? It all sat so heavily on the callow shoulders of this very likable boy with the absurd nickname. So it must have been with great anxiety that Billy Simpson stood and announced: "The State calls Charles David Helmer."

"Charles David" was briefly introduced, then quickly swept aside in favor of "Bounce." The direct examination of Bounce was straightforward, as Simpson took him down the same path as he had Pete Cafferal. The key difference in Bounce's testimony, of course, was the identification of Eaton. Even the *Basin Republican* had to admit that this identification made the testimony dramatic.[21] That big crowd no doubt strained forward and became very quiet at this key moment in the trial:

Q: Did you notice the build of any one around there?
A: I never noticed the build of anybody until after the mask dropped away from that fellow's face.
Q: What was this man doing that the mask dropped away from his face?
A: He was untying the buggy from the supply wagon.
Q: For what purpose, what was he untying it for?
A: Get it off so it would burn I guess.
Q: Was the light plain then so you could see this man?
A: Yes sir.
Q: And the mask dropped away from his face?
A: When he stooped over to take the buggy away from the wagon the mask flew away from his face.

Q: And you seen this man's face from the light of the fire there?
A: Yes sir.
Q: Who was this person?
A: Ed Eaton.
Q: How long have you known Ed Eaton?
A: I have known him ever since I was a little bit of a kid.
Q: Were you very familiar with him?
A: Yes sir. I worked under him on the round up when he was foreman.
Q: And you were familiar with his build?
A: Yes sir.[22]

Throughout the direct examination, Bounce's answers to Simpson's questions were short, and he offered only the exact information sought (meaning that Bounce was well coached).[23] Simpson asked about the same number of questions of Bounce that he had of Pete Cafferal, but the examination must have gone much faster because Bounce, whatever his mental shortcomings, had no trouble with English.

The cross-examination was another matter entirely. Whereas the cross-examination of Cafferal only covers four pages in the trial transcript, that of Bounce is fourteen pages long, with two more pages of re-direct by Billy Simpson thrown in.[24] Ridgely knew what an important witness Bounce was, and he was determined not to let him off the witness stand until his testimony had been severely diminished.

The first thing Ridgely wanted to know was where Bounce had been all summer. The transcript states that Bounce told him: "Dingeness, Washington," but Bounce probably said "Dungeness," which would refer to a town off the Strait of Juan de Fuca.[25] Bounce admitted that he went there at the "solicitation" of Sheriff Alston and that Alston had paid all his expenses. On October 12, Bounce started back to Wyoming in the company of Alston's aunt. At Frannie, Wyoming, he was met by a deputy sheriff, Rice Hutsonpiller, and then taken to Meeteetse to the ranch of Bill Hogg, where he remained until the trial began. Ridgely made sure the jury knew that Hogg was a sheepman and was probably the partner of George Taylor, the foreman of the grand jury.[26]

Ridgely very cleverly introduced the matter of the huge amount of reward money and managed to insert another reference to that ominous presence, Joe LeFors:

Q: Are you to have any of the reward money in this case?
A: Not that I know of.
Q: They have not told you anything about that?

A: No sir.
Q: You have heard them discuss the reward money haven't you?
A: I never have heard Mr. Alston say anything about it.
Q: Never heard Alston say anything about it.
A: No sir.
Q: And you have no promises as to having some of that reward money?
A: No sir.
Q: Don't expect any of it?
A: No sir.
Q: Did you ever hear Joe LeFors discuss the reward money?
A: No sir.[27]

All of these questions were just on the edge of being objectionable, but there was never such a clear violation of the rules of evidence that the prosecution had a basis for objection. And, like much of Ridgely's cross-examination, they did not so much establish facts as invoke other themes, foggy ideas that would have quickly evaporated if brought into the clear light but that might appeal to a mind seeking to justify an acquittal. In just a few minutes of cross-examination, Ridgely had implicitly asserted several subsurface contentions of the defense: This whole prosecution is a put-up job by the sheepmen, and they are doing it by purchasing witnesses with this obscene amount of reward money and bringing in mercenaries like Joe LeFors; Alston is a lackey for the sheep interests and is willing to go to any lengths to carry out his ill purposes, including capturing and controlling this poor young boy.

The cross-examination drifted briefly while Ridgely obtained general information about the last few days before the raid, when the bands of sheep were being driven from Worland. But then Ridgely returned to another of his subliminal themes:

Q: Now you say Emge had an automatic Remington?
A: Yes sir.
Q: Did he have any other guns.
A: Yes sir, he had an automatic six shooter.
Q: He had plenty of ammunition in his wagon?
A: Yes sir.[28]

Ridgely tried to push Bounce to say that he could not tell whether the firing of the automatic came from the sheepwagon or the hill, but that tactic backfired when Bounce said: "I could not tell, but it sounded between me and the wagon." Then Ridgely tried to imply that there was not enough light for Bounce to see Eaton, and this question turned out even worse:

> Q: And when you arrived at the wagon at the south side they had just
>     set it afire?
> A: Yes sir, it had just commenced to blaze up good.[29]

But when Ridgely asked Bounce to whom he first revealed that he had recognized Ed Eaton, the defense attorney hit pay dirt. Bounce said that the first time he ever declared that he had recognized Eaton was in his testimony to the grand jury.[30]

Why Bounce said this is inexplicable, except that it did provide him with an easy excuse for those who would criticize him for revealing it at all (such as his father). Ridgely already knew that Bounce had at first denied he could identify anyone, but he must have been taken aback when Bounce said he had withheld this crucial knowledge until he told the grand jury. Ridgely had represented Eaton from the beginning, and the first thing a criminal defense attorney wants to know after his client is arrested is: What have they got against him? So when Eaton was arrested immediately after Alston brought Bounce back to Basin, Ridgely had to have concluded that Bounce had identified Eaton. But if Bounce wanted to deny that, then so much the better for the defense. It all supplied fertile ground for cross-examination.

Throughout the remainder of the cross-examination, Ridgely hit Bounce time and time again with this initial denial that he had identified anyone. Ridgely would leave the subject briefly and then return to it, finding another direction to come at Bounce, another way to again challenge him. First Ridgely nailed the witness down to his story:

> Q: Didn't you ever tell any one else?
> A: I told my mother.
> Q: Didn't tell any one beside your mother?
> A: No sir.
> Q: Didn't tell the sheriff?
> A: No sir.
> Q: Sheriff Alston didn't know you had recognized anybody there?
> A: No sir, that I know of.[31]

Then Ridgely started building facts showing the inconsistency in Bounce's testimony. He established that shortly after the inquest Bounce went to Al Morton's, then to Hyattville, then to Basin. From Basin he went to Lovell and took a train to Sheridan. Sheriff Alston took him to Sheridan and paid his expenses to Sheridan and his expenses while in Sheridan. Then came the payoff, the demonstration that what Bounce was saying made no sense:

> Q: Mr. Alston had paid your expenses over there and your expenses in Sheridan right after the inquest, and you never told him anything about identifying Ed Eaton.
> A: No sir.
> Q: Never said a word to him about that?
> A: No sir.
> Q: Not a word?
> A: Not that I ever remember of.[32]

It was impeccable cross-examination technique and should have seriously compromised Bounce's credibility.

Having addressed Bounce's dealings with Alston, Ridgely went after an early conversation with Percy Metz. He established that Metz had asked everybody to leave the room "at what is now Mr. Porter Lamb's house." Only Metz and one other man were present in the room when Metz questioned Bounce.

> Q: Didn't you tell Percy Metz at that time you identified Ed Eaton?
> A: No sir.
> Q: Never said a word to him about that?
> A: No sir.
> Q: He wanted to know what you knew about it?
> A: Yes sir.
> A: And you told him?
> A: I told him all but that.
> Q: Did you tell him you was withholding anything?
> A: No sir.
> Q: Then what you told him you represented as being the truth at that time?
> A: I never told him I knew Ed Eaton was there.
> A: But you told Mr. Metz you didn't know any more did you?
> A: Yes sir.
> Q: And what you represented to him was the truth?
> A: Yes sir, I told him the truth but I never told him that.
> Q: But you told him you didn't know any more?
> A: Yes sir.[33]

Ridgely then moved away from this topic and addressed what Bounce had seen that night and what he'd done after he and Pete were released. This inquiry didn't produce any obvious dividends and very soon Ridgely came back to the identification of Eaton and hit Bounce with his hardest blow.

Q: Where did you take dinner on the Sunday following the killing?
A: I don't remember.
Q: Didn't you take dinner at I. P. Lathams place?
A: I ate dinner there I know one day, I don't know just when it was.
Q: And Mrs. Latham and Bob Goodrich and Mr. Latham were at table with you at dinner?
A: Mrs. Bob Goodrich was there too.
Q: And you were discussing this killing weren't you?
A: Not but very little, I never spoke very much about it.
Q: I will ask you if you didn't eat dinner at I. P. Latham's on the Sunday following the killing in question at which time Mr. I. P. Latham, Mrs. I. P. Latham and Bob Goodrich were present and at which time you were discussing the killing in question, and didn't Mr. I. P. Latham in the presence and hearing of Mrs. I. P. Latham and Bob Goodrich ask you this question: — Did you recognize any of the men, meaning those who committed the crime, to which question you made this answer, No sir, I could not recognize any of them, I was too scared?
A: I said that?
Q: You said that did you?
A: Yes sir.
Q: Then didn't Mr. Latham ask you this question at the same time and place in the presence and hearing of Mrs. I. P. Latham and Bob Goodrich, Couldn't you recognize any of them by their appearance, by their walk, their clothes or their voice, to which question you made this answer, No sir, I could not, I was too scared?
A: Yes sir, but I was not going to get out and say that.
Q: You had this conversation?
A: Yes sir.
Q: And the first time you ever told any one that you recognized Ed Eaton there that night was before the grand jury?
A: And I told my mother.
Q: How soon after it was it you told your mother?
A: I told my mother and then the grand jury, that is all I told.[34]

After this cross-examination, Simpson had to try to rehabilitate his witness. He was well prepared to do so, but Ridgely was also prepared to frustrate the attempt:

> Q: You may state to the jury what reasons you had for not telling that you recognized any of these people, or that you recognized Eaton at the fire on this night at Latham's place?
>
> Defendant objects as self-serving. Objection overruled. Defendant objects [*sic*].
>
> Defendant objects as immaterial, irrelevant and incompetent. Objection overruled. Defendant excepts.
>
> A: I didn't want to tell them for fear it might leak out, and I was afraid they would kill me if I told, and I didn't want to let it out.
>
> Q: Who was you afraid would kill you if you should tell it?
>
> Defendant objects as immaterial, irrelevant and incompetent. Objection overruled. Defendant excepts.
>
> A: I knew that somebody would kill me if I had told, if I gave it away.
>
> Q: Before you talked to Latham had you been warned in any manner as to keeping your mouth quiet about this or otherwise?
>
> Defendant objects as immaterial, irrelevant and incompetent. Objection overruled. Defendant excepts.
>
> A: No, only my mother.
>
> Q: What did you mother say to you about it?
>
> Defendant objects as immaterial, irrelevant and incompetent, and hearsay. Question withdrawn. . . .
>
> Q: And what reasons did you have for not telling Mr. Metz, if any, the names of the party there that night?
>
> Defendant objects as immaterial, irrelevant and incompetent, and self-serving. Objection overruled. Defendant excepts.
>
> A: Because there was a lot of people in the room, and I was afraid there might be somebody there listening.[35]

During the re-direct, Simpson also had Bounce make clear that he knew that the shooting was between him and the wagon because he could see the flash of the gun going towards the wagon "fast as the powder would blow out."[36]

The re-direct examination was effective (although it still did not explain why Bounce would not have told Alston about Eaton once he was safely in the sheriff's custody), and this apparently irked Ridgely. When he got his turn again, on re-cross, he began petulantly:

> Q: So you was afraid of your brothers Mr. Helmer?
>
> A: I didn't know but somebody might let it out.

Q: You was afraid of them?
A: No, I was not afraid of them, only they might let it out.[37]

But then Ridgely returned to the solid points he had made earlier, and
Bounce helped him again by making a questionable assertion regarding
the grand jury:

Q: Now at the time you was talking to the county attorney at the Greet
   place, or what is now the Lamb place, everybody was sent out of the
   room and the doors closed?
A: There was a board door between them.
Q: And it was closed.
A: Yes sir, loose board door.
Q: And you were afraid to tell him?
A: Yes sir. I thought the grand jury would be plenty good enough any
   time to tell it to the grand jury.
Q: Did you know there was to be a grand jury at that time?
A: I knew there would likely be a grand jury for anything like that.
Q: Did any one tell you there was going to be a grand jury?
A: No sir.
Q: Didn't say a word to you about a grand jury?
A: No sir.[38]

The prosecutors must have groaned inwardly when Bounce claimed
he knew there would be a grand jury. The attorneys did not even know
that until almost three weeks after the crime.

Based simply on a reading of the trial transcript, Ridgely's cross-examination would have to be deemed a signal success. He had brought forth
several examples of statements that made little sense and, with respect to
the remarks before the Lathams and Bob Goodrich, had shown a desire to
conceal very damaging admissions. Of course, no one would know for a
few days how the jury viewed it. The opinions of several newspapermen
were known, however. *Denver Post* reporter John I. Tierney wrote at some
length about Bounce's testimony. Under the subheading "BOY GOOD
WITNESS," he stated:

Bounce Helmer, a lad of 17 years, made a good witness for the state. He
identified Ed Eaton, one of the raiders, when the latter stooped over and
his mask swung aside. He was asked whom he told about Eaton.
    "No one but my mother," said the boy, "and the grand jury." And the
answer made a deep impression on the jury. . . .

Bounce Helmer, a lad to be trusted, was called to testify as to the occurrences at the camp when the raiders made themselves known. . . .

The herders told straight forward stories that could not be shaken or discredited in any way by the skillful cross-examination of attorney Ridgely for the defense.[39]

Tierney obviously did not think that Ridgely's cross-examination had been successful, and he was not the only reporter with that opinion. The *Big Horn County Rustler* reported:

The testimony of Bounce Helmer, the young sheep herder who, with Peter Cafferal, the Frenchman, was in charge of the south wagon, was particularly strong. Nor did the defense make anything of its attempt to discredit him with an impeaching question as to whether or not he had not told certain persons that he did not recognize any of the raiders.[40]

The *Rustler* quoted Bounce's testimony that he had only told his mother and the grand jury about his identification of Eaton, then said: "The answer of the boy made a profound impression on the jury. It bore the stamp of truth."[41]

The *Rustler*, of course, could be expected to be favorable to Bounce. But even the *Republican*, although certainly not as positive as the *Rustler*, did not claim that the cross-examination was a great success. It only stated:

On cross-examination by attorney H. S. Ridgely, Helmer admitted he had said nothing to anyone except his mother, of his recognition of Eaton.

"I was afraid," was his excuse. "I was afraid someone might kill me."[42]

The inescapable conclusion is that the bare transcript does not accurately reflect the impression Bounce made on the witness stand. Bounce was a very appealing young fellow, and when he told people that he was afraid to tell he had recognized Ed Eaton, they believed him. The fact is, Bounce had been in a terrible predicament, and people could understand why he acted as he did. A lawyer's clever questioning would not change a bit of that. And, after all, it didn't matter much *when* Bounce told that he had recognized Eaton, only whether he actually had recognized him. His testimony made sense: Ed Eaton did have a very distinctive build, standing over six feet tall and not even weighing 150 pounds. The surprising thing was that Bounce had not recognized more of the raiders.

Bounce's testimony would be further strengthened by other credible witnesses who testified to Ed Eaton's involvement with the raid. The most important of these, the next witnesses to be called that Saturday, were Bill Keyes and Charlie Faris, the two raiders who were turning state's evidence. During the first day of the trial, when the lawyers were in the throes of selecting the jury, Faris and Keyes had arrived on the noon train. Since then they had been held by the soldiers in a tent by the courthouse. In this way they could be kept out of the county jail, where the defendants were incarcerated, and the city jail, which was controlled by the defense attorney, Mayor Collins. These two witnesses were so important that they merited the personal attention of Joe LeFors, who slept in their tent.[43]

Bill Keyes was the first to testify. When bailiffs forced a passage through the crowd to bring Keyes to the stand, the jurors got their first look at a man who would bring them into the deepest confidences of the raiders themselves.[44] By that Saturday afternoon, the jurors knew all about the crime, exactly who had been killed and what had been burned and destroyed, and how and where it had all been done. But only Bounce Helmer had told them *who* had done it, and Bounce only knew the name of one of the raiders. Keyes, however, knew all of their names and most of their secrets.

Will Metz presented the testimony of Keyes and smoothly took him through his story. He had Keyes explain that his ranch occupied a central place, only seven miles from the scene of the crime and five miles from Alexander's ranch. Keyes told the jurors of the gathering of the raiders, when each arrived and with whom, Faris being the last man to appear. The evening of April 2, George Saban, Herbert Brink, Milton Alexander, Charlie Faris, Tommy Dixon, and Ed Eaton were all at Keyes' ranch. Then, Keyes testified, "they talked it over that evening about going down and doing up the sheep outfit." Around 8 o'clock, the seven men rode out of Keyes' ranch and headed north, with Saban in general command.[45]

Keyes confirmed that Saban had taken Farney Cole's automatic and he identified the gun when it was presented to him. Saban and Alexander had told Keyes the purpose of the expedition: "They gave me to understand we were to go down there, bunch the sheep and drive them over the bank and kill some of them and burn the wagon, but there was no killing to be done."[46]

Keyes testified that when they arrived at Spring Creek, the raiders broke into two groups, one consisting of Saban and Brink, the other of five men under the leadership of Alexander. Saban and Brink were to go to the north wagon and the second group to the south wagon, with a signal shot to come from those to the north.[47]

Keyes' testimony as to what happened during the raid was closely consistent with Bounce Helmer's, except that Keyes had spent less time at the north wagon than Bounce had, perhaps because some of his time was spent cutting the telephone wire. Keyes knew nothing of the killings at the north wagon, but he did directly support Bounce's testimony on one crucial point: When Pete Cafferal and Bounce were brought back to the area of the south wagon, Ed Eaton was working there and the fire from the wagon was blazing.[48]

Keyes told the jury that after the raiders left Spring Creek, they returned south, breaking up at Otter Creek about 12:30 or 1 o'clock. He explained the complicated movements of Farney Cole's automatic rifle, as Saban directed him to different hiding places.[49]

Will Metz did not wait for the defense to bring out Keyes' immunity from prosecution, although Ridgely was not going to let him present this easily:

Q: And you have been granted immunity by the State to come on the stand and tell the truth about this matter?
Defendant objects as leading and assuming. Objection sustained. Plaintiff excepts.
A: Have you been granted immunity?
Defendant objects as leading. Objection overruled. Defendant excepts.
A: I was to be indicted and thrown in jail and I was not to be prosecuted.
Q: Why were you not to be prosecuted, on what condition were you not to be prosecuted?
A: On the condition I would state to the court what we done down there.[50]

Metz closed this testimony on a point that anticipated Brinks' alibi. He had Keyes testify as to the kind of footwear Brinks was wearing the night of the raid:

Q: And these boots he wore, what kind of boots were they?
A: Just looked to me like ordinary riding boots, high heeled boots.
Q: Cowboy boots?
A: Yes sir.[51]

The cross-examination of Keyes was not the ferocious assault that might have been expected. Keyes was a cautious witness, in effect discounting his testimony before Ridgely got an opportunity to do so. Ridgely's cross-examination therefore seems general, almost rambling, with an occasional thrust when the attorney saw an opening. He asked Keyes how long he had been on Otter Creek, how many cows he ran, where his range was, and where his ranch was relative to Faris' ranch. He asked about cattle Keyes was "turning out" — that is, releasing from the ranch area to the range. Ridgely tried to get Keyes to say that he had notified different cattlemen that he was going to turn out on April 2, but Keyes replied: "No sir, I don't think so." Ridgely then tried to get Keyes to say that this was the reason the defendants were at his place, but again, Keyes responded: "No sir, I don't think so." Instead Keyes said that he had turned the cattle out because the extra help was already there. Keyes did agree that Dixon had some bulls with his herd and there was a cow and a calf that belonged to someone named Driscoll, but he denied there were any of Saban's or Brink's or Joe Henry's cattle among his herd.[52]

Ridgely wanted to know why these cattlemen were "going down to do it up," and Keyes replied: "Because they didn't want the sheep in the country, wanted to stop them going through there." The defense attorney picked at why Keyes carried a rifle and why he was turning state's evidence:

Q: The reason why you are now testifying is because you have got an agreement you won't be hung?
A: Not altogether that, they promised me when they went down there there should not be any killing.
Q: And you went on that peaceful mission with all of these guns, and there was to be no killing?
A: Yes sir.[53]

Ridgely also tried out Keyes for the "fall guy," someone to blame instead of his client:

Q: You say you fired no shot into that wagon?
A: No sir.
Q: Nor at anybody?
A: I don't know what anybody else done.
Q: Will you say how it was there were three empty exploded .30-30 shells that were picked up in the neighborhood where you were standing?
A: I can't explain it, no sir.
Q: But you were there with a .30-30 gun?
A: Yes sir.[54]

Ridgely tried to push Keyes away from his identification of the automatic rifle, but if anything Keyes' testimony was strengthened when he declared he noticed some sand on the rifle from when he put it in Otter Creek.[55]

The newspaper reports do not speak of any drama associated with Keyes' testimony. It is almost as if it had been assumed that Keyes would at least identify all of the raiders and describe the raid, and when that is about all he did, no one got particularly excited. If so, this was an ominous sign for the defense, because Keyes' testimony added facts sufficient to show the raiders guilty of felony murder. Worse, it bolstered the upcoming testimony of Faris, which would have a strong impact, a thrust not simply towards the minds of the jurors but into their hearts. The doctrine of felony murder is an abstract one that juries do not always feel an emotional commitment to follow. Charlie Faris could provide that emotional commitment.

The beginning of Faris' testimony, like that of Keyes', was not controversial. E. E. Enterline had his witness show that he had known all of the defendants for years. Faris gave his tale of what happened during the first part of April 2, how he had come to Keyes' ranch house late, not until 7 p.m., and then only on the assurance that there was to be no killing. Faris set out the calibers of the guns of all the participants, including a .30-30 for himself and Eaton and a .25-35 for Brink.[56]

The testimony of Faris for the time after the raiders left the ranch house was very similar to that of Keyes. There were, of course, some variations. Keyes had testified that Saban and Alexander had located the sheep camp earlier in the day, while Faris said that Eaton had also gone to Spring Creek. And Faris' actions at the beginning of the raid varied from those of Keyes, because Faris and Dixon took charge of Bounce Helmer and Pete Cafferal. After Faris arrived below the north wagon, Saban came to where the prisoners were being held and led Faris to the north wagon, leaving Tommy Dixon in charge of the prisoners.[57] From that point in his narration, Faris' testimony became startlingly different from Keyes'. Indeed, what Faris then told the jury was probably the most dramatic passage in the whole trial:

A: . . . Saban took me over there to the north wagon.
Q: Did you ask him anything at that time?
A: Yes sir.
Q: What did you ask him?
A: I asked him where his men were.
Q: What was his answer?

A: He said he didn't know, but thought they were dead.
Q: To what men did you refer when you asked him that?
A: The sheepmen.[58]

Faris testified that when he started up to the north wagon with Saban, he saw Eaton, Alexander, and Brink; Eaton was standing near the front of the wagon and Saban, Alexander, and Brink near the north side. Faris told of his disobedience of an order given by Saban:

A: . . . Saban told me to go back and start the fire under the south wagon and I refused to go.
A: What became of the men that were there, that is did they all remain there, and if any one left, you may tell the jury who?
Q: Eaton left.
A: Do you know why he left?
A: He left to start a fire under the south wagon.
Q: How do you know that.
A: Because he was told to.
Q: By whom?
A: By Saban.[59]

Faris then told the jury that when he first arrived there was no fire at the north wagon, but Brink soon started one:

Q: Where? At what point of the wagon did he start the fire?
A: At the hind end of the wagon, at the hind wheel.
Q: Do you know how he started it?
A: He started it with sage brush.[60]

Then Faris came to the crucial time, when Joe Allemand emerged from the wagon:

Q: Now after the fire was started Mr. Farris [sic], what was the next thing you heard or saw there at that north wagon? After the fire was started.
A: After it got to burning pretty well Allemand came out of the wagon, or a man came out of the wagon. . . .
Q: Where was he, and in what part of the wagon, and what direction of the wagon was he when you first saw him?
A: In front of the wagon.
Q: Can you estimate how far he was away from the front wagon when you first observed him?
A: Probably twelve or fourteen feet, twelve feet.

Q: Now you may tell the jury Mr. Farris whether you heard any one say anything or do anything at that time?

A: Yes sir, the first I heard was some one commanding to some one to come out and hold up their hands.

Q: What did they say?

A: Hollered Halt there, Halt, throw up your hands, and I thought this party was some one coming up from the outside.

Q: Did you at that time you heard the command see any one on top of the hill there?

A: No, not at just that time I didn't.

Q: Did you afterwards?

A: When I heard this command I took about one or two steps up the hill and I could see him then.

Q: Now when you saw him just illustrate to the jury what this man did up on the top of the hill and hold your hands?

A: He was coming from the direction of the wagon when I saw him.

Q: How was he holding his hands?

A: He was holding his hands up when I saw him.

Q: Just show it from the point it appeared to you?

A: He was in this position (witness indicating). Stooped.

Q: What happened next?

A: I heard a shot then.

Q: Who fired that shot?

A: Brink fired that shot.

Q: What became of that man who had his hands up as you observed him?

A: He fell.

Q: Did you hear any one — Did this defendant make any remark either at the time or before or after he fired the shot?

A: Yes sir, right after.

Q: What did he say?

A: He said it was a hell of a time of night to come out with your hands up.

Q: How far away were you standing from Brink when he fired the shot?

A: Probably a rod. . . .

Q: After this shot was fired you may tell the jury whether you observed anybody go up there?

A: Yes sir I did.

Q: Do you know who it was that went up there?

A: Yes sir.

Q: Who was it.

A: It was Alexander.

Q: Did he make any remark then?

A: Yes sir he did when he came back.

Q: What did he say?

A: He says it is Allemand.
Q: After Alexander came back what was next done there?
A: We prepared to leave.
Q: Did any one say anything before you left?
A: Yes sir.
Q: Who?
A: Saban.
Q: What did he say.
A: He says, that is enough, we will leave.[61]

The burden on a defense attorney when defending a capital case is a terrible one, because the lawyer invariably feels that a client's life is in his hands. When he rose to cross-examine Faris, Ridgely must have felt a very heavy weight. If the jury believed Faris, Herbert Brink would probably be convicted of first-degree murder and sentenced to die.

The cross-examination of Faris was very similar to that of Keyes, except more aggressive. Faris was a stronger witness, and Ridgely could put much more of a bite in his questioning. The first part of the inquiry, as with Keyes, was of general information relating to his ranching on Otter Creek, but shorter. Then Ridgely struck hard:

Q: What was the purpose of your going down to ditch the sheep outfit you speak of?
A: Because they were coming in on our range.
Q: That was not a sheep range in there?
A: No sir.
Q: And you went down for the purpose of destroying the sheep and burning the wagons?
A: Yes sir.
Q: And outside of that it was to be a peaceful mission?
A: Yes sir.
Q: And you went down there armed for that occasion?
A: Yes sir.
Q: And you went with the determination to accomplish your purpose of burning those wagons and killing those sheep didn't you?
A: Yes sir we went to ditch those sheep and to burn those wagons, yes sir.
Q: And what kind of a gun did you carry with you?
A: .30-30.
Q: How many shells did you take with you?
A: I probably had thirty shells.
Q: And you knew whose outfit it was you were going down to ditch and burn?

A: Yes sir.
Q: You knew it was Allemand's and Emge's?
A: Yes sir.[62]

But Ridgely then seemed to lose his focus and took Faris through many questions that were just a repetition of the direct testimony. Toward the end of the examination though, Ridgely found a clearer direction. He launched into a line of questions by which he obviously sought to lay the groundwork to accuse Faris himself of the murder. Ridgely first established that Faris' .30-30 had been loaded, then asked:

Q: And whenever you looked up you saw a man out in front of the wagon?
A: I didn't see him when I first heard this commanding, but I took a step or two up this slope and saw him then.
Q: Which way was the face with reference to the wagon?
A: With his back to the wagon as though he had come from the wagon, going from the wagon.
Q: Which side did he have to you.
A: Left side to me.
Q: And you was carrying a .30-30 gun?
A: Yes sir, I was carrying a .30-30.
Q: And any one shooting from where you were standing to strike him in the side would have to strike his left side?
A: Yes sir.
Q: And he was on the level a little above you wasn't he?
A: Yes sir, he was above me. He was above me and quartering, between the wagon and me.[63]

On re-direct, Enterline had Faris clarify that Brink was "standing further around the hill and above me." Faris also testified that Brink had been sitting or kneeling down.[64]

And then, when Ridgely declined to again cross-examine, it was over. It was almost 6 p.m., and the trial was finally recessed for the day. The attorneys were no doubt exhausted; the tension of even a short day of trial is physically draining. Even those in the crowd were probably very tired. Many had remained standing on chairs through the whole day, listening to every witness and not climbing down until after Faris was done.[65]

The next day, the *Denver Post* summarized that grueling and fascinating Saturday:

Basin, Wyo., Nov. 6 — The prosecution in the Ten Sleep murder cases today played its trump cards against Herbert Brink, one of the seven cattlemen accused of that crime, when Albert Keyes and Charles Farris, two of the accused men, who had turned state's evidence, were put on the stand. The testimony of Keyes and Farris was all that had been expected — and more; and when court adjourned, it was admitted on all sides the state had scored in an unmistakable manner.[66]

## NOTES

1.  *Rocky Mountain News*, 11/7/09.

2.  *Basin Republican*, 11/12/09. Oddly enough, the *Denver Post* reported that the town had lost interest in the trial, that only three spectators appeared on Saturday (*Denver Post*, 11/6/09, p. 3, cols 4–6). Generally, *Post* stories seem accurate, but there are other examples of statements that are blatantly wrong. It seems the *Post* reporter missed some parts of the event and then created something to fill the gap. Percy Metz alluded to the drinking of the reporter for the *Denver Post* (speech before the Park County Historical Society, 6/9/61).

3.  Trial transcript, 126, 127. In 1909, when a judge made a ruling, the attorney for the unsuccessful party had to "except" in order to later complain about the ruling to the Wyoming Supreme Court. So in each instance where Judge Parmelee ruled for the state, Ridgely would say: "Defendant excepts."

4.  *Denver Post*, 11/6/09, p. 3, col. 4–6.

5.  Trial transcript, 128, 130, 133, 136, 137, 138.

6.  Ibid, 136.

7.  Subpoena dated 11/2/09, *State v. Brink*, Case No. 443, Records of the Big Horn County Clerk of the District Court. Those subpoenaed by the defense were Billy Miller, G. B. McClellan, I. P. Latham, Mrs. I. P. Latham, Bob Goodrich, Porter Lamb, Mrs. Porter Lamb, John Meredith, Abram Rebideaux, Charley Rebideaux, Sadie Rebideaux, Henry Helms, Oscar McClellan and George C. Pickett. Those subpoenaed by the state were: William Gibson, Henry Greet, W. W. Cook, Porter Lamb, Clyde Atherly, Charles Helmer, Farney Coles, Fred Greet, W. G. Colethorpe, John D. Callahan, Charles Farris, Felix Alston, Ed Cussac, Al Morton, Lizzie Lamb, Mary Buckmaster, Rufus Barrington, Mrs. F. T. Brown, Mrs. William Goodrich, George W. Walker, M. D., John Buckmaster, William Keyes, Peter Cafferal, Samuel Brant, Fred Widmayer, S. W. Richie, George Rogers, Joe LaFors, W. D. Goodrich, Lewis Harvard, Charles Mann, Walter Nelson, and F. T. Brown. It appears that W. W. Early's name was originally on this list and then crossed out.

8.  Grand jury testimony of Porter Lamb, 3, Homsher Collection; trial testimony of Porter Lamb, 140.

9.  Trial transcript, 141, 142, 143.

10. Grand jury testimony of Porter Lamb, 4.

11. Trial transcript, 144. It should be noted that under the rules of evidence in 1909 an attorney could not impeach a witness he had called, so the prosecution could not demonstrate the inconsistencies between Lamb's grand jury and trial testimony.

12. *Denver Post*, 11/6/09, p. 3, col. 4–6; trial transcript, 149.

13. Trial transcript, 156.

14. Ibid, 157; speech of Percy Metz before the Park County Historical Society, 6/9/61; *Worland Grit*, 11/4/09.

15. *Denver Post*, 11/6/09, p. 3, col. 4–6. Billy Simpson was the father of Milward Simpson, former governor and United States senator from Wyoming and the grandfather of Al Simpson, presently the junior United States senator from Wyoming and minority whip of the Senate.

16. Trial transcript, 157–169.

17. *Denver Post*, 11/7/09, p. 5, sec. 1, cols 1–2. This description seems consistent with what Cafferal would have felt, but the *Post* articles have to be regarded somewhat skeptically because of some clear examples of outright fiction, wherein the writer dressed up the news. Most of the details in the above *Post* article are consistent with the actual testimony, but one quote attributed to Cafferal is at least an embellishment. The article said that Cafferal was asked how long he was prostrate, and Cafferal supposedly answered: "I don't know; it seemed ages, with bullets flying all around me." In fact, Cafferal was only asked on cross-examination how long he was lying in the road, and he said: "I don't know, the time was pretty long, the time you stay in things like that" (171). In response to other questions, he did indicate there was shooting "all of the time" (161, 168). There was no testimony that "it seemed ages" or about "bullets flying all around."

18. Trial transcript, 163, 164, 168, 172.

19. Ibid, 166 169.

20. Ibid, 169–173.

21. *Basin Republican*, 11/12/09.

22. Trial transcript, 186.

23. The reader should not think this was improper. The prosecution would have been seriously derelict had they not spent a long time preparing such an important witness.

24. Trial transcript, 188–204.

25. Ibid, 188. Dungeness, Washington, is a tiny town on the north coast of the Olympic Peninsula, southwest of Vancouver Island, British Columbia.

26. Trial transcript, 188, 189.

27. Ibid, 190.

28. Ibid, 190, 191.

29. Ibid, 191, 193.

30. Ibid, 194.

31. Ibid.

32. Ibid, 194, 195, 196.

33. Ibid, 196, 197.

34. Ibid, 199–201.

35. Ibid, 201, 202.

36. Ibid, 203.

37. Ibid.
38. Ibid, 203, 204.
39. *Denver Post*, 11/7/09, p. 5, sec. 1, cols 1–2.
40. *Big Horn County Rustler*, 11/12/09.
41. Ibid.
42. *Basin Republican*, 11/12/09.
43. *Basin Republican*, 11/12/09; *Cheyenne State Leader*, 11/6/09.
44. *Basin Republican*, 11/12/09.
45. Trial transcript, 205–207, 210.
46. Ibid, 208, 221, 223.
47. Ibid, 211.
48. Ibid, 214, 216, 218.
49. Ibid, 223, 224.
50. Ibid, 224, 225.
51. Ibid, 226.
52. Ibid, 226–231.
53. Ibid, 233, 239.
54. Ibid, 236.
55. Ibid, 241.
56. Ibid, 247, 248.
57. Ibid, 243, 249, 255.
58. Ibid, 255.
59. Ibid, 256, 257.
60. Ibid, 258.
61. Ibid, 258–261.
62. Ibid, 266, 267.
63. Ibid, 271, 272.
64. Ibid, 273.
65. *Basin Republican*, 11/12/09.
66. *Denver Post*, 11/7/09, p. 5, sec. 1, col. 1–2.

# Plaintiff Rests

## CHAPTER 15

S unday, November 7, must have been very welcome to all the attorneys, but especially to the prosecutors. In presenting the state's case, they had borne a great burden, and it had been an arduous three days, days filled with pressure and anxiety. The prosecuting attorneys could not exactly rest — not even Sunday is a day of rest during a jury trial — but they could relax a bit and plan how to complete their case.

They felt they had made a strong showing, and perhaps they were tempted to stop after presenting Charlie Faris' testimony. The case, though, was still quite vulnerable to the argument that Faris' and Keyes' testimony had not been corroborated; many details were substantiated only by their testimony. Besides, who knew how the jurors were thinking? If there was persuasive evidence available, it would have been irresponsible not to present it to the jury. The prosecution had to assume that John Donahue, and maybe other jurors, would take a great deal of persuading. And yet there was a danger of gilding the lily, presenting that one extra witness who would suddenly turn on the state and taint the fine showing it had already made.

Such were the convoluted and worrisome considerations the prosecuting attorneys toyed with that Sunday. Some witnesses would surely be called, those who were safe and also helpful. One was deputy William Gibson, who could testify regarding the .35 automatic rifle Saban had used in the raid. Also, several people had seen Brink and Dixon (and other riders) near Bill Keyes' place on the afternoon of Friday, April 2; all had freely testified before the grand jury. Then there was Sam Brant, the stage driver, presumably neutral, who had seen Alexander near the sheep camp that same afternoon.

John Callahan had made that important sighting of Brink heading back to Keyes' ranch, and Callahan was safe, so he would be called. Callahan was safe not only because he was not a cattleman but also because he had taken a special interest in helping Mrs. Allemand through her difficulties after her husband was killed. W. G. Colethorpe, Allemand's brother-in-law, who had heard Brink threatening Emge and Allemand, would also be safe. His employer, Fred Widmeyer, who heard some of that conversation, was more of a question. Mr. and Mrs. F. P. Brown had overheard other of Brink's statements, and they were safe witnesses because they had been friends of the Allemands.[1] Finally, both of the Goodriches, especially Billy, had important evidence to offer and most certainly would be called.

But the prosecution decided not to call several witnesses they had subpoenaed. One was Henry Greet, presumably because he would have duplicated the testimony of Fred Greet and Porter Lamb. Another was W. W. Cook, who had some interesting things to say about Alexander and Eaton but nothing directly related to the man on trial, Brink. Still another was Lizzie Lamb. After her husband's retreat, the prosecution was probably afraid of her. Besides, Anna Goodrich would cover most of what Lizzie would testify to, and if Brink took the stand and gave an alibi, Lizzie would still be available for rebuttal.

Rufus Barrington and Walter Nelson, the two men on the lumber wagon, could only duplicate what Sam Brant would say about Alexander, and as employees of George McClellan, they were not neutral. Neither was Lewis Harvard, Milton Alexander's employee; if called, he might even back off what he had already told the grand jury and actually help Alexander and Saban establish an alibi. Harvard would have been a good witness for the prosecution only if the defense had called him. He would then have been subject to leading questions on cross-examination, and the admissions that could be drawn from him would have made a real impact.

Farney Cole was another ranch hand who might be dangerous to call. His boss was turning state's evidence, however, and the prosecution decided to call him anyway, probably because his testimony was so valuable that it was worth the risk. There was one final witness who was listed but did not testify: Joe LeFors. It is intriguing to speculate why he was not called or why he was listed at all, but there is nothing in the historical record hinting at either.

In any event, Monday morning, the state proceeded, and its first witness that day was William Gibson. Right after Keyes confessed, the sheriff sent Gibson to Keyes' ranch, and, sure enough, in a chicken coop, under a box (and eggs and feathers), wrapped in a gunnysack and covered with sand, was the .35 automatic rifle. Gibson also found another gun there, but the court refused to let him tell what kind it was.[2]

Farney Cole was next called, and he repeated how Faris had sent him to Hyattville on April 2, and that when he had left the ranch right after the noon meal, Herbert Brink, Tommy Dixon, George Saban, Bill Keyes, Clyde Harvard, and Ed Eaton were there. The jury learned that Cole had owned a new .35 Winchester automatic, had left it in the corner of Keyes' living room, and found it missing when he returned to the ranch on Monday. This rifle was in the courtroom, having been identified by Keyes and then introduced in evidence through Gibson, but Cole would not swear this gun was his. Enterline did get him to admit that he did not know of any other automatic at the Keyes' ranch when he had left.[3]

The four witnesses who followed were all people who had seen Brink and Dixon Friday afternoon: George Rogers, Samuel Walter (Walt) Richie, and John and Mary Buckmaster. Each of the witnesses testified to essentially the same thing: That Friday they all had dinner (the noon meal) at Buckmasters' ranch on Otter Creek. About 3 p.m. they saw Herb Brink and Tommy Dixon riding south down the county road; Mr. Buckmaster talked to them. Around that time the witnesses also saw four or five riders near a gate on Keyes' ranch. Ridgely's cross-examination was largely confined to showing that Brink and Dixon had been riding away from Spring Creek.[4]

Sam Brant was called, and he told the jury that on April 2 he had been driving his stage route south through the Upper Nowood. He saw Milton Alexander about 4:15 p.m. riding west a mile and a quarter south of the sheep camp. Brant arrived at Otter Creek about 5 o'clock, continued south, and about 6 p.m. met John Callahan. Callahan was standing by a mailbox about three miles south of Otter Creek. Still further south Brant had passed Walter Nelson driving a lumber wagon. In the cross-examination, Ridgely concentrated on the fact that Brant had not seen Brink that day.[5]

None of this testimony was earth-shaking, but it did corroborate Faris and Keyes in important particulars — that seven raiders had gathered at Keyes' ranch, that the .35 automatic had been available to Saban, that he had used it and it was then hidden in different places, and that Alexander had scouted the sheep camp the afternoon of April 2.

John Callahan could provide corroboration, too, but his testimony was more than just corroboration; it undercut Brink's alibi. Billy Simpson took Callahan cleanly and directly through his story. On April 2, Callahan had been trapping "just below Alexander's place on the place belonging to Joe Allemand on Nowood Creek." On that day he saw Herbert Brink going north toward the Buckmaster and Keyes ranches. It was about 5:20, and Callahan had a conversation with Brink, which he reported to the jury: "When he rode by I passed the time of day with him, and I said you are riding like you are in a hurry. He said, I am, just going down to Buckmasters to see his new horse." Callahan watched Brink then go north on the county road, but rather than head toward Buckmaster's, Brink turned and "went across lots" almost directly to the Keyes ranch. About twenty minutes later, Sam Brant came along, driving the stage. Callahan testified that he had once before seen Brink in that area, about a month before at Alexander's.[6]

At first, Ridgely was circumspect in his cross-examination, asking some general questions and showing that Callahan's most recent work had been with two sheep outfits, Allemand-Emge and Driscoll-Bragg. But then Ridgely did an uncharacteristic thing, directly challenging the witness with very little to support his challenge. He continued this tactic through most of the remaining cross-examination:

> Q: And is it not true that Brink was riding on the day he went by you a brown colored horse?
> A: A dark colored horse.
> Q: I am asking you if it is not true he was riding a brown horse?
> A: I would not call it that.
> Q: Didn't you testify before the grand jury that he was riding a brown colored horse?
> A: I did not, no sir.
> Q: You didn't testify to that?
> A: I testified he was riding a dark bay horse, very dark bay horse.
> Q: And you testified to that before the grand jury?
> A: I did. . . .[7]
> Q: Is it not true Mr. Callahan you never saw Mr. Brink on that road except the time you saw him at Alexander's place?
> Plaintiff objects as being unfair to the witness. Objection overruled. Plaintiff excepts.
> A: I saw him on April 2nd as I described to you.
> Q: Is it not true you never saw him at any other time except the time you saw him at Alexander's?
> Plaintiff objects as repetition. Objection overruled. Plaintiff excepts.
> A: I saw him on April 2nd.[8]

Ridgely's confrontational tactics were not effective; with a strong witness such as Callahan they only served to underline the testimony, allowing Callahan to repeat his original statement with even more conviction. It is hard to know why Ridgely proceeded this way. One possibility is that Brink told him Callahan was lying and that Ridgely, having nothing else to use against this damaging witness, simply charged in and confronted him. Whatever the reason, the defense would have been better off if Ridgely had stopped after establishing Callahan's recent employment with sheepmen.

The prosecution did decide to call Fred Widmeyer. Widmeyer did not have much to offer, but what he did say dovetailed very well with the testimony of W. G. Colethorpe. (Percy Metz presented the direct testimony of these two witnesses, and, other than his own testimony, this was his only involvement in the trial.)

Both of the witnesses recalled a day in March, about two weeks before the raid, when Herb Brink had stopped at the Goodall-Widmeyer ranch on the Nowood. There was a conversation about Emge and Allemand bringing sheep into the valley. Widmeyer only caught part of it, being out doing chores, but just as he stepped into the door of the ranch house he heard Brink. "He said that he hoped that Allemand and Mr. Emge would not cross their sheep across the cow range. He said if they did they were liable to be something doing."[9]

Colethorpe had been in the house during the entire conversation, although Brink had been talking not to him but to a young man named Cobb and another man named Fatty Allen. But Colethorpe did have a very distinct memory of some of what he overheard Brink say: "He said, they never would get through there with their sheep, he was ready with his rifle to go out and mob the sons-of-bitches and drive them back, they would show them where they belonged."[10]

The cross-examination of Colethorpe was brief. Ridgely brought out that the witness was Allemand's brother-in-law. Colethorpe also admitted that there was "quite a little discussion at the time in the community" that Emge and Allemand were bringing sheep across the cattle range but denied that "it was heralded through the country that Emge was coming through there armed."[11]

The next two witnesses, Mr. and Mrs. Frank P. Brown, were also presented as a set, both testifying to the same conversation. Mr. and Mrs. Brown left their home in Big Trails the morning of Monday, April 5; their purpose was to see Mrs. Allemand and comfort her. On their way, they met Billy Goodrich and Herb Brink on the county road just north of Milton Alexander's ranch. They stopped and talked, and at first the conversation was about where Mrs. Allemand could be found. Then the talk turned to the raid, and Herb Brink made a statement about Allemand coming out of the sheep wagon: "He [Brink] said he [Allemand] came out and he looked around as though he was listening to something, or had heard something, and was shot and fell down, if I am not mistaken, and got up and staggered over to where he was laying when they found him." After he said this, Brink had added, "That is the supposition."[12]

When he cross-examined both Mr. and Mrs. Brown, Ridgely tried to establish that Brink, having just come from the crime scene, was simply repeating what he'd learned there. Enterline responded to this very skillfully in his re-direct of Frank Brown:

> Q: Mr. Brown did Brink tell you he had learned down there that Allemand came out and stood and looked as if he was listening and was shot and fell and staggered to where he was lying?
> Defendant objects as leading. Objection overruled. Defendant excepts.
> A: No sir he didn't.[13]

Charles Mann testified to the value of the burned sheep wagons ($225 and $175). He was hesitant to state the value of the sheep, however, finally estimating $6 per head; Mann also testified that twenty-five sheep had been shot and killed at the time of the raid and that about a dozen that had been injured later died. The witness produced a gold tooth that he said had been Joe Emge's and had been found directly beneath the face of one of the bodies in the north wagon.[14]

The Goodriches were the next witnesses, and they were surely the most significant witnesses of the day. Anna Goodrich was questioned by E. E. Enterline, and he introduced her to the jury by having her tell where she and her husband lived and where that was located in relation to Spring Creek. Mrs. Goodrich recalled that she had first heard about the raid on Sunday morning, April 4. She told her husband, Brink, and Jack Rebidaux about it and she testified that all of them were surprised. Brink then wanted to use the phone; he acted nervous and called Mrs. Brown, wanting to know if she knew "who they supposed did it." Brink went to the phone three or four times and was acting nervous and excited.[15]

Mrs. Goodrich also told the jury that on the day of the raid, Brink and Dixon had been at the ranch early, when she went to the Helmer's. But when she returned about 5 p.m. they were not there, and she did not see them again until Saturday morning. She had, however, seen George Saban at the ranch the day before the raid; it was the first time she had met him, he had never been to the ranch before.[16]

Most significantly, Anna Goodrich told the jury about a conversation she had with Brink about the raid:

A: He was to buy our ranch.

Q: Who was?

A: Herbert Brink, and he said — I asked him if he got the money from Mr. Bragg and he said Mr. Bragg was on the fight so about the raid and he didn't ask him about it, and then he said he wanted him to settle up with him this Fall.

Q: Who wanted to settle up?

A: Mr. Bragg with Mr. Brink.

Q: Now go on.

A: And he didn't ask him about the money at all, and he asked me if I knew anything about the killing and I told him I didn't, and I didn't want to know anything about it, and he said I guess you are better off not to know anything about it.

Q: Did he say anything about getting any money?

A: He said, well if Tommy and I — He didn't know whether Tommy and I [he] would get our [their] money out of it or not.[17]

The cross-examination was rather benign, perhaps because Ridgely did not want to offend the jury by being too hard on Mrs. Goodrich. If so, the defense paid a price, as Anna Goodrich's testimony was strengthened by the cross-examination. He asked what the witness thought Brink meant when he said he didn't know whether he and Tommy would get their money out of that. Ridgely was told: "I thought he meant they would not get their money out of the raid." Then he asserted to Mrs. Goodrich that at that time, "you didn't know who was even suspicioned?"[18] Anna corrected him, indicating that she had already talked to her husband about Mr. Brink.

Anna Goodrich's testimony was not as damaging as her husband's would be, but everything she said about Brink was consistent with Brink's guilt. At this stage in the trial, with all the damaging evidence presented against Herb Brink, the defense was probably glad for any witness who did not provide direct evidence of guilt. Perhaps the defense would only react strongly to a witness who did provide such direct evidence. If so, they would have cause to react very strongly to Billy Goodrich.

The direct examination of Billy went very smoothly. Enterline first elicited the usual general background information. One statement was notable: Goodrich said that Brink was wearing corduroy pants Saturday morning, April 3 (Pete Cafferal had testified that one of the raiders was wearing corduroy pants). Then Goodrich explained how he and Brink had gone to Spring Creek on Sunday afternoon because Lizzie Lamb was worried about her husband, had conversations with Felix Alston, and started back home that evening. It was during that return trip that Brink made some startling admissions to Billy:

> A: He said Felix was mistaken as to the number of tracks, that there was only seven.
>
> Q: Did you have any conversation with him about the sheriff's statement of the wagon being all surrounded, the north wagon?
>
> A: Yes sir.
>
> Q: What did you say to him about that, and what did he say?
>
> A: I said to him Felix said that that wagon was completely surrounded, and he said it was not, that there was just that many men at that wagon (witness holding up his hand with two fingers).
>
> Q: And did you then ask him anything about it when he was demonstrating to you?
>
> A: I said you must have been there?
>
> Q: What reply if any did he make to that suggestion or statement of yours?
>
> A: He said, I was.
>
> Q: Did you in the course of your conversation discuss with him Mr. Goodrich the fight at that wagon?
>
> A: He said there was not.
>
> Q: Just what did he say about the shooting from the wagon if you now remember?
>
> A: He said there was not a shot fired from the wagon.
>
> Q: In the course of your conversation with him Mr. Goodrich did he detail to you or tell you about how these wagons were captured?
>
> A: Yes sir.
>
> Q: Tell us what he said about that.
>
> A: He said there were five of them went to the south wagon, him and another fellow went to the north wagon.
>
> Q Did he tell you who the other fellow was that went with him to the north wagon?
>
> A: No sir.
>
> Q: Now you may tell the jury if he made any statement as to what he did at the north wagon about firing?
>
> A: He said the first shot he fired was right into the door of the wagon.
>
> Q: And what if anything did he say about the result of that shot?
>
> A: He said there was a hell of a racket in the stove and pots and pans.
>
> Q: Did he tell you on that occasion what was done by those five men at the other wagon?
>
> A: Yes sir.
>
> Q: What did he say they did?
>
> A: He said they captured Bounce and the Frenchman, walked them around there a while and killed some sheep.

Q: And then what?

A: Left two to guard them and the rest of them came over to the other wagon.

Q: Now if he made any statement to you as to what was done when the others came over to the other wagon what did he say was done then?

A: He said he told them to strike a light in the wagon.

Q: Go right ahead.

A: He said there was no light lit, he asked them again, there was no light lit, and he said now I am going to give you fair warning, I am going to count three and if there ain't a light lit in the wagon we will riddle the snap with bullets, and he said I counted three, there was no light lit, and we turned loose.

Q: If he made any statement to you about any one being the only person from Tensleep, what if anything did he say about that?

A: He said Saban was the only man from Tensleep.

Q: At that time were you acquainted with Milton A. Alexander?

Q: Yes sir.

Q: Do you know of any particular name, or how he is referred to occasionally?

A: They call him the "Injun" a good deal.

Q: If Brink made any statement to you about Alexander in any way, what did he say about him?

A: He said when it comes to fighting with a gun the Injun is there and over.

Q: You may state to the jury whether or not while that was going on you were discussing the raid?

A: Yes sir.

Q: In the course of the conversation with him Mr. Goodrich did you talk to him about who had set fire to the wagon?

A: Yes sir.

Q: What did he say about that?

A: He said he done it.

Q: Did he say in what manner?

A: With sage brush.[19]

Billy closed this sensational testimony by relating what Brink had said about John Callahan: "He said Callahan was the only man who had seen him go down there, and if necessary he would take care of him, or something like that."[20]

Of the statements Goodrich attributed to Brink, perhaps the most remarkable was that there had been no shots returned from the sheep-wagon. This is consistent with other testimony, but is still surprising.[21] Many witnesses referred to the first shot, the signal shot, which was presumably the one that made a "hell of a racket." Other testimony, including that from both Bounce and Brink, showed that after the two sheepherders were captured at the south wagon it was at least a few minutes, and perhaps a half hour, before they were brought over to the north wagon. Only after this did Brink and Saban shoot into the wagon.

All of which raises one of the greatest mysteries about the raid: Why didn't anyone in the wagon fire back during the time after the signal shot and before Brink and Saban "turned loose?" The men in that wagon were well armed, and Joe Emge was supposed to be a fearless man with guns. So why didn't anyone in the wagon take any aggressive action (or any other kind, for that matter)?

The answer to this mystery may be found in other testimony. Fred Greet and Bounce Helmer spoke of being awakened by a shot, followed by a fusillade, which they believed came from an automatic rifle. Porter Lamb had a similar recollection except he didn't remember the first shot. Bill Keyes said he heard several shots from the north wagon area after the signal shot, and Faris testified to hearing rapid shots "right afterward."[22] This testimony, though, is inconsistent with the idea that the automatic was not fired until some time later, after Bounce and Pete were brought over to the north wagon. It is conceivable, however, that there were two occasions when Saban opened up with the automatic (probably joined by Brink). If so, Emge and Lazier may have already been dead or disabled before Bounce heard those terrible commands to "strike a light."

Such speculation is intriguing. But the concrete reality of the direct testimony of Billy Goodrich was that it was devastating to Herbert Brink, especially given the solid evidentiary showing the prosecution had already made. There was a difference with this testimony, however: The defense had some answers to Billy Goodrich.

At first, Ridgely's cross-examination was very general, the primary point being to show that the information Brink gained about the raid was from what he had learned at the scene. Then he asked Billy whom he had told about Brink's admissions. Billy mentioned his wife, Porter Lamb, and the grand jury. Ridgely then got down to the real thrust of his questioning and started asking Billy whether he had any interest in the case. Billy assured him he did not, that he wasn't to receive any money for his testimony, not a cent. Finally, Ridgely established that Billy had stopped at Porter Lamb's house over night after having testified before the grand jury.[23] The trap was set and Ridgely sprung it:

Q: I will ask you if you didn't stop at Porter Lamb's overnight on your way home from Basin last Spring where you had been in attendance upon the grand jury as a witness and did you not in a conversation with Porter Lamb at his ranch that night in which conversation you were discussing the Spring Creek raid tell him in substance as follows: That Felix Alston had told you that you would get the fattest pocket book you ever had for giving your testimony?

A: I don't remember of telling Porter Lamb any such thing.

Q: Do you say you didn't?

A: I say I didn't.

Q: And you know Frank Helmer?

A: Yes sir.

Q: Do you recollect of his being to your ranch along the latter part of last July?

A: He was there several times during July.

Q: Did you not have a conversation during the latter part of July this year at the ranch where you were then, with Frank Helmer in which conversation you were discussing the Spring Creek raid and your testimony before the Grand Jury and didn't Frank Helmer at that time ask you in substance this question: How much are you to get out of this for such evidence and to which you replied, Felix Alston said I am to have my share of the reward?

A: No sir, I didn't.

Q: You never had any such conversation?

A: I never had any such conversation with Frank Helmer. . . .

Q: Do you know Oscar McClellan?

A: Yes sir.

Q: Do you recollect talking with him on the road there to Big Trails from your ranch about two weeks after this occurrence?

A: No sir I don't recollect any such thing.

Q: Did you not on the Sunday about two weeks after the occurrence of the killing at Spring Creek while travelling on the road in your field between Big Trails post office and the ranch where you were living in company with Oscar McClellan while discussing the Spring Creek raid ask him this question: Do you have any idea who was mixed up in the killing, and to which he answered, I do not, nor do I want to know, to which you replied, I am glad the fellows here, meaning Dixon, Brink and Garrison, were not in it, as they were at home that night?

A: I don't remember whether I did or not.

Q: Will you swear you didn't?

A: No sir, I won't swear that I didn't.

Q: Were you at home that Friday night the killing occurred?

A: Yes sir.[24]

The *Denver Post* reported that Goodrich responded to the "fattest pocket book" accusation "in a weak voice" and that his denial of the statement of Frank Helmer was also weak. The *Post* reporter concluded: "Goodrich left a bad impression in his answers to these questions."[25]

Those observations probably had merit, and yet the treatment given by the *Post* to the rest of his testimony shows that Goodrich's presentation still had an impact. Some of the headlines from the *Cheyenne State Leader* give a similar view: "WITNESS SWEARS BRINK CONFESSED TO HIM HIS PART IN TEN SLEEP RAID." "William Goodrich Testifies That Prisoner, After Viewing Remains of Slain Sheepmen, Related to Him His Complicity."[26]

After Goodrich testified, there was an odd procedural arrangement whereby the defense recalled two witnesses for more cross-examination. One was Felix Alston, and he was asked if he had not told Porter Lamb, "There was two thousand dollars in it to anyone that could tell you the names of any one that would squeal, if pinched." The prosecution objected to the propriety of this questioning, however, and the judge sustained the objection.[27] The second recalled witness was Dr. Walker, and Ridgely again bickered with him over whether a pencil was the size of Allemand's wound, but, as before, no distinct resolution was made.[28]

The prosecution briefly recalled Sheriff Alston so that the clothes Allemand wore at his death could be put in evidence.[29]

The last witness presented by the state of Wyoming was Adeline Allemand, Joe's widow. Her testimony was very short. The ostensible reason for it was to solidify the value of the sheep killed.[30] The real reason was to show that Joe Allemand was not just a dirty trespassing sheepherder who deserved killing. He was a man married to a pretty young woman, and his death had robbed her of a husband and their two little boys of their father.

The next notation in the trial transcript signifies that the state had completed its case and believed that it had presented evidence sufficient to justify a conviction: PLAINTIFF RESTS.

## NOTES

1. Trial transcript, 312.
2. Ibid, 274, 275.
3. Ibid, 276–281.
4. Ibid, 281–290.
5. This paragraph is based upon Brant's trial testimony, 290–294 of the trial transcript.

6. Trial transcript, 294–297.

7. Trial transcript, 298, 299. The trial notes prepared by the prosecution indicate that Callahan testified before the grand jury that Brink was riding a "dark bay horse." Homsher Collection.

8. Trial transcript, 300, 301.

9. Ibid, 302–306.

10. Ibid, 305.

11. Ibid, 306.

12. Ibid, 307–315.

13. Ibid, 309, 313.

14. Ibid, 317, 319, 320. It was never ascertained how Mann had come into possession of the tooth or how he knew it was Emge's.

15. Ibid, 321–325.

16. Ibid, 323, 324.

17. Ibid, 326.

18. Ibid, 329.

19. Ibid, 337–339.

20. Ibid, 340.

21. Ridgely tried to push several witnesses to say that firing came from the wagon, but no witness ever so testified. Keyes specifically stated that no firing came from the wagon while he was there (trial transcript, 236). In the author's opinion, the fact that a few spent shells were found in the north wagon has no great significance, any more than do spent shells in modern four-wheel-drive vehicles. Such shells just accumulate over a period of time from hunting and target shooting. Still, this is consistent with a statement Saban is supposed to have made that Emge appeared at the door of the sheep wagon, was defiant, and started shooting with his automatic rifle (*Cheyenne State Leader*, 11/16/09). Assuming the accuracy of the report (which was at least hearsay), these statements are not credible. Not only are they inconsistent with much of the evidence, but they were made by a man who badly wanted to avoid the opprobrium of society at large.

22. Ibid, 215, 251

23. Ibid, 340–347.

24. Ibid, 347–349.

25. *Denver Post*, 11/19/09, p. 6, col. 3–5.

26. *Cheyenne State Leader*, 11/9/09.

27. Trial transcript, 350.

28. Ibid, 332.

29. Ibid, 353.

30. Ibid, 355.

# The Defense Proceeds CHAPTER 16

The prosecution rested in the middle of the afternoon of Monday, November 8. The defense attorneys apparently felt they could not proceed immediately, and they requested a delay until the next morning. The defense needed much more than a little extra time, however. Only five witnesses were called in the defense presentation, witnesses the *Cheyenne State Leader* characterized as "seemingly immaterial."[1]

It was a bleak sign for the defense when Ridgely waived his opening statement. The prosecution had used its opening statement effectively, to form a structure for the entire case and spill out all the facts to fill that structure. By contrast, as the *Rustler* noted, this waiver by the defense "was an unusual proceeding, since the jurors as well as the prosecution were left in the dark as to the line of procedure the defense would undertake."[2]

The first witness called was George Pickett. Mr. C. A. Zaring questioned Pickett, and it was the first time an attorney other than Ridgely spoke for the defense. Pickett was a juror in the inquest held right after the raid and had observed the bullet holes in Allemand. Asked what the size of the bullet hole was at the point of entrance, he replied: "Well I would not know. As near as I can guess I believe it was about the size you could shove an ordinary lead pencil into, something like that."[3]

He was then asked what, in his judgment, was the caliber of the bullet that made the wound. The prosecution objected that Mr. Pickett had not been shown competent to render this kind of opinion, and the court sustained the objection. Zaring then tried to qualify his witness, but all Pickett could say was that the only experience he had was from hunting, and even there he had not made a careful observation of wounds made by guns of various sizes. Still, Pickett was again asked his opinion as to the size of the bullet. There was again an objection, and it was again sustained. Zaring tried yet again and elicited that Pickett had once before seen the effect of a gunshot on a human body. So there was one more attempt to have Pickett testify as to the size of the bullet and this time, probably to the surprise of Zaring, Judge Parmelee allowed the witness to answer. The predictable response: ".30-30."[4] Of course, what the defense was trying to show was that the bullet hole corresponded to the .30-30 carried by Faris and not to the .25-35 carried by Brink.

The first question E. E. Enterline asked the witness on cross-examination was, "What is the size of a .30-30?" Mr. Pickett did not know, and he did not know even how to tell the exact measurement. He further admitted that in some cases a soft-nosed bullet might expand while going through clothing, but he had never seen the clothing Allemand was wearing and could not state the effect of a bullet's first going through a coat, jacket, shirt, and overshirt.[5]

On redirect, when Zaring tried to rehabilitate Pickett, he only emphasized the ignorance of his witness. Pickett knew that the .30-30 caliber was larger than a .25-35, but he did not know the difference between them.[6]

Putting such a witness on the stand probably did the defense more harm than if no witness had been presented at all. If, in such an important case and on such an important point, the defense could not present a witness any better than George Pickett, it very much underlined their inability to refute the prosecution's charges.

Mr. Zaring then called Henry Helms to the stand. Helms testified that he resided in Red Bank Basin, less than a mile from William Goodrich's residence, that he was acquainted with Goodrich's reputation for truth and veracity, and that it was "kind of bad." The cross-examination was by Will Metz; he asked Helms who had told him Goodrich's reputation was "kind of bad." Helms said George McClellan, Charles Wells, and A. L. Coleman, but he couldn't relate any specific time or place when statements had been made by any of these men. Metz then showed that Helms, McClellan, and Coleman were all in the cattle business.[7]

Frank Helmer was the third witness called by the defense. His opinion was similar to that of Henry Helms': Goodrich's reputation for truth and veracity was "bad." In addition, however, Helmer confirmed that Goodrich had told him, "Felix Alston said I should have my share of the reward."[8]

The cross-examination of Helmer began as Helms' had, with the witness listing a number of cattlemen who had bad things to say about Goodrich.[9] Then Enterline elicited more detail about Helmer's conversation with Billy Goodrich, and it became apparent that Helmer had told Billy that he should not testify at all because the defendants were friends.

More than that, it also became apparent that Helmer tried to discourage his son, Bounce, from testifying. Enterline called up that April 5 visit by the witness and Bill Garrison and obtained a helpful admission: Helmer said he was going to tell Bounce to testify to "just what he knew and nothing else," but he admitted that he did not doubt the veracity of his son.[10]

On re-direct, the witness testified that there was no trail leading from the county road between the Allemand mailbox (where John Callahan was on April 2) and the Keyes' ranch. The implication was that Brink could not have cut cross-country, as Callahan testified he had. Enterline was not going to let that impression stand:

> Q: Do you mean to testify Mr. Helmer that you cannot after leaving that mailbox go over to Keyes without going to Buckmaster's?
> A: Oh yes, you can go through sagebrush and through the junipers. I can go across there or any one who is familiar with the country.
> Q: Do you not go across there?
> A: I can go across there, but there is no trail.[11]

Porter Lamb was the next witness called by the defense. It quickly became clear that the prosecution had very good reason to question Lamb's allegiance. Lamb was called to relate what Billy Goodrich had told him after his appearance before the grand jury. Mr. Zaring had difficulty formulating the proper question, but eventually he obtained the testimony he wanted: "We talked a great deal during the evening about this, and he told me that he was to get the fattest pocket book for giving his evidence that he had ever had."[12] This testimony was not a great surprise after the cross-examination of Billy Goodrich and so would have a limited additional effect. But when Enterline cross-examined Lamb, he was able to turn the testimony in favor of the state:

> Q: What did he tell you that Brink had told him?
> A: He told me first that he denied the thing or knowing anything about it before the grand jury, then he told me he told the whole story, or what he knew about it.
> Q: Didn't he tell you he was reluctant to testify against these parties?
> A: Yes sir.
> Q: Didn't want to testify against them?
> A: Yes sir.
> Q: On account of their being friends to him?
> A: I don't remember what he said was the cause, but he said he didn't want to testify against them. . . .

Q: Didn't he tell you that Brink had told him that he and another fellow had taken one of the wagons?

A: He didn't give me the particulars of the raid, but he told me that Brink had told him about it.

Q: Did he tell you Brink had told him who were in it?

A: I don't remember. I think he did. I think he said that Brink had told him, but I don't think he told me.[13]

When the fifth of the defense witnesses was called to the stand, it was still morning. That witness was Big Horn County State Senator George B. McClellan. Zaring first had McClellan supplement Pickett's testimony; McClellan told the jury that the .30-30 was a larger caliber than a .25-35 by five one-hundredths of an inch. Then McClellan joined Helms and Helmer in stating that Goodrich's reputation for truth and veracity was bad.[14]

Enterline quickly went after McClellan, accusing him of advising Goodrich to leave the country. McClellan was not a man to be intimidated, though, and he refused to accede to Enterline's accusation. There was a struggle between these two strong-willed men, and a reading of the transcript calls up the image of a wrestling match. Finally, Enterline pulled from McClellan the admission he sought:

Q: So you told him then to leave the country, or words to that effect?

A: I didn't tell him to leave the country. I had no right to tell him anything about it.

Q: He was asking your advice about it?

A: Exactly.

Q: Then you had the right to tell him?

A: I told him what I would do in his place.

Q: What did you tell him you would do if you were in his place?

A: Told him I would leave the country.[15]

The cross-examination continued in this combative vein, with McClellan eventually admitting that a person could proceed from the Allemand mailbox to Keyes' ranch by horseback, that he (McClellan) had taken a great interest in the defense of the case, and that he objected to sheep being brought into that country.[16]

When McClellan finished, it was just before noon. The defense had issued subpoenas for many other witnesses. The testimony of some had become moot because of admissions made by prosecution witnesses. It would not be necessary to call either of the Lathams or Bob Goodrich because Bounce Helmer had admitted he had made a statement before them, nor would it be necessary to call Oscar McClellan because Billy Goodrich did not deny he had talked to Oscar about the whereabouts of Brink and Dixon. There were other subpoenaed witnesses, however, whose testimony was presumably still viable: Billy Miller, John Meredith, Lizzie Lamb, Abram Rebideaux, Charley Rebideaux, and Sadie Rebideaux.[17] Joe Henry was available and had been an important part of the alibi Brink had given the grand jury. And then, of course, there was Herbert Brink himself. But Ridgely was not about to put Herb Brink on the stand. The prosecution had already anticipated his alibi, and if Brink testified differently than he had before the grand jury, William Hardin, the attorney who transcribed the grand jury testimony, was standing by to accuse him of perjury.[18] More than that, Ridgely surely knew that Brink would not be an effective witness — putting Brink on the stand would have removed all doubt as to his guilt.

The problem, as the newspapers later noted, was that the defense had not rebutted any of the testimony of Faris or Keyes, nor had there been any testimony showing where Herbert Brink had been on April 2 or what he had done.[19] Nevertheless, the defense was finished; it rested its case. It was a stunning development, and a bold headline in the *Cheyenne State Leader* expressed the response of most observers: "ASTONISHINGLY WEAK DEFENSE SET FORTH IN BEHALF OF BRINK."[20]

The *Basin Republican* forwarded an explanation that was probably what the defense would have said:

> The fight waged by the defense was purely legal and Brink's fate was put into the balance against the admissibility of the confession of Charles Farris, who turned state's evidence along with Albert Keyes. It was in preparation for a battle along those lines that all of Tuesday afternoon and added hours until midnight went by before instructions to the jury were agreed upon by opposing attorneys.[21]

What the *Republican* did not say is that the defense had to fight a "purely legal" battle, relying upon the instructions to the jury, because the factual presentation had gone so badly that it had no choice.

Attorneys' battles over jury instructions are a part of the trial the public rarely sees, but these battles can be crucial. Typically, the attorneys repair to the judge's chambers, each side with its own set of proposed instructions, and each tries to get the trial judge to adopt its version. This procedure generated titanic struggles in *State v. Brink*, as the *Republican* article shows. In a criminal case, the defense has a great advantage. Most trial courts lean toward the safety of giving defense instructions because the court cannot then be appealed. But in *State v. Brink*, this advantage did the defense lawyers no good. Their predicament was such that they had to contend for instructions which were clearly not the law and Judge Parmelee rejected most of their contentions.

The first instruction that would be read to the jury was not objected to, but it still had significant consequences. This was the "felony murder" instruction. It stated that anyone who kills a human being "in the perpetration of . . . arson" is guilty of first-degree murder.[22] Under this instruction, *all* of the raiders were guilty of first-degree murder, because a human being had been killed in the perpetration of arson.

The defense did object to an instruction that declared that Herbert Brink could only be found guilty of murder in the first degree, murder in the second degree, or not guilty.[23] In other words, the jury was not going to have the power to find Herbert Brink guilty of arson or the lesser homicide crime of manslaughter. Judge Parmelee apparently reasoned that if Brink committed arson, he was guilty of murder, and that there was nothing in the evidence to show guilt of anything but the more serious homicides.

The judge also decided to give, over the objection of the defense, a "conspiracy" instruction, whereby Herbert Brink could be found guilty of first-degree murder if he was one of those who assembled together "to commit a wrongful act" that was incidental to the raid. He would be guilty even if the murder was not specifically intended but merely "probable in the nature of things."[24] The objection of the defense should come as no surprise; in light of the evidence, this instruction was almost a direction of guilt.

The most spirited debate, though, probably came over the instructions requiring corroboration of the testimony of accomplices. The defense did not mind the basic instruction requiring such corroboration, nor the one declaring that the testimony of one accomplice could not corroborate that of another accomplice (such as Faris for Keyes), but it disliked very much the following directive:

> You are instructed that it is not necessary that the testimony of an accomplice be corroborated, circumstantially and in detail, but the corroboration is sufficient, if the corroborative evidence of itself, and without the aid of the accomplice's testimony, in any material matter, tends to connect the defendant with the commission of the offense for which he is charged, but it need not be sufficient of itself to establish the defendant's guilt.[25]

Judge Parmelee overruled the defense objections and decided that this instruction, together with thirty-six others, would be read to the jury in the morning.[26]

Sometime during November 9, Will Metz found a few minutes to write a quick letter to his wife. He was very confident: "We have finished our side of the Brink case and have made a very strong case. Every one who heard it says that we will surely convict him of murder in first degree, except those who don't want to see him convicted."[27]

His confidence would be tested very soon. The next morning, Wednesday, November 10, after Judge Parmelee read all the instructions to the jurors, the final arguments began. Will Metz led off for the prosecution. There were no limits to the length of any of the speeches, and they would go on throughout the day. It was an age of oratory — indeed, the principal speaker for the defense, J. L. Stotts of Sheridan, was hired for his oratorical ability. He had not spoken one word during the body of the trial. The closing arguments, unfortunately, were not transcribed, but most of the remarks are found in the two Basin newspapers (the *Rustler* provides excellent detail of the prosecution's arguments and the *Republican* of the defense arguments).

Metz began boldly, asserting that "we can see the hand of an overruling Providence. . . ." "It was the impelling motive from above that loosed his [Brink's] tongue and made him tell all the details of this most foul crime. The secret within his bosom was too big, too monstrous to be held."[28]

Metz traced Brink's movements throughout April 2, finally bringing him to that fateful hill over Spring Creek, where he sat in the dark watching a burning sheep wagon. During this early part of Metz's argument, Adeline Allemand came into the courtroom carrying her nine-month-old baby. She was dressed in what the *Denver Post* described as "deep mourning," and every person in the courtroom must have watched her as she worked her way toward the front of the courtroom. She sat just behind the railing separating the crowd from the attorneys. As Will Metz continued to speak, the jurors watched the little boy coo and wave:[29]

> He has set fire to the sheep wagon and as the glow from the flames mounts higher and higher he is waiting there with rifle cocked, finger on trigger, for his victim.
>     Presently from the wagon comes the form of Joe Allemand. He peers into the outer circle of darkness, listening — listening, as the murderer Brink told Mrs. Brown was his attitude. He advances a step and the word of command rings out, "Throw up your hands." He obeys.

A few hours ride away is the good wife with the month old babe on her bosom. Why did he not forsake the camp that ill-fated night and go to his home. Oh, that he had and this foul murder stayed and the breadwinner left to the wife and her helpless offspring. . . .

Then out rang the shot and the wife was made a widow, the children orphans. And with the bloody exultation of the depraved fiend, the murderer, Brink, prisoner at the bar, exclaimed boastfully, "This is a hell of a time of night for a man to come out with his hands in the air."[30]

While Metz was delivering this final argument, Brink watched and listened to him, as if mesmerized by everything the attorney was saying. Perhaps he found specially fascinating a demonstration the prosecution conducted for the jury. Metz had Billy Simpson put on Allemand's coat and assume a posture with his hands up. From the evidence presented and the location of the various shells, the prosecution was able to fix the positions of both Brink and Faris. Metz argued that the course of the bullet made a straight line from Brink to the entry wound to the exit marked by holes in the coat, and that it was a physical impossibility for Faris to have made the wound from his position that night.[31] During this demonstration, Mrs. Allemand "averted her head and her frail, black-garbed figure shook with emotion."[32]

Metz referred to the nine lawyers appearing for Brink and asked: "With this cloud of counsel about him, where has there been one word of denial of testimony fixing the guilt of this defendant?"[33]

The prosecuting attorney asserted that when Brink told Anna Goodrich that he and Tommy Dixon might not get their money out of it, he "confessed himself a hired assassin, a midnight killer for hire."[34] The attorney was on thin ice here; other than Anna Goodrich's interpretation of a statement by Herb Brink, there was no evidence to show that the raiders were paid by anyone.

Metz closed with an appeal to the jurors to do their "full duty" and declared that "the safety of the entire community depends upon your returning a guilty verdict."[35] It was a dramatic speech, and when Will Metz sat down he was well satisfied; a few days later he wrote his wife, "I made *the* speech of my life."[36]

Metz's argument had been long, and it was not until afternoon that the next speaker, J. L. Stotts began. Stotts was generally critical of the state's case, but he particularly focused on Charlie Faris. The *Republican's* account:

"If you want to know who the murderer of Joe Allemand was," he said, "go back to last Saturday and recall the picture of the low-browed rascal, Faris, who, not satisfied with three murders on his blood-stained hands, would now come in here and swear away the lives of five others."

"Mark you the devilish gleam in his eye, the look of a man who would kill in the dark, and then contrast his appearance with the face of the defendant in this case."

"Of such material is the state's case against the defendant. Two self-confessed murderers, for that they are under the instructions the court has given you, come in here, and with the promise of the state that they shall escape the hangman's noose, they would swear away the lives of others to purchase their own miserable existences."[37]

Stotts touched on a theme that Ridgely would discuss in greater detail, declaring that the testimony of the witnesses for the prosecution "was not corroborated in a single material point."[38]

The *Republican* wrote of an incident that occurred during Stotts' argument:

While Judge Stotts was commenting on the witnesses he spoke of Cowlthorp's evidence that Brink had said he would take his rifle and help drive the sheepmen from the range. The witness referred to, who was sitting in the front row interrupted the speaker with:
"Yes, I can get more evidence if you" —
"You've had your turn in Court, sir," thundered Judge Stotts."[39]

The *Republican* clearly was impressed by Stotts' oratory and cited an example:

In his argument Judge Stotts drew a thrilling picture of an open grave and a gallows. With his voice scarcely above a whisper he personally called members of the jury by name and asked for whom was the open grave, for whom was the gallows — who was going to pull the rope, — fill the grave?: With all his power, later, after leading up to it with an eloquent passage he said, "Are you going to give this man's life away?"[40]

Stotts was obviously a potent presence, and his speech probably made the prosecuting attorneys worry that the jurors would be swayed. The criticism of Stotts' presentation would be that it was long on emotion but short on facts. Ridgely followed Stotts, though, and his argument was a much more factual, lawyerly, closely reasoned offering.

Ridgely's argument was a challenge to the credibility of all the principal prosecution witnesses, especially Keyes and Faris. He declared that no one said Brink shot Allemand except Faris and that the Faris confession was not corroborated. (The defense seemed to contend that in order to convict Brink, the prosecution had to prove that he pulled the trigger, but as to Keyes and Faris, they were "self-confessed murderers" because they were part of the raid.)

Ridgely supported his claim of lack of corroboration by making a "critical resume" of all the evidence. He said Faris "was in the place from which a bullet would penetrate the left side where the point of entrance of the death wound was located." Ridgely assumed he had completely impeached Billy Goodrich because Billy's neighbors had said Billy had a bad reputation for truth and veracity. He asserted that neither Anna Goodrich, Bounce Helmer, Mrs. Brown, nor John Callahan had told the truth.[41]

In this way, Ridgely was able to argue that even under Instruction No. 28, the corroboration did not even "tend to connect the defendant with the commission of the offense." Ridgely thereby supported Stotts' argument that the state had not proved a single material allegation of its information. He told the jury: "You cannot in justice to your oath return any but a verdict of not guilty for my client." In response to Metz's accusation that there had been no denial of the charges, Ridgely said: "My answer is that there has never been any necessity to." Ridgely closed by reading to the jurors the instruction stating that the burden of proof was always on the state and never shifted to the defense.

E. E. Enterline gave the final address of the day. Enterline was angry. He was not out of control, but he had that motivating irritation that sometimes seizes a trial lawyer when he believes his opponent has made an unfair argument. Enterline declared that the only defense offered by counsel for Brink was "vituperation and vilification of the state's witnesses and abuse of the state's attorneys. . . . When a lawyer descends to such practices, he abuses his license as an advocate."[42]

Enterline then completely reviewed all of the testimony, emphasizing the corroboration supplied by each witness. He proceeded to deliver a "savage excoriation" of Brink, according to the *Rustler*. He told how Brink, "with the cunning of cowardice," had pulled up sagebrush, piled it beneath the rear of the wagon "where his precious body would be shielded from harm," lit it and withdrew out of danger. "This is the kind of a fighter the assassin, Herbert Brink is. No man need be afraid of him in the daytime, but at night, ah, that is different."[43]

Enterline finished with a forceful appeal: "Justice demands a verdict of guilty be returned against the defendant." Then, shortly before 6 p.m., Judge Parmelee handed the written instructions to the jury. The bailiff, George Mead, took charge of the jurors and they were locked up for the night.[44]

This is always the worst time for the trial lawyer. Suddenly, there are no more arguments, no more objections, no more strategy, nothing more to be done for the client. Metz, Ridgely, Enterline — each felt the desolation of a future that was no longer fluid. There was nothing more they could do; if their best had not been good enough, then their client would lose. There is little of the fatalist in the trial lawyer, but it would serve him well when the jury is out and all that can be done is to wait and to wait and to wait. Some of the newspapers were declaring that only a verdict of guilt was possible,[45] but such predictions were small comfort to a prosecution team that had known of many juries reaching impossible results in cases much less volatile than this sheep raid case, in which only one man need dissent for a defense victory.

At least, in *State v. Brink*, the wait was not long. The next morning the jury announced it had reached a verdict.

## NOTES

1.  *Cheyenne State Leader*, 11/9/09.
2.  *Basin Republican*, 11/12/09; *Big Horn County Rustler*, 11/12/09.
3.  Trial transcript, 356.
4.  Ibid, 357, 358.
5.  Ibid, 358, 359, 360.
6.  Ibid, 361. The diameter of a .30-30 bullet is thirty one-hundredths of an inch (.30), while that of a .25-35 is twenty-five one-hundredths of an inch (.25).
7.  This paragraph is based upon the testimony of Henry Helms; trial transcript, 361–366.
8.  Ibid, 367.
9.  The men listed were A. L. Coleman, Chas. Wells (who also ran sheep), Tom Mills, George McClellan, and Oscar McClellan.
10.  Ibid, 372–374.
11.  Ibid, 375–376.
12.  Ibid, 378.
13.  Ibid, 379.
14.  Ibid, 381.
15.  Ibid, 383, 384.

16. Ibid, 384–386.

17. See Note 6, Chapter 15.

18. Subpoena dated 11/5/09 to W. E. Hardin, *State v. Brink*, Case No. 453, Records of the Big Horn County Clerk of the District Court.

19. See *Big Horn County Rustler*, 11/12/09; *Denver Post*, 11/9/09; *Cheyenne Daily Leader*, 11/10/09.

20. *Cheyenne State Leader*, 11/9/09.

21. *Basin Republican*, 11/12/09.

22. Instruction No. 1, *State v. Brink*.

23. Instruction No. 10, *State v. Brink*.

24. Instruction No. 24, *State v. Brink*.

25. Instructions No. 26, 27, and 28, *State v. Brink*.

26. *Big Horn County Rustler*, 11/12/09.

27. Letter of 11/9/09 from Will Metz to Jennie Metz, Metz Collection.

28. *Big Horn County Rustler*, 11/12/09.

29. Denver Post, 11/10/09, p. 13, col. 2; *Basin Republican*, 11/12/09.

30. *Big Horn County Rustler*, 11/12/09.

31. *Worland Grit*, 11/11/09.

32. *Basin Republican*, 11/12/09.

33. *Denver Post*, 11/10/09, p. 13, col. 2.

34. *Big Horn County Rustler*, 11/12/09. It is possible that Saban or Alexander paid money (although Faris or Keyes would have said something about it, if so), but it seems more likely that Brink was simply referring to the fact that he and Tommy would not get their money from Bragg because of the raid.

35. Ibid, 11/12/09.

36. Letter of 11/14/09 letter from Will Metz to Jennie Metz, Metz Collection.

37. *Basin Republican*, 11/12/09.

38. Ibid.

39. Ibid.

40. Ibid.

41. This discussion about Ridgely's argument is taken from the 11/12/09 articles in the *Big Horn County Rustler* and *Basin Republican*.

42. *Big Horn County Rustler*, 11/12/09.

43. Ibid.

44. Ibid.

45. See, for example, the *Thermopolis Record*, 11/13/09.

# The Verdict

## CHAPTER 17

There is no more dramatic event than a jury's return of the verdict. Even when a verdict resolves matters of little moment, there is something heart-stopping about this ancient ritual. In *State v. Brink*, for lawyers and witnesses and those hundreds of people who had invested so much in the case — and, of course, for Herbert Brink — the tension and anxiety must have been unbearable, a time of sheer terror.

All through the night of November 10, there had been rumors floating about Basin that the jury had made this vote or that. The jurors were put in a tiny log cabin "back of the Roger house." Small groups of people walked by the house on Park Avenue and paused by the little cabin. Sometimes they would see figures outlined on the window curtain in the cabin, men apparently arguing. But if they tarried too long, Mr. Mead, a gruff man whom the *Cheyenne Leader* described as "a stalwart mountaineer, an old timer," would say something such as, "I guess you have seen enough," and these gatherings of curious people would have to move along.[1]

The jury had deliberated until at least midnight. The next morning, the jurors arose earlier than usual, before 7 a.m., and they told Mead they had arrived at a verdict. Word was sent to all the participants, and at 8:45 Judge Parmelee arrived at the courtroom and mounted the bench. The jurors were already seated. The foreman, ominously for Brink, was that Burlington beekeeper, W. H. Packard, and he held the verdict and the court's instructions under his arm.[2]

The *Big Horn County Rustler* gave an excellent description of what happened then:

> The defendant, Herbert Brink, was brought in and took a seat at the other side of the table opposite his counsel. Jailer Walter Smith, for the first time since the trial opened, occupied a seat directly behind Brink.

The prisoner's face showed signs of worry and a sleepless night, but otherwise he preserved a calm demeanor.

"Gentlemen of the jury, have you agreed upon a verdict?" asked Judge Parmelee.

"We have, your honor," said Foreman Packard, advancing with the papers, which he handed to the judge.

Judge Parmelee read the verdict over slowly and handed it to Clerk Russell.

The silence in the court room was intense, even painful, as the clerk pronounced the words "guilty of murder in the first degree."[3]

Within the courtroom there was no demonstration; it was as if everyone was too stunned to react.[4] According to the *Cheyenne State Leader*, Brink "sat with reclining head as the verdict was issued and apparently was unmoved at hearing his fate."[5] The *Denver Post* said Brink's "face paled only for an instant and there was a slight twitching of muscles of his hands," but otherwise he "met the gaze of the hundreds in the courtroom without flinching."[6]

The court and counsel completed the routine requirements after a jury's verdict: The jury was discharged, and Ridgely was given ten days in which to file a motion for new trial. Brink was returned to the jail.[7]

The reaction may have been subdued in the courtroom, but it certainly was not in the press. Every newspaper covering the trial carried its biggest headline on the front page. Even the *Denver Post* featured the story on its first page, along with the byline of John I. Tierney:

### BRINK GUILTY OF MURDER, SAYS JURY
**First Degree Verdict is Reached in Ten Sleep Case**
MEANS DEATH PENALTY
Others Accused May Try to Avoid Hanging by Pleading Guilty in Second Degree[8]

Headlines in other newspapers were similar: "BRINK IS GUILTY"; "BRINK'S LIFE FORFEIT FOR MURDER OF JOE ALLEMAND"; and "THIS MORNING THE JURY RETURNED WITH A VERDICT OF MURDER IN FIRST DEGREE."[9]

For all the conflict associated with the case, the jury had not had a difficult time reaching its verdict. There were only five votes: The first showed eight for first-degree murder, two for second-degree murder, and two for acquittal. On the second ballot, eight voted for first-degree murder and four for second-degree murder. The third saw another shift, so that ten voted for first-degree murder and two for second. Another ballot brought the tally to eleven for first-degree murder and only one for second, and on the fifth and last ballot, the vote was unanimous for first-degree murder. This was shortly after midnight, and the jurors went to bed.[10]

The prosecuting attorneys hardly paused to savor their victory; within two hours of the verdict, the case of *State of Wyoming v. Thomas Dixon* was begun. They knew they still had four cases to try, and their intent was to plow straight forward until all the Spring Creek Raid cases were completed. On the other hand, the defense was already looking for a compromise. The murder statute under which Brink was convicted required that the convicted person "shall suffer death."[11] The *Post* observed that this caused "consternation" to the defendants and their cattlemen supporters.[12]

It is not known why Tommy Dixon was selected as the next defendant to stand trial. A more logical choice would have been Saban, and there had been talk of proceeding next with *State v. Saban*.[13] Tom Dixon was not considered one of the ringleaders nor one of the more culpable defendants. The *Rustler* even parenthetically observed, "have you noted that everyone has a good word to say for Dixon?"[14] The state had earlier offered him the opportunity to plead guilty to arson, but Tommy refused to turn on his friends and said: "Let her go as she lays"; he stated he would take his medicine with the rest of the defendants.[15] Perhaps, though, the prosecution was still hoping to obtain a last-minute plea of guilty and a confession from Dixon to strengthen the cases against Saban and Alexander, the leaders.

The jury selection for the *Dixon* case was very similar to that in *Brink*. It proceeded rapidly (the jury was selected by 3 p.m.); the defense used all its twelve peremptory challenges, the prosecution only two of its peremptories, and the jury finally selected was a body of neutrals, top-heavy with farmers.[16]

They were:

W. H. Lewis, carpenter, Byron
Hyrum Perry, farmer, Byron
W. S. Smith, Basin
H. H. Burkett, teamster, Cody
P. E. Everett, farmer, Cody
Chas. E. Parker, banker, Cody
W. J. Jones, barber, Basin
Andrew Black, farmer, Kane
John B. Farmer, Byron
Byron A. Sessions, farmer, Byron

J. J. Davis, cattleman, Sunlight

Nephi Robertson, farmer, Cowley.

If anything, this jury might have been more favorable to the prosecution than the *Brink* jury had been; there were no jurors from Shell,
Hyattville, Ten Sleep, or any of the Nowood area. The jurors who resided
closest to the scene of the crime were those from Basin.[17] There were a
couple of surprises. One was that J. J. Davis, a cattleman who had been
challenged peremptorily in the *Brink* case, was left on this jury by the
prosecution. The other was that W. H. Lewis, one of the jurors who had
found Brink guilty of first-degree murder, was not challenged by the
defense.

After the selection of the jury, time was needed to prepare opening
statements, so the case was adjourned until the next morning.[18] There
was another reason the prosecution did not push to immediately submit
an opening statement. The focus of the action was shifting from the
courtroom to private negotiations seeking to settle all the remaining cases.
A proposal had been made by the prosecution to allow each of the
remaining defendants to plead guilty to a lesser offense than first-degree
murder, although the state did not want to relieve Brink from the death
sentence.[19]

That evening there was a conference of the defense attorneys, the
defendants, and some of the cattlemen supporting the defendants.[20]
Dissension had been brewing among defense counsel, and that evening it
came to a head. Even in the earliest days of the *Brink* trial, J. L. Stotts had
wanted to negotiate with the prosecution and try to reach a compromise
for pleas of guilty to offenses less serious than first-degree murder. Ridgely,
however, took a much tougher line. He was a trial lawyer and thought he
could fight it out and win. He supported the defendants in their fervent
belief that the charges were unjust and should be contested and beaten.[21]

Brink's conviction of first-degree murder should have discredited
Ridgely, but the prosecution, by insisting that Brink's death sentence
stand, probably bolstered him. The defendants perhaps thought: What
have we got to lose by fighting on?

There were other complicating factors. One was that the first trial had
been terribly costly and the defense's funds were almost gone.[22] But the
more wrenching consideration was Brink's emotional state. He was not
handling the situation well. When Brink was brought back to his jail cell
after his conviction, he was supposed to have gone "plumb wild." An
observer said he "took on at a great rate" and that "Brink evidently thought
that they were going to hang him that same day."[23]

Brink's friends felt they had to stick with him. The *Republican* reported what happened when the prisoners considered the prosecution's proposal:

> These [proposals] were rejected because the overtures did not carry with them safety for Brink. Indeed, when the plan was broached, Brink, with tears streaming down his face, is said to have uttered to Mr. Ridgely, "For God sake, Ridgely, save the boys and hang me."
>
> "No," cried George Saban, "if you [Brink] can't be saved, we will all hang on the same tree."[24]

The upshot was that Ridgely's position prevailed — the defense was going to fight it out unless the prosecution offered a much more favorable deal. Stotts resigned from the defense team and prepared to leave Basin (as did W. L. Walls, although it is not known if this was because he agreed with Stotts).[25]

The next morning the defense did make a counterproposal, apparently proposing relief for Brink and, for the other defendants, dismissal of the murder charges in exchange for guilty pleas to arson.[26] The prosecuting attorneys held a powerful hand, knew it, and were not about to accept such an offer. It was rejected out of hand, and Dixon's trial began.

E. E. Enterline again presented the opening statement for the state, and it was very similar to his presentation in the *Brink* case. There were some additional elements, though. Enterline cited the admissions Tommy Dixon had made to Billy Goodrich, including Dixon's statement that either Saban or Brink killed Allemand. Enterline also said that the prosecution would introduce significant new evidence in the form of declarations made by another raider,[27] probably a reference to some of the statements made by Alexander, although there is no way of being certain of this.

There is no way of knowing because the trial ended after one witness. Felix Alston was again the lead-off witness, and the primary difference from his earlier testimony was on cross-examination. Ridgely questioned him at much greater length, with the intent of showing that the automatic firing heard by witnesses was from Joe Emge's rifle.[28] When Alston stepped down, the defense made another settlement move and instead of resuming the trial after the lunch break, the court called a recess to accommodate negotiations.

Things had changed dramatically in the defense camp. The cattlemen supporting the defendants had decided that following Ridgely was a path to disaster, and they took control of the negotiations. Stotts was even brought back to help with the settlement discussions (his luggage was already on the train).[29] It was the cattlemen, though, who did most of the talking, first calling a conference of the defendants and defense attorneys to convince them that a more realistic posture had to be taken. The *Denver Post* described what was done:

> The leader at the conference on behalf of the cattlemen was Milo Burke, one of the wealthiest stockmen in Wyoming. With him were State Senator George B. McClellan and W. T. Whaley, the latter being father-in-law of Saban, and a director in the Basin State Bank. The cattlemen pointed out that the evidence against all of their friends was of a character that would convince every jury as it had convinced the Brink jury. It was time to deal with the state on the best terms obtainable in order to save the lives of the remaining four. The lawyers for the defense had very little to say and when the stockmen made it plain that there would be no more money advanced in fees they undertook the commission imposed upon them and sought the state's attorneys. All afternoon the negotiations were carried on and even in these preliminaries, the cattlemen assumed the leading part. They declared to the state's attorneys that they would not be placed in the false position of defending men whom the community at large believed to be guilty of the crime charged.[30]

As shown in the *Post* story, the cattlemen conferred with the prosecuting attorneys, as well as with the defendants. The prosecutors were reluctant to move very far from their initial proposal, not simply because their position was so strong but because the woolgrowers, who had supported the prosecution from the beginning, demanded severe penalties.[31]

Around 6 p.m., at the end of an afternoon of very tough and sometimes heated negotiations, a compromise was finally reached. It was agreed that Dixon and Eaton would plead guilty to arson and Saban and Alexander to second-degree murder. Their penalties would be decided by Judge Parmelee. As to Brink, it was felt that his penalty and that of Alexander and Saban should be similar, and the prosecution agreed to petition Governor Brooks that the death sentence be commuted.[32]

Both sides felt they had pushed the other side to make concessions, and each was right. The prosecution, as well as the defense, had something to gain from the arrangement. The pleas meant four more convictions for serious crimes, convictions that bore a rough correspondence to the degree of guilt. Another important consideration: Guilty pleas would stop the hemorrhaging from the county coffers.[33] Will Metz wrote his wife about the negotiations and perhaps he magnified his part a bit: "I brought about the final conclusion in those cases by laying down the ultimatum to Milo

Burke and Geo B McClellan. I convinced them that we would convict their friends of murder in the first degree & hang them all, unless they compelled them to come in & plead guilty, and I assure you, they went to work."[34]

It may have been that a discussion with Will Metz was the impetus for McClellan and Burke to take the initiative they did. More likely, these cattlemen independently came to their conclusions, and when Metz and the other prosecuting attorneys spoke to the cattlemen the afternoon of the 12th, they were preaching to men already converted.

The sentencing took place early the next morning, Saturday, November 13. The weather, so bright and beautiful that fall, had finally broken, and it was cold and snowy. The bad weather did not keep spectators away, though; the news had spread, and the courtroom was crowded. The five men were brought in, each accompanied by a deputy: Joe LeFors had charge of Dixon; Frank James, of Eaton; the jailer, Walter Smith, was with Saban; Sheriff Alston, with Alexander; and the undersheriff, Ed Cussack, with Brink. The reporting papers described it as a sad event (although the *Republican,* in a strange observation, praised Ridgely's strategy by which "the lives of all the cattlemen were saved").[35]

All of the defendants showed the effects of the ordeal, but Saban seemed the most affected. The *Republican* referred to Saban as "pale" and "ashy" and having aged twenty years overnight, "a broken hearted and broken spirited man."[36] Brink's eyes were red and moist, and it appeared he had been crying for hours. At first Alexander seemed the least affected, but when Brink was sentenced his eyes, too, filled with tears.[37]

Before the proceedings even began, Judge Parmelee walked over to Herbert Brink, and there was an earnest discussion. Brink looked the judge "unflinchingly in the eye, as if to read his every thought." Then the judge assumed the bench. The first order of business was the change of pleas, and each defendant withdrew his "not guilty" plea. Dixon and Eaton pled guilty to arson, Saban and Alexander to second-degree murder. In doing so, Alexander asserted that he had not fired the shot that killed Allemand.[38]

Judge Parmelee then announced the sentences at which he had arrived, and he did so in the same order the pleas had been received. Tom Dixon was sentenced to not less than three nor more than five years in the penitentiary. Eaton received the same sentence.[39]

The judge then asked Saban to stand. Saban did not respond, and Judge Parmelee called his name again. The jailer reached over and touched Saban and he started, as if his thoughts had been far away, and he finally rose to his feet. The judge asked him if he had anything to say, and Saban said in a low and halting voice: "I wish to say that I never shot anyone — never shot a living human being in my life." After hearing Saban, Parmelee pronounced sentence: not less than twenty years nor more than twenty-six in the Wyoming penitentiary. Alexander received the same sentence.[40]

Finally, it was Brink's turn, and he, too, was asked if he had anything to say. Brink stood up and told the judge: "I wish to say that I did not kill Allemand and was far from shooting any man with his hands in the air." Parmelee delivered the sentence: "Herbert Brink, it is the sentence of the court that you be taken to the penitentiary and that on January 14, before the hour of sunrise, you be hanged by the neck until you are dead."[41]

The *Rustler* described the scene:

> The situation was impressive. Strong men were seen to wipe away a tear. A great lump came into the throat of the reporter, as the pity of it all seemed to rush in upon him.
>
> It was all over. The sheriff and his deputies again took the prisoners in charge. Brink walked up to the judge and had another long earnest talk. Friends came up and shook the hands of the prisoners. There were tears in the eyes of many, and others, so overcome were they by emotion, could only take the hand of the prisoner and look the sorrow they could not otherwise express.
>
> The prisoners were then taken back to the jail and the court (for so wags the world) proceeded with other business.[42]

In this second conversation with Judge Parmelee, Brink was supposed to have told the judge that it was Faris and not he who shot Allemand.[43] Alexander also claimed that Faris was the one who shot Allemand.[44] Of course, neither of these gentlemen was willing to submit himself to cross-examination on the point. To this day there are people who express doubts that Brink was the one who pulled the trigger.

The jurors certainly had little doubt, however. The jury must have believed Faris to have come to a verdict of first-degree murder, with its mandatory death penalty, as easily as they did. Percy Metz never questioned who shot Allemand: "He [Brink] was guilty of murder here, he was a degenerate, he was anything and everything that was bad. He is one of the scum of the earth types who came west, and was really the trigger happy fellow who started all the killing."[45]

Which raises the most persuasive reason why there should be little doubt that Brink and not Faris shot Allemand. Faris did not have the character of a cold-blooded killer. Brink did. Both before the raid and long after, Brink's life revealed a human being without conscience.

## NOTES

1.  *Cheyenne State Leader,* 11/12/09.
2.  *Big Horn County Rustler,* 11/12/09.
3.  Ibid.
4.  Ibid.
5.  *Cheyenne State Leader,* 11/12/09.
6.  *Denver Post,* 11/11/09, p. l, col. 1.
7.  *Big Horn County Rustler,* 11/12/09.
8.  *Denver Post,* 11/11/09, p. 1, col. 1.
9.  *Big Horn County Rustler,* 11/12/09; *Cheyenne State Leader,* 11/11/09, *Worland Grit,* 11/11/09, respectively.
10. *Big Horn County Rustler,* 11/12/09; *Cheyenne State Leader,* 11/12/09. The *Rustler* provided the information regarding the balloting. To have obtained this kind of detail, the *Rustler* must have interviewed one or more of the jurors.
11. See Wyoming Compiled Statutes 1910, 5789.
12. *Denver Post,* 11/11/09, p. 1, col. 1.
13. *Denver Post,* 11/10/09, p. 13, col. 2.
14. *Big Horn County Rustler,* 11/9/09.
15. *Denver Post,* 11/13/09, p. 1, col. 3.
16. *Denver Post,* 11/12/09, p. 2, col. 5; Record of Challenges, *State of Wyoming v. Thomas Dixon,* Case No. 435, Records of the Big Horn County Clerk of the District Court. Thirty men were selected from the panel; W. H. Lewis, Hyrum Perry, A. A. Pully, M. H. Warner, Harrison Shoemaker, W. S. Smith, H. H. Burkett, Clause Andrieu, M. H. La Follett, Fred Houston, W. E. Morris, L. Moncur, John H. Smith, E. B. Powelson, P. E. Everett, C. C. Berelyhmer, C. H. Gardner, Chas. E. Parker, James McKinney, W. P. Rice, Angus Beaton, John W. Myers, W. J. Jones, Andrew Black, John B. Farmer, Byron A. Sessions, J. J. Davis, Dan A. Winslow, C. W. Lambert, and Nephi Robertson. Of these, Rice was probably challenged for cause by the defense, Warner, Winslow, and Gardner were probably challenged for cause by the prosecution, Morris and Myers were challenged peremptorily by the prosecution, and Pully, Andrieu, LaFollett, Houston, Shoemaker, Moncur, Smith, Powelson, Berelhymer, McKinney, Beaton, and Lambert were challenged peremptorily by the defense. The remainder were accepted as jurors.
17. *Denver Post,* 11/12/09, p. 2, col. 5.
18. *Big Horn County Rustler,* 11/19/09.
19. Speech of Percy Metz before the Natrona County Historical Society, 11/2/61.
20. *Denver Post,* 10/12/09, p. 2, col. 5.

21. See the *Big Horn County Rustler*, 11/19/09; the *Denver Post*, 11/12/09, p. 2, col. 5, and 11/13/09, p. 1, col. 3.

22. *Denver Post*, 11/12/09, p. 2, col. 5.

23. *Sweet Smell of Sagebrush*, 98.

24. *Basin Republican*, 11/19/09.

25. *Big Horn County Rustler*, 11/19/09; *Denver Post*, 11/12/09, p. 2, col. 5.

26. Speech of Percy Metz before the Natrona County Historical Society, 11/2/61.

27. *Big Horn County Rustler*, 11/19/09; *Denver Post*, 11/12/09, p. 2, col. 5.

28. Ibid.

29. *Big Horn County Rustler*, 11/19/09.

30. *Denver Post*, 11/13/09, p. 1, col. 3.

31. *Basin Republican*, 11/19/09; see also the *Denver Post*, 11/11/09, p. 1, col. 1, wherein it is stated that the woolgrowers wanted Saban to be tried, as they believed him to be the primary instigator.

32. *Denver Post*, 11/13/09, p. 1, col. 3; speech of Percy Metz speech before the Natrona County Historical Society, 11/2/61; *Big Horn County Rustler*, 11/19/09.

33. *Big Horn County Rustler*, 11/19/09.

34. Letter of 11/19/09 from Will Metz to Jennie Metz, Metz Collection.

35. *Big Horn County Rustler*, 11/19/09; *Basin Republican*, 11/19/09.

36. *Basin Republican*, 11/19/09.

37. *Big Horn County Rustler*, 11/19/09.

38. Ibid.

39. Ibid; Sentence, *State v. Thomas Dixon*, Big Horn County Case No. 435; Sentence, *State v. Ed Eaton*, Big Horn County Case No. 449.

40. *Big Horn County Rustler*, 11/19/09. The *Republican*'s version of this is a bit different, but the *Rustler*'s report is probably the more reliable. Of all the newspapers reporting about the raid, the stories from the *Rustler* seem the most complete and accurate. See also Sentence, *State v. George Saban*, Big Horn County Case No. 444; Sentence, *State v. Milton A. Alexander*, Big Horn County Case No. 433.

41. Ibid.

42. Ibid.

43. *Basin Republican*, 11/19/09.

44. The *Cheyenne State Leader*, on 11/16/09, said that Milton Alexander saw Faris about to shoot Allemand and shouted: "His hands are in the air, Faris. Don't!" This is inconsistent with what Dixon told Goodrich (that either Saban or Brink shot Allemand) and, implicitly, with Bounce Helmer's testimony. Bounce heard someone shout "get them hands up," and surely would have heard Alexander's alleged statements. Alexander was much closer to Bounce than either Brink or Saban had been.

45. Speech of Percy Metz before the Natrona County Historical Society, 11/2/61.

# The Aftermath

## CHAPTER 18

The trials were done. In the ordinary case, those convicted and sentenced go to prison and serve their terms out of the public gaze. They are quietly released years later without notice by an uncaring public. But this was not the ordinary case; it was an event that marked the anguished struggles of a society growing up. The stretching and tearing would continue, as the young and exuberant people of the Big Horn Basin tried to adjust to a new order and clean up the untidy remnants of the old.

With the trials over, one of the first things Governor Brooks wanted to do was remove the militia from Basin. The same day the defendants were sentenced, Brooks telegrammed Felix Alston: "Reduce guard to limit of safety keeping enough to ensure protection. Show Gatchell this order."[1] Brooks had never been enthusiastic about the presence of the militia, believing that an adverse public reaction might offset any gain in maintaining order. The law enforcement people of Big Horn County, however, did not share Brooks' apprehensions about the militia, and they did not believe that all the danger was past. Felix Alston quickly wired back the governor, pointing out that under Wyoming law, Brink, as a prisoner under death sentence, could not be transferred to the penitentiary for a week. He requested that the soldiers remain another week, and the governor acceded.[2]

One of the reasons law enforcement officials welcomed the continued presence of the militia was that the troops had conducted themselves so well; there was uniform praise for their deportment.[3] Judge Parmelee, in a letter to Governor Brooks, told the governor that the troops were well behaved even though "the situation must have been trying to some of them, and doubtless there were occasions when the individual resentment of the soldiers ran high."[4]

On Sunday morning, the day after the sentencing, a remarkable scene was played out. Judge Parmelee visited the jail and talked quietly with each of the sentenced men. The *Republican*, already deeply impressed by the judge ("wise, conscientious, impartial and learned in the law"), spoke of his actions in awed tones, describing how the judge met the men "as a father would meet an unfortunate son . . . on a high and sacred plane." The *Republican* closed its article with a paragraph that heralded the response of the cattlemen to their crushing loss: "That the judge left the little room a saddened man no one can doubt. Yet out of it all stands preeminent the loyalty which pledges eternal fidelity between men in whom years of association had bred that friendship that qualls at no sacrifice."[5]

The prosecutors certainly did not sense any nobility arising out of the defendants' predicament; they felt only that the prosecution had struck a great blow for law and order. Congratulatory letters went back and forth from several people to Governor Brooks. The French government was, of course, informed of the excellent results.[6]

The prosecuting attorneys moved very quickly to complete the agreements with Faris and Keyes. On Monday morning, Percy Metz filed papers entitled "nolle pros," by which all criminal charges against Charles Faris and Albert Keyes were dismissed. Bills of sale were also made out for all the property held by Faris and Keyes in Big Horn County. The county, probably with the assistance of woolgrowers' funds, was buying out the ranch operations of the two men.[7]

At noon that same day, November 15, Keyes, Faris and his wife and baby, and Billy and Anna Goodrich and their child arrived at the train station. The *Republican* made an oblique reference to "the attitude of the public toward Faris, Keyes and Goodrich occasioned by developments at the proceedings Saturday morning."[8] The newspaper seemed to be alluding to Brink's statement that Faris had shot Allemand, and it apparently assumed that the general public believed Brink. Whether or not Brink was believed, there was certainly deep anger felt by cattlemen toward these witnesses. If it was not clear enough to Billy Goodrich, another event made it irrefutable: On Wednesday night, the night the jurors were deliberating, Goodrich's sawmill at his ranch was burned to the ground.[9]

Bill O'Neal states that when this small party entered the depot, they were "treated like lepers." People refused to speak to them, either walking away or pointedly looking out windows.[10] The *Cheyenne State Leader* in an editorial said Faris and Keyes were being "crushed beneath the burden of public contempt," that they were "guilty but by the law made guiltless." The tenor of the *Leader* editorial was not at all favorable to Faris and Keyes, alluding to Benedict Arnold.[11] All these people knew they could not return home to the Upper Nowood. They had been cast out as surely as

Cain. And so the three ranchers and their families somberly boarded the train for Billings. The *Rustler* said: "It is understood they are all going further west, where they expect to locate."[12]

The week of November 15 was a hectic one for Percy and Will Metz. They were trying another murder case, *State v. Paseo*, (Lorenzo Paseo was the man the posse caught just before the *Brink* case began). Will Metz was very proud of his son's performance. In a letter to Percy's mother, Jennie, Will said that Percy "threw away his notes and went at it hammer & tongs and made a splendid argument."[13]

At the end of that week, on Saturday, November 20, the five defendants finally left Basin for the state penitentiary in Rawlins. Early that morning, many people visited the raiders at the jail, perhaps as many as a hundred, and several brought fruit and flowers. A "splendid dinner" was served at noon in which the Mexican, Paseo, participated. Paseo had been convicted of first-degree murder and sentenced to death, and the raiders took him to their bosoms as a kind of soul brother.[14]

When the prisoners arrived at the train depot, there was a big crowd to see them off (the *Sheridan Enterprise* said 500 people).[15] The crowd was augmented by the militia, which also left Basin that day, and deputies taking the men to the penitentiary, as well as the usual run of passengers. It was not an unruly crowd, and there were no demonstrations. It was as if the people were there to see soldiers off to a war. More flowers and more fruit were produced, and a "huge basket" was taken onto the train. As the party walked the length of the platform, the convicted men were given parting handshakes and words of sympathy.[16]

Percy Metz was disgusted by the whole spectacle. Fifty-two years later he said: "And down to the train came their friends and relations with flowers — I think Bowers and some of the outfits in Denver made quite a killing on flowers to give these fellows — it was unbelievable."[17]

In 1909, a train trip from Basin to Rawlins was taken by proceeding north, not south.[18] The first leg of the journey was to Billings, Montana, and from there to Sheridan. From Sheridan, the train trip wound east, back through Montana, to South Dakota, and then south to Nebraska and back to Wyoming. The prisoners were not delivered to the penitentiary until November 23.[19]

The *Republican* printed sympathetic articles telling of Herbert Brink during this trip. The newspaper quoted Brink, who lamented: "I did not feel at Basin as I do now and I tell you, my boy, it's a hard and bitter fate to think about."[20] Another article told how he offered financial assistance and comfort to the condemned murderer, Paseo.[21]

Even after the prisoners were safely in the penitentiary, the pot was stirred. On December 3, the *Republican* prominently announced that Allemand's widow was again a bride. A front-page story told of the November 24 marriage of Ada Allemand to John Callahan, whose testimony figured prominently in the *Brink* case and whose devotion to Mrs. Allemand was "marked and remarked while they were in Basin." The opening sentence of the article read: "Trailing the heels of the Tensleep trials in which the death of Joseph Allemand was legally avenged comes Cupid to the heart of the widow of the slain flockmaster to solace affliction with affection."[22] Although the *Republican* would not make such observations, this story probably produced comments from some of the newspaper's more ardent followers that her broken heart certainly healed quickly and that maybe that great display of grief two weeks before her marriage, which so swayed the jury, was not wholly genuine.

In the same edition, the *Republican* carried an even more prominent article about the high cost of the raid cases. Each item of expense was carefully detailed: the attorney fees (which the *Republican* declared would surely be doubled or tripled before all was said and done); the costs of hiding Goodrich, Cafferal, and Helmer; the sheriff's expense account; the militia expenses; the jail expense; and, of course, the witness and jury fees. It would come to at least $25,000 (a staggering sum in 1909), said the *Republican* and possibly more.[23] Again, this was a story that carried a stern but unstated undertone, the real message being that the expenses had been extravagant and inappropriate, perhaps even a waste of money in a bad cause.

Only one day after these two articles were published, Gebhart and Anderson, the publishers of the *Republican,* wrote Governor Brooks to ask who had been awarded the $500 reward offered by the state. They noted there was "naturally considerable interest in the matter, and we would like to print it as well."[24] The response from the governor's office was that no one had yet been awarded the money.[25] Initial reports stated that Felix Alston would claim the reward money and was going to share it with his deputies.[26] But Alston declared that he would not take the state or county reward because he had only been doing his job.[27] Later, he formally waived any claim to this money in favor of Joe LeFors. It is not clear whether LeFors received $500 or $1,000, but the public part of the reward money all went to him.[28]

The real question is what was done with the private reward money? Four thousand dollars had been offered by woolgrowers and another $1,000 by Joe Allemand's brother. Because these parties did not have to answer questions by prying newspapermen, the disbursement of reward monies, whether to Faris, Keyes, Goodrich, or others, could be completely concealed. It was. The *Republican* never learned how the private monies were disbursed, and it is not known to this day.[29]

But the *Republican* could not be deterred as to the attorney fees claimed by Will Metz. Metz announced that he was taking the $2,500 that had been set aside when the Spring Creek raid cases began, feeling he had earned it. He asked for no further money, however. On December 10, the *Republican* printed an article, originally run in the *Cody Enterprise*, in which Judge Metz's actions were clearly disapproved of, though the story was not as harsh as those printed in May. A later article stated that the attorney fee question was such a political problem that Will Metz had assured leaders of the Democratic Party that only $2,500 would be taken.[30]

And then, for a while, the Spring Creek raid actually faded from public attention. The five men began their atonement, and, at first they quietly served their time. Brink was no longer subject to a death sentence; as expected, Governor Brooks had commuted his sentence to life imprisonment.[31] The only ripple from the raid came from some of the militiamen who had served in Basin. In May 1910, Henry May of Cody wrote Governor Brooks and told him that the members of Company E had never been paid and that many of them had lost their jobs when they returned home.[32] Governor Brooks had to tell Mr. May that if Big Horn County did not pay (and Big Horn County could not; on December 28, 1909, it had to disapprove $520.60 in expenses because of lack of funds), the guardsmen could not look to the state of Wyoming either, unless the legislature authorized some money.

Shortly thereafter, another sidelight from the trial appeared: Joseph L. Stotts filed suit in Big Horn County on July 26, 1910, against George H. Saban, Milton A. Alexander, Thomas Dixon, Herbert Brink, Ed Eaton, Joe Henry, and W. T. Whaley. The gist of the petition was that the defendants had retained Stotts, agreed to pay him $4,500, had only paid $1,750, and owed him $2,750.[33] The defendants had probably been unhappy with Stotts because of his soft line and were slow to pay him. The record, though sparse, indicates that a compromise was reached. Stotts had other problems collecting his fees; immediately after the trial he had prepared suit papers against Faris and Keyes, asserting that they owed him $2,000 for services rendered (presumably before they turned state's evidence).[34] There is no record of how this matter was resolved.

The most significant event of 1910 was the election, in which both Alston and Metz were up for re-election. Metz's opponent was R. B. West, one of the attorneys who had represented defendants from the raid. Alston won and Metz lost, and the remarkable thing was how the various precincts voted. Some were quite predictable. The Shell precincts voted very heavily against both Alston and Metz, and West beat Metz badly in Ten Sleep. There were, however, some unexpected results. Ten Sleep, for instance, gave as many votes to Alston as to his opponent (a man named Eyre). In the Spring Creek precinct, Alston won big, although Metz lost big. Probably the strangest vote was from Red Bank (Bear George McClellan's precinct) where it was an even vote between Alston and Eyre and Metz beat West 19 to 14.[35]

These election results underline how many people quietly disapproved of the raiders' violent tactics. Throughout the event, from a time before the raid and during the investigation and the trial, cattlemen overestimated the support for the raiders.

The real tale of the 1910 election was found in the returns from some of the bigger towns. Metz lost badly in Greybull, Basin, and Worland. Alston, however, won Basin and Worland and only lost by a small margin in Greybull.[36] (These voters apparently did not approve of Percy's zealous enforcement of the alcohol and gambling laws.[37])

After the election the *Republican* crowed mightily; it was almost a Republican sweep. In addition to the county attorney's office, the County Commission was changed from Democratic control to Republican, and all the legislative offices went to the Republicans.[38] The *Republican* did not acknowledge Alston's victory and ignored another race in which the Democratic candidate did well. Joseph M. Carey, running for governor on the Democratic ticket, did well not only in Big Horn County but also in most Wyoming counties (he was running not against B. B. Brooks, who did not seek re-election, but against W. E. Mullen) and was elected.[39] This would have great significance for Alston and Metz in ways that were not to the *Republican*'s liking.

One came very soon. In April 1911, the new Governor Carey appointed Felix Alston warden of the Wyoming State Penitentiary.[40] Felix journeyed south to Rawlins to take control of a penitentiary which held a number of men he had helped put there, including the five Spring Creek raiders. Not long after he took over as warden, two of the raiders tried to break out. They did so not by climbing a wall but by filing a writ.

Saban and Alexander retained Samuel King, a Salt Lake City lawyer, and W.E. Mullen, Carey's campaign opponent, who had been the attorney general of Wyoming. On April 12 these lawyers filed petitions for writ of

coram nobis. These were verified petitions; that is, Saban and Alexander
swore under oath that they were true.[41]

Each petition began with a chronology of the initial procedural steps
in the case (information, arraignment, plea), but then each began to shade
the facts so that they very much favored the defendants. One paragraph
in particular offered facts faithfully reflecting the perspective of cattlemen.
It said that in 1909 many people in Big Horn County were engaged in
raising either cattle or sheep, and that

> for several years prior to said time there had been a vast amount of trouble
> and controversy between the cattle and the sheep owners over their
> range rights. It was repeatedly charged and alleged that many of the sheep
> owners and grazers wrongfully and in violation of the settled rights of
> the cattle owners, and with a fixed and determined purpose, invaded the
> range owned and occupied by the cattle owners, thereby destroying their
> range, ruining their homes and rendering habitation in certain localities
> impossible, and bringing ruination to their business, and many of the
> sheep men made counter charges against the cattle men.[42]

The prosecution would contest all of these assertions but the first one:
There had certainly been a "vast amount of trouble" between the cattlemen and the sheepowners.

The petition stated that the report of the three deaths at Spring Creek
aroused the sheepmen of the county and "inflamed their minds" against
cattlemen. When the defendants were arrested, there was great hostility
toward them and threats of mob violence. The petition further argued that

> the sheep men and their allied interests . . . raised vast sums of money to
> assist in the prosecution of said causes and employed many and able
> counsel and shrewd, designing and artful detectives for the purpose of
> securing a conviction of this petitioner and the others herein named,
> whether said conviction was right or proper. That said sheep men . . .
> brought about in said Big Horn County a practical reign of terror.[43]

It was asserted that just before the *Brink* case began, "practically the entire
population of the town of Basin . . . was in constant fear of murders, riots
and mob violence."[44]

There was more. The petitions spoke of the National Guard's being
called in because county officials "became alarmed for the general safety
of the people of the community and they called upon the Governor of the
State of Wyoming for protection." These soldiers were "heavily armed and

were ordered to be ready for trouble at any moment and to shoot to kill in the event of any trouble being commenced," and they told the defendants that "threats had been made to dynamite said jail and to kill the inmates thereof." Saban and Alexander swore that their friends were being threatened with death and bodily injury if they didn't testify for the prosecution and "that there was large sums of money to be paid to them if they would testify against this petitioner and the other accused parties." Both stated that their friends and attorneys "counseled, insisted and advised" them to plead guilty and said that only the "immediate departure from said town and his immediate sentence would prevent an open outbreak and prevent the taking and sacrificing of human life and the life of this petitioner."[45]

Then came the payoff: "Laboring under the influence of such fears, intimidation, duress and terror, he was driven and compelled to enter a plea of guilty as aforesaid and that such plea was extorted from him in violation of his rights as a citizen of the State of Wyoming."[46]

In sum, George Saban and Milton Alexander swore they were coerced into pleading guilty and they wanted to withdraw their pleas and have a trial.

The new county attorney, R. B. West, as a former lawyer of the raiders, knew he had a conflict of interest and quite properly called in E. E. Enterline to oppose the petitions. Enterline quickly filed a rejoinder to dismiss the petitions, saying that the defendants knew of the alleged coercive conditions at the time of the trial yet failed to ask for a change of venue and that neither of the defendants had asserted a valid defense to the charges to which they pled guilty.[47] Both Enterline and Alston filed affidavits stating that the whereabouts of Keyes, Faris, and Mr. and Mrs. Goodrich were not known. Keyes was last in the dominion of Canada, Faris' location was completely unknown, and the Goodriches were last located somewhere in California.[48] The point of these affidavits was that if a trial were required, the state could no longer produce these essential witnesses.

Judge Parmelee gave short shrift to the petitions, apparently viewing them as nothing more than clever exercises in revisionist history.[49] Alexander promptly filed an appeal to the Supreme Court of Wyoming. This appeal was heard, and the April 23, 1912, opinion is printed in the official reports.[50] The Supreme Court had no problem affirming Judge Parmelee. The stated legal reasons were that neither Alexander nor his attorneys had suggested at the time of the trial that Alexander needed additional protection for the exercise of his rights, and it was not alleged that Alexander was not guilty of second-degree murder. But the more basic reason was that even in faraway Cheyenne the Supreme Court knew something about the history of sheep raids in Wyoming, and the judges just could not swallow the idea that these cowboys were being victimized.

In the early fall of 1912, Herbert Brink did something that should have prevented his release from prison for a very, very long time. At that time a former prisoner, Frank Wigfall, was being returned to the penitentiary.[51] He had been released only a few months earlier after serving fourteen years for rape. Wigfall remained around Rawlins but he then raped an old lady, who was white.[52] Her race was significant because Wigfall was a black man. By the standards of 1912, he had committed a particularly heinous crime, one against which even other prisoners could express revulsion. Even before he was returned to the penitentiary there was talk of a lynching.

He arrived only about a day before final and brutal action was taken. Several prisoners, including Brink and Lorenzo Paseo (who, by then, had his death sentence commuted to life imprisonment[53]), formulated a plan. Very early on the morning of October 2, Brink overpowered the guard who held the keys to Wigfall's cell. Then several men invaded the cell, pulling Wigfall out and quickly carrying him up the stairs to the galleries. A noose was fitted on Wigfall's neck, and Paseo threatened him with a knife when he declined an invitation to jump. It is not clear exactly how Brink was involved, but Billy Simpson believed that Brink "put the rope over the negro's neck and kicked him off the cell runway."[54] Whether or not it happened just that way, Wigfall was lowered by a rope around his neck and hauled up and down until the desired result was obtained.

After the lynching there was at first no official action. But shortly afterward there was more trouble with the prisoners, during which Paseo tried to escape and was shot dead. Then about ten men were put in solitary confinement because of the lynching, including Brink and some men who had nothing to do with it. Brink was the first of these ten to be released, supposedly because he was needed so badly in the blacksmith shop. No other official action was taken against him.

In contrast to Brink, the other four raiders were exemplary prisoners. All four were trustees, given special privileges and positions based upon their trustworthiness. Saban organized a prison baseball team. He was also one of the players, although it must have been difficult for him because he was missing parts of fingers from both hands. It was a good team, though, and Warden Alston took it into Rawlins, where it won a game. The team began to unravel when balls and chains were put on two of the players because they ran away. Then Joseph Seng, the catcher, was executed; as the author of the *Sweet Smell of Sagebrush* observed, "the ball team didn't amount to much after they hanged the catcher."[55]

Tommy Dixon drove the wagon that carried supplies to the prison, and during the time he was incarcerated, his record for good time was perfect. "Good time" was an arrangement utilized by Alston whereby a prisoner could earn a reduction in his sentence of ten days per month for good behavior.[56]

The parole board met in January of 1912, and Dixon and Eaton sought a commutation that would allow them to be pardoned or paroled.[57] Several letters were written on their behalf although there was one, from Lewis Jacobs, a Ten Sleep sheepman, apparently opposing their release.[58] Favorable action was not taken, and the reasons were supplied in a letter Governor Carey wrote Dixon:

> Mr. Dixon, I want to state that I have a great deal of sympathy for you. Everything I have heard about you since you entered the penitentiary, has been to your credit. . . . I do not believe that at heart you are a criminal or that you ever were a criminal, but you, with others were engaged in an unlawful act which resulted in the commission of a serious crime. I have always felt that some time or other the sheep men and the cattle men of Big Horn county, would almost with unanimity ask that you and your associates should have such commutation of sentence as would relieve you of much longer service in the penitentiary. Until this time comes the Board of Pardons, I do not believe, would feel like modifying your sentence.[59]

For Ed Eaton it would be the only chance he would have for release from prison. In May of 1912 he went with a road gang to the Big Horn Basin. Only a short time later he was bitten by a tick, and on June 1, in Meeteetse, he died of spotted fever.[60] He was buried in the Ten Sleep Cemetery. Tom Dixon did not suffer such a sad fate; indeed, just a month and a half after Eaton's death, a disaster at the penitentiary resulted in good fortune to Dixon. On July 19 there was a major fire at the prison broom factory. Tom Dixon (and others, including Milton Alexander) fought the fire hard all through the night. Because of this, the Board of Pardons commuted Dixon's sentence, and he was released on November 1, 1912.[61]

Shortly thereafter, agitation for the release of Saban and Alexander began in earnest. In November Governor Carey wrote letters to prominent sheepmen telling them that there had been appeals for executive clemency on behalf of Saban and Alexander and asking their opinions on the subject. Carey was a cattleman and sympathetic to the raiders, but he was also a very cautious politician, continually testing waters before entering. In December, Fred Bragg and A. M. Brock responded, and both men were surprisingly magnanimous. Bragg, speaking as president of the Big Horn County Woolgrowers Association, felt that the parole of these men would be well received and would create "a better feeling between the cattlemen and sheepmen of this section." He thought it would be a good Christmas present to their wives and children.[62]

Other sheepmen, however, were not willing to forgive and forget, including David Dickie of Meeteetse and Lewis Jacobs of Ten Sleep. Many unsolicited letters were written to the governor; some objected to probation or parole, and several recommended it. Frank Gapen of Basin wrote the governor on December 15, 1912, to tell him how offended he was by the petitions being circulated in favor of Saban and Alexander. He thought that these men had perjured themselves in connection with the coram nobis petition; Gapen stated he heard Judge Parmelee say he positively knew these allegations to be false. (Gapen wrote the governor again just six days later asking that his earlier letter not be made public because he belonged to a cattle association.[63])

Probably the most persuasive letter came from Billy Simpson. He stated that reports that a number of sheepmen were in favor of pardons were false, and he said that none of the prosecutors would sign an application for pardon. Simpson declared that pardons would be a "calamity to the public and to the administration of justice" and urged Carey to read the transcript of the trial.[64]

The last letter sent to Carey in 1912 was from M. A. Alexander. The letter, simply a polite statement expressing concern over the exact time his case would be heard, is remarkable if only for Alexander's handwriting. The letter is written on a prison letter form, but the hand is so strikingly elegant, stylish even, that it transforms this pedestrian document into an unusually handsome one.[65]

Unfortunately for Alexander, the governor had to reply that it was not to Alexander's advantage to have the case taken up at the next meeting of the Board of Pardons, because opposition was developing. Carey again repeated his theme that if there came a time when the people of the Big Horn Basin, "with comparative unanimity," asked for parole, he would be glad to give his approval.[66]

Despite this setback, favorable letters and petitions continued to roll in. Dr. Walker wrote from his new residence in Stockton, California.[67] A Reverend Moore, Bishop Burke of Cheyenne, and John Donovan wrote several letters on behalf of Saban, numerous residents from the Nowood area wrote, and an Upper Nowood petition was filed seeking pardons for Alexander and Saban. The latter contained many familiar names, such as Charley Wells and George and Oscar McClellan. Other petitions were received from the Rawlins area (98 names), Basin (42 names) and Cody (336 names!).[68]

Interestingly, two trial jurors' names appear in these petitions, W. S. Lewis of Basin and John Rutrough of Cody. Lewis was a juror in both the *Brink* and *Dixon* cases, and it had been surprising that the defense attorneys left him on the jury in the second case (they had probably heard he was sympathetic to the defense). The presence of Rutrough shows that the prosecuting attorneys had good reason for concern when they grilled him so long before allowing him to stay on the *Brink* jury. These signatures are probably those of the jurors who initially voted to acquit Herbert Brink. However, the dreaded John Donahue of Hyattville appeared on no petitions.

Some opposition did continue to be expressed, and Governor Carey continued to refer to "comparative unanimity." The governor stated several times that he expected and hoped for a resolution from the Big Horn County Woolgrowers Association recommending probation or parole of Saban and Alexander.

The woolgrowers met in the spring of 1913, but no resolution was forthcoming. The governor's theme was obviously wearing on George Saban, as seen in a careful but pointed letter he wrote to Carey on March 25, 1913. Saban noted that there never would be a time when some sheepmen would not object. But, he said, "I have been the same as paroled for two years, I do not think there will be any objections." Saban was referring to the fact that he had been on the road camp for two years and had been accorded unusual liberties, including living with his wife.[69]

No paroles or pardons came through for Saban or Alexander in the first eleven months of 1913, and in December Saban had become a desperate man. The death of John Donovan probably contributed to his despair. Donovan was a wealthy man from St. Joseph, Missouri, and he had taken the plight of George Saban as his special cause. He went so far as to structure an unusually favorable business arrangement in New Mexico for Saban, should he be released.[70] But in November 1913, Donovan died.

Then, on December 15 or 16, Felix Alston wired D. O. Johnson, a guard, to return Saban to Rawlins. By this time, Saban must have been thoroughly disgusted with Governor Carey's refusal to assume responsibility — the frequency of his insistence on "comparative unanimity" did make Carey appear to be a 1913 version of Pontius Pilate, frantically washing all guilt from his hands — and the prisoner decided to act. Johnson came to Colter (south of Worland) to pick up Saban, who requested to go to Basin to transact business at a bank.[71] Johnson drove him to Basin, arriving about 5 p.m., where he obtained a room at the Antlers Hotel for the evening. Saban then said he had to go to the Basin State Bank and left Johnson. But if he went to the bank, it was only briefly to obtain money to facilitate his escape. About 9 o'clock that evening, Saban persuaded a man named Ora Allen to drive him to Laurel, Montana, for a charge of $100. Saban told Allen that he was a free man. After driving through the night, Allen left Saban at 6 o'clock the next morning.

It was not until 2 o'clock that afternoon that Johnson learned Saban had gone to Montana and sounded the alarm. It was far too late.

This incident caused a great furor. Mr. Allen was criminally charged, but the county attorney (then W. S. Collins, another former defense attorney for the raiders) dismissed the case, saying there was insufficient evidence and that the real culprits were Johnson, the guard, and the state of Wyoming for giving Saban so much freedom. The two Basin newspapers started sniping at one another again, leading the *Rustler* at one point to write: "The *Republican*, by a process of reasoning peculiar to that con-scienceless organ, has almost convinced itself that the real guilt in the whole affair rests with the editor of The *Rustler*."[72]

There were two men who were especially irate about Saban's escape. One was Governor Carey, who expressed surprisingly strong anger. In one letter he declared that Saban had made "the mistake of his life" and that he (Carey) had intended to "help Saban in a way that my successor will not do."[73] In another he indicated that Saban had let him down, that "George Saban ran away," and that "he intended to abandon his family."[74]

The other man who was irate was the new district judge. The Big Horn Basin had become four counties; Park (with Cody as county seat), Washakie (Worland), Hot Springs (Thermopolis), and the remaining part of Big Horn County (still Basin). In 1911 the legislature recognized the need to create a new judicial district encompassing only the Big Horn Basin. In early 1913, a new district judge was named, and Governor Carey took the second action that so distressed the *Republican*: He appointed Percy Metz. Percy was supposed to be the youngest district judge in the country.[75]

The new Judge Metz demanded a full investigation of the escape. In the end, though, nothing could be done. Many people felt there was some sort of complicity by someone, but with a halfhearted prosecutor and circumstances firmly pointing only to gross stupidity, the furor finally fizzled out.

Saban's escape did not seem to hurt Alexander and Brink's prospects for release. Indeed, it was used as an argument in favor of an early release: There are three men out, it was said, who were convicted of essentially the same crime as Alexander and Brink, so those two should also be released. It was the summer of 1914, however, before the big push began. The letters and petitions sent to Governor Carey primarily sought clemency for Brink, probably because so much had already been submitted for Alexander. There were, however, several letters (and perhaps another petition) forwarded on behalf of Alexander. The letters emphasized what a devoted father Alexander was and how his two boys needed him. (Letters that had been written on behalf of Saban had a similar emphasis.) The most fervent and constant correspondent was Alexander's wife, Myra. She had moved to Cheyenne, and her whole life was devoted toward getting her husband out of prison.[76]

Herbert Brink had some feminine assistance, too, although the great bulk of his support came from cattlemen. There is a February 1914 letter from Miss Dorolis Rebideaux of Reno, Nevada. She wrote the governor of her hope that Brink could be released soon and coyly confessed: "Yes, Governor Carey. To be candid with you He is my Sweetheart."[77]

In June 1914, there was an avalanche of mail recommending Brink's probation or parole. This correspondence was obviously the result of an organized effort on Brink's behalf, but the amount was still impressive. There were 78 letters written for Brink and 173 names on petitions.[78] Most of the letters were very similar, making exactly the same points. A typical one reads as follows:

> Dear Gov. Carey,
> Regarding Herbert Brink, who was sentenced to prison for life, I have known him for the last several years. I have been a resident of _____ for the last twenty years.
> I believe that he has been punished sufficiently, and that the demands of the law have been *appeased*. If pardoned I am sure he would again be a good citizen. This is the opinion of most of the citizens of this county.[79]

If any of these people were aware of Herbert Brink's activities while in prison, they ignored such knowledge. For Herbert Brink, the man, had been transformed into Herbert Brink, the symbol, and when that happens, facts cannot compete with feelings.

By late 1914 opposition to the release of the remaining raiders was almost entirely muted. The way of the wind was shown by a December 1, 1914, letter from Carey to Myra Alexander in which the governor hinted that he might act even if the Board of Pardons did not make a favorable recommendation. Governor Carey was spared that dilemma, however, when, on December 9, 1914, the board unanimously recommended parole for Milton Alexander and Brink. The condition of the paroles was that neither man could live or do business in Big Horn County.[80]

Mrs. Alexander then wrote the governor and asked if the condition applied to Washakie County as well as Big Horn County, as the Alexander ranch was no longer in Big Horn County but in the newly created Washakie County.[81] Carey immediately responded that sheepmen had withdrawn their objections to the parole of Mr. Alexander and Brink on the condition they not return to the Big Horn Basin. The governor noted that the Alexanders could still keep their property, but he recommended that "for his [Alexander's] good keep entirely out of the Big Horn Basin."[82]

So on December 14, 1914, Milton Alexander and Herbert Brink were discharged from the penitentiary. The Spring Creek raid was finally over. What remained were the broken hearts, the broken dreams, and the broken faith of the people of the Upper Nowood.

## NOTES

1.  Telegram of 11/13/09 to Felix Alston, Sheriff, Sheep Raid File.

2.  Telegram of 11/13/09 from Felix Alston to Gov. B. B. Brooks (3 p.m.); see also the 11/15/09 letter from P. A. Gatchell, Adjutant General, to the Hon. B. B. Brooks, and the 11/20/09 letter from P. W. Metz to the Hon. B. B. Brooks; all in Sheep Raid File.

3.  Letter of 11/14/09 from Felix Alston to Gov. B. B. Brooks, and the 11/22/09 letter from C. H. Parmelee to Hon. B. B. Brooks, Sheep Raid File.

4.  Letter of 11/22/09 from C. H. Parmelee to Hon. B. B. Brooks, Sheep Raid File.

5.  *Basin Republican*, 11/19/09.

6.  See, for example, the 11/15/09 letter from Felix Alston to Gov. B. B. Brooks, the 11/20/09 letter from Percy Metz to Governor Brooks, and the 11/24/09 letter to the Hon. Bon H. de Saint Laurent, Consul for France, Chicago; all in Sheep Raid File.

7.  *State v. Keyes* and *State v. Faris*, Case Nos. 411, 412, 413, and 421, Records of the Big Horn County Clerk of the District Court; *Big Horn County Rustler*, 11/19/09. The records of the Washakie County Clerk, originally Big Horn County Records, show a November 15, 1909 deed from C. E. Shaw to Eva Faris (20 Deeds 281) and one on May 12, 1910, from Mrs. Faris to George Greet (24 Deeds 28). The county apparently purchased the personal property of these men, the cattle, horses, and equipment, but did not directly purchase the land owned.

8.  *Big Horn County Rustler*, 11/19/09; *Basin Republican*, 11/19/09.

9.  *Cheyenne State Leader*, 11/16/09.

10. O'Neal, *Cattlemen vs. Sheepherders*, 146, 147.

11. *Cheyenne State Leader*, 11/17/09.

12. *Big Horn County Rustler*, 11/19/09.

13. Will Metz letters to his wife Jennie, 11/14/09 and 11/19/09, Metz Collection.

14. *Sheridan Enterprise*, 11/23/09; *Worland Grit*, 11/25/09; *Basin Republican*, 11/26/09.

15. *Sheridan Enterprise*, 11/23/09.

16. Rhodes, *The Rest That Came*, 46; *Worland Grit*, 11/25/09; *Sheridan Enterprise*, 11/23/09.

17. Speech of Percy Metz before the Natrona County Historical Society, 11/2/62.

18. The southern terminus of this stretch of the Chicago, Burlington and Quincy Railway was a point a few miles south of Worland; it was several years before the line was built through Wind River Canyon. Davis, *Sadie and Charlie*, 18, 19.

19. *Worland Grit*, 11/25/09; Rhodes, *The Rest That Came*, 46; letter of 11/24/09 from Felix Alston to Hon. B. B. Brooks, Sheep Raid File.

20. *Republican*, 11/26/09 (from 11/23/09 *Sheridan Enterprise*).

21. *Basin Republican*, 12/3/09.

22. Ibid.

23. Ibid.

24. Letter of 12/4/09 from Gebhart and Anderson to Hon. B. B. Brooks, Sheep Raid File.

25. Letter of 12/6/09 from Secretary to the governor to Messrs. Gebhart and Anderson; Sheep Raid File.

26. *Denver Post*, 11/13/09, p. 1, col. 3.

27. O'Neal, *Cattlemen vs. Sheepherders*, 147.

28. Letter of 2/11/10 from W. L. Simpson to the Honorable B. B. Brooks; 3/13/10 statement by Felix Alston, Sheep Raid File. The early reports of the reward money referred to $500 (see Chapter 5 herein), but the December 3 *Republican* article referred to entitlement to $1,000 and indicated that $500 would come from Big Horn County and $500 from the state of Wyoming.

29. I sought this information from the papers of the Wyoming Woolgrowers' Association and National Woolgrowers' Association donated to the University of Wyoming. These papers, unfortunately, do not quite go back to 1909 and 1910. Besides Faris, Keyes, and Goodrich, others who may have received reward money were Alston's deputies and even Percy Metz. See Will Metz, 11/19/09 letter to his wife, Metz Collection. Billy Simpson was also mentioned as a possible recipient, but he declined, not even applying for any monies. *Worland Grit*, 12/2/09.

30. *Basin Republican*, 12/10/09, 12/24/09.

31. Gov. B. B. Brooks' Records, Petitions for Pardon (Brink) File, Wyoming State Archives, Cheyenne. The date of the commutation was December 18, 1909.

32. Letter of 1/17/10 from Henry A. May to Hon. B. B. Brooks, Sheep Raid File.

33. Petition, *Stotts v. Saban*, Case # 1007, Records of the Big Horn County Clerk of the District Court.

34. Letter of 11/27/09 from J. L. Stotts to Metz & Metz, Basin, with an enclosed draft of a petition; Metz Collection. The surprising thing is that Stotts enlisted the messrs. Metz to assist in this collection. By modern ethical standards, this action is very questionable.

35. *Basin Republican*, 11/11/10.

36. Ibid.

37. Vera Saban, in *He Wore a Stetson*, discusses at pp. 47–51 the unpopularity of Percy Metz's actions against gambling as well as such things as citing the houses of prostitution for selling liquor.

38. *Basin Republican*, 11/11/10.

39. Larson, *History of Wyoming*, 320.

40. Rhodes, *The Rest That Came*, 46; *Sweet Smell of Sagebrush*, 125.

41. Speech of Percy Metz before the Natrona County Historical Society, 11/2/61; *Alexander v. State*, Brief of Plaintiff in Error, Case # 682, before the Wyoming Supreme Court; see Petition of George Saban, Defendant Herein, for Writ of Error Coram Nobis. The State of Wyoming vs. George Saban, Case No. 444, Records of the Big Horn County Clerk of the District Court.

42. Paragraph 9, *State v. Saban*.

43. Ibid.

44. Ibid.

45. Ibid, Paragraph 10–12.

46. Ibid.

47. Motion to Quash and Dismiss Proceedings, *State v. Saban*.

48. Affidavits of E. E. Enterline and Felix Alston attached to Motion to Quash and Dismiss Proceedings, *State v. Saban*.

49. April 23, 1911 Order, *State v. Saban*.

50. *Alexander v. State*, 20 Wyo. 241 123 Pac. 68.

51. This account is based primarily on the narrative found in *Sweet Smell of Sagebrush*, 145–151.

52. Rhodes, *The Rest That Came*, 48.

53. Gov. B. B. Brooks' Records, Petition for Pardon (Lorenzo Paseo), Memoranda (commuted July 9, 1910), Wyoming State Archives, Cheyenne.

54. Letter of 4/13/33 letter from Wm. L. Simpson to E. E. Enterline, American Heritage Center Collection of Wm. L. Simpson, University of Wyoming (Acc. No. 26).

55. *Sweet Smell of Sagebrush*, 118, 130; letter of 11/19/12 from Governor Carey to Fred Bragg, Gov. Joseph M. Carey Records, Petition for Pardon File (Alexander and Saban), Wyoming State Archives, Cheyenne; prison records of George Saban, Wyoming State Archives, ("Description of Prisoner"). The fingers were apparently lost as the result of imprudent ropework with cattle.

56. *Sweet Smell of Sagebrush*, 118, 131; penitentiary records of Thomas Dixon (No. 1440), Wyoming Department of Commerce, Archives and Records Division, Cheyenne.

57. See penitentiary records of Thomas Dixon and Ed Eaton and letter of 12/18/11 letter from Governor Carey to T. W. Dixon; Gov. Joseph M. Carey Petition for Pardon (Ed Eaton) File; and Gov. Joseph M. Carey Petition for Pardon (T. W. Dixon) File, Wyoming State Archives, Cheyenne.

58. See Note 56. Jacobs' letter is not available, but a year later he wrote and opposed the early release of Saban and Alexander. See letter of 12/26/12 from Governor Carey to Lewis Jacobs, Petition for Pardon (O. J. Reynolds) File, Wyoming State Archives, Cheyenne.

59. Letter of 12/28/11 from Governor Carey to T. W. Dixon, Petition for Pardon (T. W. Dixon) File, Wyoming State Archives, Cheyenne.

60. Penitentiary records of Ed Eaton. Jack Gage stated that Eaton went to Meeteetse after his release and died there when he was bitten by a tick (*Ten Sleep and No Rest*, 219). In fact, he was never released — he just happened to be in Meeteetse with the road gang when he died.

61. Commutation by Gov. Joseph M. Carey, 11/25/12 "Discharge Notice," Penitentiary Records of Thomas Dixon.

62. Letter of 12/5/12 from Fred Bragg to Gov. J. M. Carey, Petition for Pardon File (Milton Alexander). The following discussion is based upon this file and the Petition for Pardon File (George Saban) found in the Wyoming State Archives.

63. Petition for Pardon (Alexander) File.

64. Ibid, letter of 12/26/12 from W. L. Simpson to Hon. Frank Houx, Petition for Pardon (Alexander) File.

65. Letter of 12/31/12 from M. A. Alexander to Hon. Gov. J. M. Carey, Petition for Pardon (Alexander) File. There is another possibility: that Mr. Alexander could not write and the letter was penned by a prison scrivener.

66. Letter of 1/1/13 from Governor Carey to M. A. Alexander, Petition for Pardon (Alexander) File.

67. Letter of 1/9/13 from Dr. G. W. Walker to Hon. J. M. Carey, Petition for Pardon (Alexander) File.

68. Petition for Pardon (Alexander) File.

69. Petition for Pardon (Alexander) File: *Big Horn County Rustler*, 12/14/13.

70. Saban letter of 3/25/13, Petition for Pardon (Alexander) File; letter of 7/7/13 letter from John Donovan to Gov. Joseph M. Carey; Petition for Pardon File (George Saban).

71. This discussion is taken primarily from the 1/2/14 issue of the *Big Horn County Rustler*, which contains excellent detail.

72. *Big Horn County Rustler*, 1/23/14.

73. Letter of 12/19/13 letter from Governor Carey to John Donovan, Petition for Pardon file (George Saban).

74. Ibid; letter of 12/29/13 letter from Governor Carey to Mr. J. C. Schneider, Petition for Pardon (George Saban) File.

75. Saban, *He Wore a Stetson*, 63. It could be speculated that Saban's escape affected Carey's choice, but there is no evidence one way or another.

76. This discussion derives from letters found in Carey's Petition for Pardon (Alexander) File.

77. Letter of 2/26/12 letter from Miss Dorolis S. Rebideaux to the Honorable Joseph M. Carey, Governor, Petition for Pardon (Brink) File.

78. Petition for Pardon (Brink) File.

79. Among the people who wrote Governor Carey were: R. P. Anderson (Proprietor, *Basin Republican*), Thos. W. Spratt, W. S. Collins, Fred Bragg, C. E. Shaw, Ray S. Hake (Worland), Ira Jones (Thermopolis), Alti Pendergraft (then sheriff of Washakie County), J. C. Frison, Joe Henry, John Luman, David Picard, Geo. P. McClellan (writing on State Senate stationary), H. N. Carstensen, Frank Helmer, Mark Warner, F. M. Sheldon (brother-in-law of Joe Allemand), Milo Burke, George Sutherland, A. S. Mercer, Jr., Roy Shriver, Henry Helms, Lewis Harvard, Geo. E. Greet, Porter Lamb, and Charles Wells.

80. Letter of 12/9/14 from Governor Carey to Mrs. M. A. Alexander, Petition for Pardon (Alexander) File.

81. Letter of 12/24/14 to Governor Carey from Myra Alexander, Petition for Pardon (Alexander) File.

82. Letter of 12/26/14 from Governor Carey to Mrs. Myra Alexander, Petition for Pardon (Alexander) File.

The Baseball Team. The prison baseball team about 1911. George Saban is standing in the back row and the catcher, Joseph Seng, who was executed shortly after this picture was taken, is the man sitting second from the left. Courtesy Jack Seaman.

The Goodriches. Billy and Anna Goodrich, in a photograph taken in the middle 1950s and originally printed in *Ten Sleep and No Rest*. Courtesy Jack Gage, Jr.

Bounce Helmer. This photograph of Bounce Helmer was taken about the same time as that of the Goodriches and is also from *Ten Sleep and No Rest*. Courtesy Jack Gage, Jr.

Percy Metz. This 1950s photograph of Judge Metz was originally printed in *Ten Sleep and No Rest*. Courtesy Jack Gage, Jr.

Herb Brink. The raider as an old man; also a Jack Gage picture taken about the same time as the others. Courtesy Jack Gage, Jr.

The Monument. The historical marker on Wyoming State Highway 434. It was erected in 1989 as a result of Clay Gibbons' efforts. Photograph by the author.

Another photograph of the Highway 434 marker, one that also shows a marker where the south wagons stood. Photograph by the author.

# Epilogue

The Spring Creek raid has passed into legend. It was an earth-shaking event for people of the time, a happening like Pearl Harbor or the death of President Kennedy — people remembered where they were when they first heard. They measured events as before the raid and after the raid. As the years rolled by, it remained such a topic of interest that every old-timer laid aside some treasured tale showing his special knowledge of the raid. It seems, too, that every child who grew up in the Nowood country after the raid tried to find a way to get an old-timer talking about the raid. These children have become today's old-timers, and all of them seem to remember those special conversations in which they were told "the real story" by someone who was alive in 1909.

The fascination persists. On April 2, 1989, the eightieth anniversary of the raid, there were dedication ceremonies for monuments at the sites of the north wagon and the south wagon.[1] A young man from Worland, Clay Gibbons, had become absorbed with the raid. He undertook a major effort to research documents from the time and uncovered the original survey notes, which allowed the location of the exact places where the wagons set.

On August 10, 1990, the Washakie County Bar Association staged a re-enactment of *State v. Brink*. It was done as part of Wyoming's centennial celebration, and the Worland lawyers used the original transcript and donned period costume to bring the trial to life. The courtroom in the Washakie County Courthouse was packed with people who wanted to learn more about the raid and the trial that followed from it.

The trial of Herbert Brink, though, did not simply live in legend; it had very concrete and enduring consequences. The convictions of Brink and his compatriots were the first, last, and only time in Wyoming that cowboys were convicted for a raid on a sheep camp, but they stopped the killing. Only two other raids occurred afterward. One was in July 1911, when 150 sheep belonging Henry Ruble were killed on Black Mountain. The authorities expected to make some arrests but evidently did not.[2] The second was in Sublette County in February 1912; and sixty sheep were killed and wagons were burned.[3] The woolgrowers' association was determined to stop all such activity and vigorously backed the prosecution of the three cowboys arrested. They were acquitted, but the message was clear: Those damn sheepherders weren't going to let a cowboy have any fun at all.

Friction between sheepmen and cattlemen did continue, however, and it wouldn't stop until 1934 with the passage of the Taylor Grazing Act. It is hard to fathom why it took so long for the federal government to pass an act establishing a leasing system. People had been talking for years about such a system. Immediately after the *Brink* case, Judge Parmelee discussed the causes of the raid and gave his opinion that further trouble could be stopped by leasing the range.[4] Percy Metz proudly noted that he had taken part in the organization of the grazing act, attending a meeting at Glenwood Springs, Colorado, that Congressman Taylor himself attended.

But the significance of the Spring Creek raid and the Brink trial went beyond the immediate enforcement of the law. Every part of the United States began as a frontier society, and every part has grown out of that condition. In the Big Horn Basin, the last of the frontier in the continental United States, the transition came very late and very painfully. Will Metz, the day the *Brink* verdict came in, said: "It is significant of the beginning of a new era, of a period where lawlessness in any form will be no more tolerated by citizens than in the more densely settled communities of the east."[5]

The *Cheyenne Tribune* put it another way: "The *Tribune* trusts Big Horn County will never again be called upon to answer for such a crime. The sooner the six-shooter and Winchester are entirely eliminated from everyday life in Wyoming, the sooner the boys will grow into manly, courageous, law abiding men."[6]

The case of *State v. Brink* signified the end of the frontier in Wyoming. It was a painful but necessary event. Men with the character of cowboys are essential to a frontier society and Americans cherish the romantic image of the wild, restless, and brave cowboy. But that image becomes less romantic when the cowboy is on his horse trampling your garden. It was up to people like Percy Metz to suppress this rowdy symbol.

Of all the people associated with the Spring Creek raid, Percy Metz was surely the most fortunate. He may not have believed it on that dismal April 3, 1909, but he was born under a lucky star. Percy Metz remained a district judge for the next forty years. For what must have seemed forever, in Wyoming's Fifth Judicial District "judge" meant Percy Metz and "Percy Metz" meant judge. In the very early years of his tenure, he became wealthy. He and his father invested in the Good Drilling Company, and in 1916, from the Elk Basin field alone, he received over $35,000 — when $35,000 was a fortune.[7] The state of Wyoming paid district judges a comfortable wage, but with his other earnings he was able to richly indulge his passions for travel and the outdoors. He died in 1964 at age eighty.

His father, William Metz, continued to practice law in Sheridan and became a member of the Wyoming House of Representatives in 1913.[8] A reporter from the *Sheridan Press* found him still practicing law and wrote a story about Will's role in the prosecution of the Spring Creek raiders.[9]

Felix Alston served for many years as the warden of the Wyoming State Penitentiary and died sometime in the 1950s in California.[10] His friend Joe LeFors continued working for the Wyoming Woolgrowers for a few years but then retired in Buffalo and wrote his autobiography, *Wyoming Peace Officer*. LeFors died there in 1940, but his book wasn't published until 1953.[11]

Bounce Helmer herded sheep most of the rest of his life. He would readily discuss the raid and if purchased a drink or two would go on at some length. He was married briefly and had one child. Bounce retired in Cody in 1953 and died in the summer of 1956.[12]

Pete Cafferal went back to France shortly after the raid, but he got in trouble because of the death of young Lazier. The details are unclear, but Pete was blamed because he had persuaded Lazier to come to Wyoming, and in some way the boys' parents construed their son's death to be Pete's fault.[13]

The Callahans (John Callahan and Ada Allemand) moved to Washington state, and their descendants still live there. In 1989, an old man journeyed from Washington to the banks of Spring Creek for the dedication of the monument at the site of the raid. That old man had been the little baby who waved and cooed at the jury in 1909.[14]

As to the men who turned state's evidence in 1909, not much is known. Keyes disappeared from the ken of Big Horn County; that location somewhere in Canada (mentioned by Sheriff Alston in his 1911 affidavit) is the last known reference to Keyes. Faris is supposed to have become a preacher in Bozeman, Montana, and to have died in Manhattan, Montana.[15]

Billy and Anna Goodrich returned to the Upper Nowood in 1918 and resumed ranching. There was still resentment toward Billy, but the strongest feelings had faded, and by then sheep and sheepmen had become common in the Upper Nowood. Billy died in 1960 and Anna in 1974.[16]

There were, of course, many other people associated with the prosecution of the raid, but time and space make it impossible to discuss all of them. A walk through the Ten Sleep Cemetery will show what became of most of them — most of those associated with the defense, too. But one man who is not buried there is George Saban.

If Percy Metz was born under a bright and lucky star, then George Saban was born under a dark one. George would never allow his children to see him in convict clothes, but after his escape they never again saw him in other dress, either.[17] He disappeared, and all that returned to Wyoming were rumors of his presence in faraway places: Alaska, Aruba, Guatemala, Cuba, Mexico, and Argentina.[18]

Mrs. Saban remained in Wyoming, and she was embittered. She could hardly speak the names of Faris and Keyes, and when she did the words were hissed out, as if they were swear words.[19] Other members of the family also suffered deeply. James Saban, one of George's sons, never got over his father's departure. Whenever he heard something about George, he would drop everything and go to that place and search for his father. Sometimes he was gone for weeks, but he never found his dad.[20]

By the best information, George Saban died in Argentina, probably in the 1930s. The story is that some bandits stole horses of his, and when he followed them he was shot dead.[21]

Herbert Brink, too, lived a terribly unfortunate life. After his release from prison, he resumed living with his half-sister, by whom he already had two children.[22] (In the last few months before he was paroled, Mrs. P. Olsen [Fannie Olsen] wrote Governor Carey several letters on behalf of Brink; Mrs. Olsen was apparently this half-sister.)[23] Another child was born, but then Brink refused to support any of his children and went to Canada. He was returned to the United States and re-entered prison on February 11, 1922. Brink was paroled again in 1928, but he violated that parole also and returned on December 31, 1932.[24]

After the last return, there was talk of pardoning Brink, and the former prosecutors discussed this prospect. A bad mark against him were the ugly rumors as to Brink's treatment of his children (Percy Metz declared that he raped his daughter), and the prosecutors decided it was best to leave Brink in prison — by then that was all he knew.[25]

It is tempting to write Brink off as the "worthless pup" Percy Metz called him, but human beings, it seems, are endlessly complicated. While in prison, Brink made several craft items of horsehair. One of them, a bridle in the possession of Richard Bullard of Ten Sleep, is a breathtaking creation. Horsehair weaving requires something on the order of four hours for every inch, and Bullard's bridle has a couple of feet of material. The details — intricate, carefully worked details — show a well-developed artistic sense. The leather work is also excellent.[26]

Brink finally completed his sentence and was released on October 26, 1943.[27] He became a ward of the state (he was living in Saratoga, Wyoming, when Gage wrote *Ten Sleep and No Rest*), and he died in the late 1950s, the last of the defendants to pass on.[28] The closest Brink ever came to admitting fault was when he told Jack Gage: "In those days I thought I was right, but I guess I wasn't."[29]

The fate of Tommy Dixon is unclear. There are statements that he went insane in Montana and others that he was killed in an oil field accident in Oklahoma a number of years before 1940.[30]

As to Milton Alexander, though, we know exactly what became of him. At first, he remained away from the Big Horn Basin as required. On February 3, 1917, however, Governor John Kendrick pardoned Alexander, enabling him to return to the Upper Nowood.[31] In 1920 the Alexanders sold their ranch, and during the 1920s Milton acted as the town marshall of Ten Sleep. People still remember him from that time as a quiet, dignified man. He died in Worland on January 24, 1931, and is buried in the Ten Sleep Cemetery.[32]

One of the supporters of the raiders who is also found at the Ten Sleep Cemetery is George McClellan. He became Washakie County's first state senator and in about 1918 moved to Worland, where he bought into the Ford dealership and renamed it the "Wild Bear Garage."[33] He sold Model Ts and Model As until returning to the ranch in 1929. He died on October 18, 1934.[34]

One of the most surprising developments was the merger of the *Basin Republican* and the *Big Horn County Rustler*. In 1928, apparently deciding Basin couldn't support two newspapers, they joined to form a publication with one of the most colorful names in the country: the *Basin Republican Rustler*.[35] This newspaper, which had its genesis in Bonanza in 1889, still publishes.

Of course, there have been vast changes since 1909, but the Upper Nowood has probably changed as little as any part of the Big Horn Basin. A drive from Ten Sleep to Nowood (taking the Spring Creek road) shows that the Upper Nowood is still beautiful. In early April, the meadowlarks still sing and the phlox bloom, and glorious spring still comes in May. For all the bitterness and agony of the raid, the land endures.

NOTES

1. *Sun Country Review, Northern Wyoming Daily News*, March 26,1989.

2. *Big Horn County Rustler*, 7/14/11.

3. O'Neal, *Cattlemen vs. Sheepherders*, 149, 150; Wentworth, *America's Sheep Trails*, 543.

4. *Worland Grit*, 12/2/09.

5. *Cheyenne State Leader*, 11/12/09.

6. *Worland Grit*, 11/25/09 (reprinted from the *Cheyenne Tribune*).

7. Davis, *Sadie and Charlie*, 52.

8. Lawrence M. Woods, *Wyoming Biographies* (Worland: High Plains Publishing Company, 1991), 133.

9. Newspaper article from Vertical File (Ten Sleep Raid), Wyoming State Historical Research and Publications Division, Cheyenne.

10. Speech of Percy Metz before the Natrona County Historical Society, 11/2/61.

11. Joe LeFors, *Wyoming Peace Officer*, Preface and Acknowledgement.

12. Gage, *Ten Sleep and No Rest*, 222; *Cody Enterprise*, 1/22/53.

13. Gage, *Ten Sleep and No Rest*, 221.

14. *Sun Country Review, Northern Wyoming Daily News*, March 26,1989.

15. Arlene G. Robinson, "*Ten Sleep Raid*," available in the Miscellaneous Files (WPA # 1307), Wyoming State Archives, 2. This article is dated April 1940. See also Gage, *Ten Sleep and No Rest*, 220.

16. Letter of 8/19/69 from Anna Goodrich to Marlene and Bob Orchard (copy in the author's possession); interview of Kent Orchard, grand-nephew of the Goodriches, January, 1992.

17. Letter of 12/10/12 from John Donovan to Gov. Joseph M. Carey, Petition for Pardon (George Saban) File.

18. Gage, *Ten Sleep and No Rest*, 221; interview of Jack Seaman, grandson of Mr. and Mrs. George Saban, February 1992.

19. Interview of Jack Seaman, October 1991.

20. Taped interview of Alberta Seaman, Oral History Number 704, Wyoming Department of Commerce, Archives and Records Division, Cheyenne. This interview is usually found with the tapes of the speeches of Percy Metz and is also available at the Washakie County Museum and Cultural Center, Worland.

21. Interview of Jack Seaman, January 1992. There is supposed to be a photograph of a tombstone in Argentina that is George Saban's grave.

22. Rhodes, *The Rest That Came*, 48.

23. Petition for Pardon (Brink) File.

24. "Convicts Discharged or Removed," Penitentiary Records of Herbert Brink (No. 1443).

25. Speech by Percy Metz before the Natrona County Historical Society; 4/13/33 letter from William Simpson to E. E. Enterline, Simpson Collection.

26. I have seen the Bullard bridle and have been told that others of Herbert Brink's handiwork exist in the Ten Sleep area.

27. "Convicts Discharged or Removed," Penitentiary Records of Herbert Brink.

28. Speech of Percy Metz before the Natrona County Historical Society, 11/2/61; Gage, *Ten Sleep and No Rest*, 219. Gage spoke of Brink as being alive in 1956, and Metz, in 1961, indicated that Brink had recently died.

29. Gage, *Ten Sleep and No Rest*, 220. While in prison, Brink filled out a form that asked for "causes of crime." Brink stated: "Listening to some one else" (Brink Penitentiary Records).

30. Gage, *Ten Sleep and No Rest*, 219; Rhodes, *The Rest That Came*, 46; O'Neal, *Cattlemen vs. Sheepherders*, 148; Robinson, : "Ten Sleep Raid," 3.

31. "Convict Discharged or Removed," Alexander Penitentiary Records.

32. *Worland Grit*, 1/29/31.

33. Pendergraft, *Washakie: A Wyoming County History*, 154, 135.

34. Interview of Howard McClellan, December 1991.

35. Interview of Eric Adams, present owner of the paper, by the author, January 1992.

# Appendix

I. (From Note 7, Chapter 5):

A CLEVER BURLESQUE

**A Worland Barber Made the Victim of a Practical Joke**

We love fun, us Western folk, and waste but little sentiment in having it. Scarce three weeks had elapsed since the Spring Creek tragedy when it was made the subject of a laughable burlesque, successfully played.

Worland has a barber who can easily give all of the so-called "yellow rags" of journalism west of the Missouri, and east of it, inclusive, several pointers on "scoops" in the publication of sensational news with few facts behind it. Holman had for several days been gossiply busy with his customers in unloading upon them a variety of lurid reports regarding the Spring Creek affair, and every story he published by word of mouth was so improbable and utterly lacking a coloring of truth that several young men around town decided to give him a lesson in the value of silence when he had no reliable knowledge of the information he was scattering abroad.

The plans arranged worked harmoniously from the start. Holman was told that six men in the Tensleep country were to be arrested on the night of the 16th, and that ten Worland men were to be deputized to take them into custody.

At 10 o'clock that evening Marshal Salisbury waited on Holman and informed him that by order of law he had been chosen a deputy sheriff to join the deputies that would go to Tensleep. In a short time a party of fictitious officers was made up, including Cy Salisbury, Ray Hake, George Simons, Joe Bernasek and — Holman set out for Tensleep, all apparently well equipped for serious business. In the meantime a party of five armed with guns containing blank cartridges preceded the deputies (?) and located themselves in a dry gulch seven miles east of town. The Worland deputies ambled along leisurely on the way to Tensleep, apparently unconcerned about the stern duties that had fallen to their lot.

When within sixty feet of the gulch a sudden, flashing volley of musketry burst upon them, and Salisbury and Hake with simulated groans of agony and a broad smile tumbled as gracefully as possible from their horses. The attacking party in the gulch continued blazing away vigorously with their harmless weapons. Seeing the plight of his fallen companions Holman made a hasty retreat that has rarely been excelled in the desperation of its speed. At 12:30 with his face blanched with terror he rode into town and woke up several families with his pitiful cries for help, which were laughingly unheeded. All the saloons in town were visited and their inmates ("loaded" with horrifying (!) descriptions of the ghastly tragedy that had been enacted in which three men he was sure ! certain !! positive !!! had been killed. At Nelson & Hampton's he found George Simons stretched on the pool table with his face blotched with red ink; and was told that he was dying. Holman's illusions, which had been painfully real, causing him intense mental anguish, were dispelled when Hake and Salisbury, the supposed dead men, and members of the attacking party came boisterously through the front door laughing loudly over their joke.

II. Partial list of people subpoenaed by Grand Jury (from Note 2, Chapter 7):

George Saban, Charles Leavitt, M. A. Alexander, Charles Helmer, Ed Davis, Wm. Gibson, H. K. Sweeney, H. N. Carstensen, Mike Lynch, Walter Nelson, Harry Robertson, P. O. Fish, Ellward Harvey, George Sutherland, Jake Goodrich, C. H. Gardner, Edward Goodall, Geo. D. McClellan, Homer E. Jarvis, B. W. Helmer, Arthur McVay, Mrs. Wm. Goodrich, W. A. Miller, Frank Yorkshire, Henry Greet, Sidney Ingram, John Robinson, W. W. Cook, Mrs. J. E. Goodrich, Ben Helmer, John Buckmaster, E. O. Pickett, Carrie Everett, Porter Lamb, Charles Runge, W. Keyes, Ed Eaton, Mrs. George Saban, Thomas Dixon, Joe Henry, Jesse Thompson, Al Martin, Oscar Arnett, Mrs. O. W. Arnett, Samuel Brant, J. C. Frison, R. W. Barrington, Charles A. Mann, Farney Cole, Mark H. Warner, Harry R. Johnson, Frank Tulley, Fred Widmeyer, O. McClellan, Elmer Chatfield, Lewis Harvard, Clyde Harvard, W. D. Goodrich, D. Peterson, Geo. C. Pickett, Fred Greet. G. A. Coleman, S. W. Richie, W. G. Colethorpe, P. P. Alspough, Mike Bader, Joe Helmer, Geo. Rogers, Mary Buckmaster, John D. Callahan, Lizzie Lamb, W. W. Early, A. LeFrac, Chas. Farris, Mrs. Chas. Farris, Mrs Chas. Mann, and Virgil Chabot. From the endorsement of names of known witnesses on the indictment of Herbert Brink. Case No. 419, records of the Big Horn County Clerk of the District Court.

III. Panel of Trial Jurors (From Note 15, Chapter 13):

J. W. Thurmond and Clause Andrieu of Marquette; Nefi Robertson, Fred Hammond, C. E. Neilson, and B. W. Salisbury of Cowley; Byron A.

Sessions, Hyrum Perry, John B. Farmere, and E. B. Powellson of Byron; W. H. Packard, M. H. Lafollett, Alra E. Slover, Ole Oleson, and Elmer E. Yarnell of Burlington; J. H. Johnson, L. Moncur, and Chas. Duncan of Lovell; C. C. Shaw, J. C. Stoddard, and Dan A. Winslow of Worland; Andrew Black of Crystal; G. W. Black, C. C. Ellis, F. W. Ackerman, J. L. Brown, W. J. Jones, C. R. James, J. T. Hurst, W. K. Lewis, and W. S. Smith of Basin; O. F. Hurd of Rothwell, Lee A. Walters and J. A. Swensen of Kirby; James McKinney of Cloverly; James Smith of Cooke, Montana; Wm. Lewis of Greybull; John Peterson, W. P. Rece, Frank Young, Rufus Wilson, Mark Ward, Ernest Babcock, and Oscar Irdall of Meeteetse; P. F. Worley, John H. Smith, and Albert E. Clifford of Ionia; Jacob Becker, R. W. Burington and W. J. Harman of Nowood; Angus Beaton and Chas. Walters of Manderson; H. H. Carstensen, J. L. Van Buskirk, and M. H. Warner of Ten Sleep; C. H. Gardner and W. E. Morris of Hyattville; James Wortz of Crosby, John H. Graves of Wapiti; W. J. Buckner of Four Bear; W. W. Rhea of Shell; Joseph Leishman and F. M. Sheldon of Big Trails; Bert Bair, W. G. Goodwin, Orin T. Tucker, and Wm. Grant of Thermopolis; H. E. Dutton of Otto; Simon Snyder of Valley; W. H. Van Alstine of Bonanza; J. E. Brown of Clark; Harrison Shoemaker of Powell; H. D. Hendrick of St. Joe; B. W. Austin of Fenton; and Robert Carroll of Penrose. These names were taken from a list of jurors on the panel apparently compiled by the prosecution. This list was found among papers in the collection of Lola Homsher at the American Heritage Center, University of Wyoming. The list is incomplete, containing only 76 names; the *Basin Republican* on November 5, 1909, indicated that almost all of the 100 jurors summoned appeared. In the Metz paper, no names from Cody are set out nor at least one from Hyattville, John Donahue.

# Directory of Names

Note: Unless otherwise indicated, the descriptions refer to the situation in 1909.

**Abplanalp, Sid:** A cattleman who ranched in the Dry Farms area above Big Trails.

**Ainsworth, Frank:** First came into the Big Horn Basin in 1879, settled on Crooked Creek and ran 500 sheep.

**Alexander, Milton:** A prosperous cattleman who ranched on the Nowood south of Otter Creek; one of the seven men indicted.

**Allemand, Joe and Ada:** French sheepman on Spring Creek and his wife; had been married about ten years and had two sons.

**Allen, Ora:** Man who gave George Saban a ride from Basin, Wyoming, to Laurel, Montana in 1913.

**Alston, Felix:** Sheriff of Big Horn County; later warden of the Wyoming State Penitentiary.

**Arnett, Oscar:** Cattleman who, with George Sutherland and James Richardson, ran the Paradise outfit near Ten Sleep.

**Atherly, Clyde:** Big Horn County surveyor.

**Bedford, Jack:** Small cattleman who was killed with Dab Burch in 1892, apparently by range detectives who thought he was a rustler.

**Bragg, Fred:** Rancher who ran both sheep and cattle on the Nowood above Deep Creek.

**Brant, Sam:** Drove the stage through the Upper Nowood.

**Brink, Herb:** Cowboy bunking at the Billy Goodrich ranch; one of the seven men indicted.

**Brooks, B. B.:** Governor of Wyoming; a sheepman from Casper.

**Brown, Eliza and Frank:** Lived on a small place in Big Trails and were friends of the Allemands.

**Buckmaster, John and Mary:** Lived near where Otter Creek flowed into the Nowood.

**Burch, Dab:** See Jack Bedford.

**Burke, Milo:** Came into the Ten Sleep area in 1882 as foreman of the Bar X Bar; later ran his own outfit.

**Cafferal, Pete:** French camp tender for Emge and Allemand; captured by raiders, testified at trial.

**Callahan, John:** Trapper in the Upper Nowood; earlier worked for Emge and Allemand.

**Carter, Dana:** Early physician who practiced out of Basin; cattlemen sympathizer.

**Chatfield, Elmer:** Owner of a ranch on Spring Creek later purchased by the Taylor brothers; employed George Rogers.

**Cole, Farney:** Ranch hand who worked for Bill Keyes.

**Coleman, Al:** Lived on a small ranch where the south fork and north fork of Otter Creek emerge from the Big Horn Mountains.

**Colethorpe, W. G.:** Employed by Goodall and Widmeyer; brother-in-law of Joe Allemand.

**Collins, W. S.:** Mayor of Basin; defense attorney for the raiders.

**Cusack, Ed:** Deputy sheriff, apparently the chief deputy of Felix Alston.

**Dixon, Tommy:** Cowboy who bunked on the Billy Goodrich ranch; one of the seven men indicted.

**Donahue, John:** Rancher and farmer from Hyattville, on Brink jury (not to be confused with John Donovan, a benefactor of George Saban).

**Early, W. W.:** Upper Nowood rancher near Big Trails who testified before the grand jury.

**Eaton, Ed:** Cowman who had been the foreman at George Saban's Bay State Ranch; tall, thin; one of the seven men indicted.

**Emge, Joe:** Prosperous rancher who had run cattle but joined with Joe Allemand to run sheep; lived next to Allemand on Spring Creek.

**Enders, Peter:** Big Horn county clerk.

**Enterline, E.E.:** Sheridan attorney hired by Big Horn County as a special prosecuting attorney.

**Faris, Charles:** Rancher on Otter Creek; one of the seven men indicted.

**Fiscus, Walter:** Proprietor of the Ten Sleep hardware store.

**Franc, Otto:** Early rancher who established the huge Pitchfork Ranch on the Greybull River in 1879 and 1880; a cattle baron.

**Frison, Jake:** Cattleman who ranched on the north bank of Ten Sleep Creek, near the Bay State Ranch of George Saban.

**Gantz, Louis:** Sheepman who was raided on Shell Creek in 1905.

**Garrison, Bill:** Cowboy who bunked with Billy Goodrich; his bunkmates were Herb Brink and Tommy Dixon.

**Gibson, William:** Deputy sheriff who found firearms in Bill Keyes' chicken coop.

**Goodrich, Billy and Anna:** Ranched at Big Trails; provided room and board to Herb Brink, Tommy Dixon and Bill Garrison.

**Goodrich, Jake and Ade:** Ran a cattle ranch on the Upper Nowood just above Otter Creek; Ade was previously married to Frank Helmer and was Bounce Helmer's mother.

**Greet, Frank and Fred:** Twin brothers who ran a cattle ranch at the mouth of Spring Creek where it joins the Nowood.

**Harvard, Clyde:** Cowboy who worked for Bill Keyes.

**Harvard, Louis:** Cowboy who worked for Milton Alexander.

**Helmer, Charles David:** Better known as "Bounce"; worked for Allemand and Emge as a sheepherder.

**Helmer, Frank:** Known as "Double H" (also the name of his ranch), a cattle rancher on Crooked Creek; Bounce Helmer's father.

**Henry, Joe:** Old-timer with ranch on the Nowood.

**Ingram, Sydney:** Cowboy who worked for George Saban.

**Keyes, Albert:** Known as "Bill Kize," a rancher on Otter Creek; one of the seven men indicted.

**Lamb, Porter and Lizzie:** Had just purchased the Greets' Spring Creek property and were moving in on April 2, 1909.

**Lazier, Jules:** French citizen, nephew of Joe Allemand who was with Allemand and Emge in the north wagon the evening of April 2, 1909.

**LeFors, Joe:** Fabled detective; the Wyoming Woolgrower's top investigator who assisted Felix Alston after the raid.

**Linton, Alex:** Chairman of the Big Horn County Commission.

**Luman, John:** Early rancher who brought cattle into the Hyattville area in 1881; one of the cattle barons.

**Lynn, J. L.:** A sheepman who ran a big herd in the Big Horn Basin and was raided on Shell Creek in 1907.

**Mann, Charles:** Joe Emge's brother-in-law who testified at the Brink trial about the value of the burned property.

**McClellan, George:** The "Bear" — large, boisterous rancher above Big Trails, on Red Bank; a leader among cattlemen.

**McClellan, Oscar:** George's brother but small, quiet, and scholarly; ranched on the Nowood above Big Trails.

**McVay, Arthur:** A hot-headed young cowboy who worked for the Paradise outfit near Ten Sleep; always rode white horses.

**Metz, Percy:** Twenty-five-year-old county attorney.

**Metz, William:** Sheridan attorney, Percy's father, who was hired by Big Horn County as a special prosecuting attorney.

**Miller, William C.:** Cattleman who ranched on the Nowood above Ten Sleep on Broken Back Creek; close friend of George Saban.

**Minnick, Ben:** Sheepman murdered in 1903 near Black Mountain; apparently mistaken for his older brother, William.

**Morrison, Lincoln:** Prominent sheepman shot and wounded in 1904 on Kirby Creek.

**Morton, Al:** Deputy sheriff, sent to scene of raid by Sheriff Alston on April 3, 1909.

**Nelson, Walter:** Worked for George McClellan; driving a lumber wagon the evening of April 2, 1909, near the scene of the raid.

**Packard, W. H.:** Burlington farmer and beekeeper; Mormon bishop who was the foreman of the Brink jury.

**Parmelee, C. H.:** Presiding judge at the Spring Creek raid cases.

**Pickett, George:** Ten Sleep–area rancher who testified in the Brink trial for the defense.

**Rebidaux:** Family that lived on the Nowood above Big Trails, just below Oscar McClellan.

**Rhodes, Marvin:** Basin resident who presided over the Masonic funeral of the victims of the raid; later wrote about the raid.

**Richardson, James:** See Oscar Arnett.

**Ritchie, Samuel Walter:** Ranch hand who worked for both Oscar and George McClellan.

**Ridgely, H. S.:** Principal defense attorney for the raiders.

**Robertson, C. F.:** Mayor of Worland and defense attorney for the raiders.

**Robinson, William:** Cowboy who testified before the grand jury.

**Rogers, George:** Cowboy who worked for Elmer Chatterfield.

**Runge, Charles:** Had worked for George Saban just before the raid; testified before the grand jury.

**Rutrough, John:** Sheepman from the Cody area; sat on Brink jury.

**Saban, George:** Prominent and prosperous cattleman, proprietor of the Bay State Ranch near Ten Sleep; one of the seven men indicted.

**Seng, Joseph:** Executed in 1911 at the Wyoming State Penitentiary; catcher on the prison baseball team organized by George Saban.

**Shaw, Charles:** Sold cattle ranch near Ten Sleep to Emge and Allemand; testified before grand jury.

**Simpson, William:** ("Billy"): Attorney from Cody who was hired as a special prosecuting attorney by Big Horn County.

**Stotts, J. L.:** Orator who was one of the defense attorneys for the raiders; from Sheridan.

**Sutherland, George:** See Oscar Arnett.

**Taylor, George:** Sheepman from Meeteetse; foreman of grand jury.

**Torrey, Col. J. L.:** Big cattleman who ran a horse ranch near Shell with George Saban.

**Walker, Dr. George:** Hyattville physician who examined the bodies after the raid and testified on behalf of the prosecution; not to be confused with the secretary of the Wyoming Woolgrowers Association, George Walker.

**Walls, W. L.:** Raider defense attorney from Cody; Percy Metz's opponent in the 1908 county attorney race.

**Warner, Mark:** Hyattville cattle rancher frequently mentioned as being one of the most dedicated cattlemen.

**Wells, Charles:** Sheep and cattle rancher who established himself very early on Box Elder Creek.

**West, R. B.:** Raider defense attorney; Big Horn county attorney, 1911–1913.

**Whaley, W. T.:** "By Dumb" Whaley, a cattleman who settled near Shell in 1890; father-in-law of George Saban.

**Widmeyer, Fred:** Ran an outfit near the junction of Cherry Creek and the Nowood with Ed Goodall; testified at trial.

**Wigfall, Frank:** Black man lynched at the Wyoming State Penitentiary in 1912, by fellow prisoners, including Herb Brink.

**Zaring, C. A.:** Basin attorney, one of the raider's defense attorneys.

# Bibliography

## ARTICLES

Harrison, Lowell H. "The Cattle-Sheep Wars." *Mississippi Valley Historical Review,* Vol. 46, No. 4 (March 1960).

Judge, Bill. "Tensleep Raid." *Frontier Times* (Summer 1962).

Kurt, Charles. "Massacre at Big Horn Basin." *Official Detective Stories* (December 1941).

Larson, Alfred. "The Winter of 1886–87 in Wyoming." *Annals of Wyoming,* Vol. 14, No. 1 (January 1942).

Nelson, Andre. "The Last Sheepman-Cattleman War." *True West* (May 1988).

Robinson, Arlene G. "Ten Sleep Raid." Available in Miscellaneous Files (WPA #1307), Wyoming State Archives, Cheyenne, Wyoming.

Author unknown. "C. Dana Carter, Pioneer Doctor." Unpublished biography available at the Wyoming Department of Commerce, Archives and Records Division, Cheyenne, Wyoming.

## BOOKS, PAMPHLETS, AND MANUSCRIPTS

Ainsworth, Mrs. Bert. *To the Wilds of Wyoming, Pioneers of the Big Horn Basin in Wyoming.* College Place, Washington: self-published, 1983.

Davis, John W. *Sadie and Charlie.* Worland, Wyoming: Washakie Publishing, 1989.

———. *Worland Before Worland.* Worland, Wyoming: Northern Wyoming Daily News, 1987.

Edgar, Bob, and Jack Turnell. *Brand of a Legend.* Cody, Wyoming: Stockade Publishing, 1978.

———. Lady of a Legend. Cody, Wyoming: Stockade Publishing, 1979.

Frison, Paul. *Apache Slave.* Worland, Wyoming: Worland Press, 1969.

———. *Great Days of the Cattle Kings, 1879–1886, Big Horn Basin, Johnson Co., Wyoming.* Worland, Wyoming: Paul Frison.

———. *Under the Ten Sleep Rim.* Worland, Wyoming: Worland Press, 1972.

Friends of the Old Pen. *Sweet Smell of Sagebrush: A Prisoner's Diary, 1903–1912.* Rawlins, Wyoming: Friends of the Old Pen, 1990.

Frye, Elnora L. *Atlas of Wyoming Outlaws of the Territorial Penitentiary.* Laramie, Wyoming: Jelm Mountain Publications, 1990.

Gage, Jack. *Ten Sleep and No Rest.* Casper, Wyoming: Prairie Publishing Company, 1958.

Gard, Wayne. *The Great Buffalo Hunt.* Lincoln, Nebraska: University of Nebraska Press, 1959.

Larson, T. A. *History of Wyoming*. Lincoln, Nebraska: University of Nebraska Press, 1959.

LeFors, Joe. *Wyoming Peace Officer, An Autobiography*. Laramie, Wyoming: Laramie Printing Company, 1953.

Lindsay, Charles. *The Big Horn Basin*. Lincoln, Nebraska: University of Nebraska Press, 1932.

McCracken, Harold. *The Charles M. Russell Book*. Garden City, New York: Doubleday & Company, 1957.

Mercer, A. S. *The Cattlemen's Invasion of Wyoming in 1892 (The Crowning Infamy of the Ages)*. Norman, Oklahoma: University of Oklahoma Press, 1954.

Nelson, Dick J. *The Big Horn Basin*. San Diego, California: Dick J. Nelson, 1957.

O'Neal, Bill. *Cattlemen vs. Sheepherders*. Austin, Texas: Eakins Press, 1989.

Pendergraft, Ray. *Washakie: A Wyoming County History*. Basin, Wyoming: Saddlebag Books, 1985.

Rhodes, Marvin B. *The Rest That Came: A History of the Ten Sleep Raid*. Basin, Wyoming: Unpublished manuscript available at the Wyoming Department of Commerce, Archives and Records Division, Cheyenne, Wyoming.

Rollins, George Watson. *The Struggle of the Cattlemen, Sheepmen and Settler for Control of Lands in Wyoming, 1867–1910*. New York, New York: Arno Press, 1979.

Saban, Vera. *He Wore A Stetson: The Story of Judge Percy W. Metz*. Basin, Wyoming: Big Horn Book Company, 1980.

Smith, Helen Huntington. *The War on Powder River, the History of an Insurrection*. New York, New York: McGraw-Hill, 1966.

Stephens, Press, and Gretel Ehrlich, eds. *The Shell Valley, and Oral History of Frontier Settlement*. Cody, Wyoming: Rustler Printing and Publishing, 1986.

Walker, George S., comp. *Sheep Owners of Wyoming, 1910 Directory*. Cheyenne, Wyoming: S. A. Bristol, 1910.

Wasden, David John. *From Beaver to Oil*. Cody, Wyoming: Pioneer Printing & Stationery Company, 1973.

Wentworth, Edward Norris. *America's Sheep Trails*. Ames, Iowa: Iowa State College Press, 1948.

Woods, L. Milton. *Moreton Frewen's Western Adventures*. Boulder, Colorado: Roberts Rinehart, 1986.

———. *Wyoming Biographies*. Worland, Wyoming: High Plains Publishing, 1991.

## COLLECTIONS

S. A. Guthrie Collection, American Heritage Center, University of Wyoming.

Lola Homsher Collection, American Heritage Center, University of Wyoming.

Percy W. Metz Collection, American Heritage Center, University of Wyoming.

Wm. L. Simpson Collection, American Heritage Center, University of Wyoming.

## GOVERNMENT REPORTS AND RECORDS

Biennial Report of the Wyoming Adjutant General, 1909–1910.

Gov. B. B. Brooks' message to the Eighth State Legislature (January 11, 1905).

Powell, John Wesley. *Report on the Lands of the Arid Region of the United States.* Washington, 1879.

Records of the Big Horn County, Wyoming, Clerk.

Records of the Big Horn County, Wyoming, Clerk of Court.

Records of the Washakie County, Wyoming, Clerk.

Records of the Wyoming Supreme Court.

*Tabulation of Adjudicated Water Rights of the State of Wyoming, Water Division Number Three.* Cheyenne, Wyoming. State Board of Control, 1978.

Wyoming Department of Commerce, Archives and Records Division, Files of Gov. B.B. Brooks and Gov. Joseph M. Carey.

Wyoming Department of Commerce, Archives and Records Division, Penitentiary Records.

## LEGAL AUTHORITIES

*Alexander v. State,* 20 Wyo. 241, 123 P. 68.

*Clay v. State,* 15 Wyo. 42, 86 P. 17.

Wyoming Revised Statutes, 1899, §4950.

Wyoming Statutes, 1977, §6-2-101.

## MISCELLANEOUS

Diary of Otto Franc.

Notes and papers of Paul Frison.

Speeches of Percy W. Metz .

Transcript of the trial, *State v. Brink,* Wyoming Department of Commerce, Parks and Cultural Resources, Archives and Records Management Section.

Preliminary Map showing site of Spring Creek raid, April 2, 1909, based on the notes of a survey on April 26, 1909, by Clyde W. Atherly, by the Northwest Chapter of Professional Land Surveyors of Wyoming, 1989.

## NEWSPAPERS

*Basin Republican*
*Big Horn County Rustler*
*Billings Gazette*
*Buffalo Bulletin*
*Cheyenne Daily Leader*
*Cheyenne Tribune*
*Cody Enterprise*
*The Denver Post*
*Deseret News Weekly*
*Evanston News Register*
*Garland Guard*
*Greybull Standard*
*Lander Clipper*
*Lovell Chronicle*
*Meeteetse News.*
*Northern Wyoming Daily News*
*Rocky Mountain News*
*Sheridan Enterprise*
*Thermopolis Record*
*Worland Grit*

# Index